COMPLETE GUIDE FOR SUPERVISORS OF STUDENT EMPLOYEES IN TODAYS ACADEMIC LIBRARIES

David A. Baldwin and Daniel C. Barkley

LIBRARIES
UNLIMITED
A Member of the Greenwood Publishing Group
Westport, Connecticut • London

Library of Congress Cataloging-in-Publication Data

Baldwin, David A. (David Allen), 1946–
    Complete guide for supervisors of student employees in today's academic libraries /
    David A. Baldwin and Daniel C. Barkley.
        p.   cm.
    Includes bibliographical references and index.
    ISBN 978-1-59158-335-6 (alk. paper)
    1. Student library assistants—United States.   2. Academic libraries—United States—
    Personnel management.   I. Barkley, Daniel.   II. Title.
    Z682.4.S89B33   2007
    023.3–dc22   2007013534

British Library Cataloguing in Publication Data is available.

Library of Congress Catalog Card Number: 2007013534
ISBN: 978–1–59158–335–6

First published in 2007

Libraries Unlimited, 88 Post Road West, Westport, CT 06881
A Member of the Greenwood Publishing Group, Inc.
www.lu.com

Printed in the United States of America

The paper used in this book complies with the
Permanent Paper Standard issued by the National
Information Standards Organization (Z39.48–1984).

10 9 8 7 6 5 4 3 2 1

Contents

Introduction

> I am only one; but still I am one. I cannot do everything, but still I can do something;
> I will not refuse to do something I can do.
>
> —Helen Keller

Dave Baldwin and Dan Barkley are friends and library colleagues who share the belief that student employees are a critical part of any successful academic or research library staffing. They perform a myriad of tasks, duties, and responsibilities that permit the library to operate effectively 100 hours or more each week as most FTE librarians and staff work more conventional business hours. Our ability to do that depends squarely on the shoulders of a group to which we pay so little attention. We contend that the supervision of student employees is no less difficult than supervising full-time staff members. Sure, we can hire them and let them go for little or no justification. If one of them gets a little difficult to work with, cut your losses and let him go. Let someone else deal with an eccentric student. Pay no attention to the fact that the library can serve to ground students, give them a stable environment and work group, and give some of them their very first real work experience. Their mere presence enriches our work lives. The fact that you have picked up this book tells us that you agree that the supervision of students is a worthwhile activity. We also hope that you will gain from the years of experience we bring to this text. Student employees are a valuable part of the library's staffing and they are lucky to have you as their supervisor. Go for it.

I

Today's Academic Libraries— Bricks and Bytes

The library is the temple of learning, and learning has liberated more people than all the wars in history.

—Carl Rowan

TODAY'S ACADEMIC LIBRARIES

Few institutions have undergone more change in the past 35 years than the academic library. Those changes have been brought about by dramatic technological advances in recent years and guided in large part by the baby-boomers, the generation born since World War II. The administrators, faculty, and staff in today's academic libraries are of all age groups including many who were college students in the 1960s and 1970s. The libraries' administrators are in large part from these generations, whose professional education either did not include changes brought by computers or whose coursework only hinted at the forthcoming changes. The administrators have had a trial by fire. The transition from a place-bound library with card catalogs and printed indexes to the virtual library with its electronic resources has been remarkably smooth. It is interesting to talk, not only to students who were born after the first personal computer, but to librarians who don't remember libraries before computers. The mix of pre- and post-computer librarians, together with the ever-changing group of student employees, make the academic library a challenging, interesting, and exciting place to work. Most notable are changes brought on by the development of international bibliographic databases and the development of the Internet. Academic libraries have experienced a gradual, yet dramatic, shifting of work assignments from professional to nonprofessional to clerical to student staffing. Duties performed by librarians not that long ago have been transferred, first to staff members. Examples of these duties are acquisitions; copy cataloging; directional; and, in some cases, reference assistance;

circulation desk supervision; interlibrary loan; reserves; IT; and the supervision of many of these library activities. Many of these traditional librarian responsibilities are now being performed by highly effective staff. The work that was being accomplished by staff members, especially nonexempt staff, was also critical to the library's functioning in the new information environment. That work was gradually transferred to part-time student employees. This transfer of meaningful work to student employees resulted in the need for more effective student employment supervision practices and made that supervision an even more important librarian and staff responsibility.

LIBRARIES RESPONSE TO CHANGE

The real heroes of the digital revolution in higher education are librarians; they are the people who have seen the farthest, done the most, accepted the hardest challenges, and demonstrated most clearly the benefits of digital information. In the process, they have turned their own field upside down and have revolutionized their own professional training. It is a testimony to their success that we take their achievement for granted.

—Edward L. Ayers and Charles M. Grisham. "Why IT Has Not Paid Off as We Hoped (Yet)." EDUCAUSE Review, November/December 2003, p. 43.

All positions have been transformed by the changes wrought by library automation. Librarians are required to focus their efforts on improving access to information through database development/management and on the interpretation of information for users. Librarians must also devote time to library and university committee work and to professional activities. Library faculty must meet requirements for tenure and promotion, including publication. Clerical, technical, and professional staff members are now required to perform high-level technical and public service duties that previously had been part of the librarian's duties. These changes are not in themselves bad but they do raise issues of pay equity and sometimes require job audits, leading inevitably to higher pay for nonlibrarian staff members. As a result of the shifting of job duties to staff members, their duties and responsibilities often get reassigned to student employees who are being required to assume more complex technical and service responsibilities. And students are generally up to the task and this group of library employees plays an increasingly more important role in the ability of today's academic library to respond to technological change. Job responsibilities of staff at all levels are impacted by online systems and increasing user demand.

Today's technical services staff are required to perform complex acquisitions, cataloging, and processing tasks as well as mastering terminal/system operations. Improved access has resulted in increased demands for assistance in not only finding but also interpreting information. Reference and information desks must be staffed by knowledgeable personnel to assist library users in effectively using the library's systems and resources, and increasingly the number of questions and demand on professional assistance declines as the systems are more effective in meeting user needs. Interlibrary loan staff must respond to greater numbers of requests and staff members in the circulation department are required to be skilled in the use of an automated circulation system.

Libraries can respond effectively to the information explosion, the technological challenge, and the research and information needs of faculty, staff, and students on campus and of users from the community only with librarians, staff, and student employees working together. Success hinges on the effective use of a large segment of the library's staff resources—student employees.

STUDENTS AS PART OF THE WORKFORCE

Student employees are a very real part of any college or university library work-force. In 2003, student employees represented 22.3 percent of Association of Research Libraries university member libraries' staffing. In 1986, they represented 23.0 percent of all FTE staff. Since 1986, the mean number of staff in these libraries has remained constant at 265. The changes in staffing, however, are that the number of professional staff (librarians) has increased by over 5 percent while the number of other staff has declined by nearly 5 percent. There was an average of 67 FTE professional staff reported at 106 ARL university libraries in 1986 and 137 staff. In 2003, there were an average of 81 librarians and 125 staff in 113 ARL university libraries. FTE student assistants declined slightly from 61 to 59. In academic libraries, the number of student employees, in real numbers, often exceeds the number of regular staff. Because of their numbers, their cost, and their importance, it follows that academic libraries need to place a high priority on the effective management of student employment.

Mean	Prof Staff	% Total Staffing	Staff	% Total Staffing	Student Asst	% Total Staffing	Total Staff	Univ Libraries
1986	67	25.3%	137	51.7	61	23.0%	265	106
1987	68	25.7%	134	50.6%	63	23.8%	265	106
1988	70	25.7%	140	51.5%	62	22.8%	272	107
1989	72	25.9%	142	51.1%	64	23.0%	278	107
1990	74	26.5%	144	51.6%	61	21.9%	279	107
1991	72	26.0%	142	51.3%	63	22.7%	277	107
1992	71	26.1%	138	50.7%	63	23.2%	272	108
1993	72	26.7%	134	49.6%	64	23.7%	270	108
1994	74	27.1%	136	49.8%	63	23.1%	273	108
1995	73	26.8%	136	50.0%	63	23.2%	272	108
1996	73	27.0%	131	48.5%	66	24.4%	270	109
1997	73	26.8%	130	47.8%	69	25.4%	272	110
1998	74	27.6%	129	48.1%	65	24.3%	268	111
1999	73	27.0%	132	48.9%	65	24.1%	270	111
2000	76	28.4%	127	47.4%	65	24.3%	268	112
2001	80	30.0%	128	47.9%	59	22.1%	267	113
2002	79	29.9%	127	48.1%	58	22.0%	264	114
2003	81	30.6%	125	47.2%	59	22.3%	265	113

WHAT DO STUDENT EMPLOYEES DO?

Visit any library at a college or university, day or night, weekday or weekend, and you will most assuredly discover that student employees are working at circulation, information, reference, special collections, documents, or periodicals desks. If you look closely, you will see students assisting patrons, shelving materials, or working as security staff. Stop by the director/dean's office and you will likely be greeted by a student employee. In the nonpublic areas, you will find student assistants engaged in a wide variety of technical and clerical tasks. If you happen to come into the library in the evening or late at night, you will be hard put to find a staff member on duty except perhaps in circulation or reference areas.

Do the student assistants run this library? No, but the library would not operate efficiently without them. Student employees are a critical part of the staffing of today's academic library. Do students do only the work that staff won't do? No, student assistants now perform very technical and demanding work as well as providing for the coverage needed for long hours of access to collections and services. Student employees are depended upon to perform all manner of job duties formerly reserved for "regular" staff employees.

RESPONSIBILITIES OF STUDENT EMPLOYEES IN PUBLIC SERVICES

Student workers are most heavily depended upon in the provision of circulation-related services. The charging, discharging, and file maintenance tasks required in circulation are most often performed by student employees. The most experienced students are often given additional supervisory and training responsibilities, as well as facilities management duties during late and weekend hours. Automated circulation systems pose no problems for most computer-savvy students and they have been in use long enough that even the most senior student employees weren't working in the library when these functions were manually performed. Reshelving and stacks maintenance are accomplished almost entirely by student workers. Who hasn't worked in a library where it was decided that instead of having the shelves run East and West, it would be oh so nice if they ran North and South? Guess who is charged with moving those shelves and all of the books on them? Yes, student workers are enlisted to reconfigure entire library floors as well as to shift books within the stacks on a regular basis. Student employees are also involved in the management of periodicals and newspaper collections, and map and media collections, as well as assisting users in their use. The management of microform files and equipment and providing assistance in their use are typical student worker duties.

In Reference departments, student assistants are often employed to handle all of the stacks maintenance and the most senior student workers may be trained to provide ready reference either at information desks or with librarians and staff at the reference desk. Student employees are often called upon to assist users during the late night hours. In branch libraries and government publications units, student employees are involved in virtually all of the public and technical service activities. Most often, student workers are given responsibility for overseeing operations during late night and weekend hours. Academic libraries, especially in urban areas, without the benefit of campus security patrols in their buildings often rely on student workers to make regular rounds in the stacks and study areas. These student assistants are identified as library security staff or proctors and are charged with building security. Campus or local police are usually summoned to deal with incidents.

Student employees are often employed by libraries, or by computer centers in collaboration with libraries, to assist users in computer pods in the library. These students may be stationed at help desks or assigned to roam large computer pods to offer assistance as needed. These services have required libraries to establish whole new classification schemes for student employees in recognition of these duties.

RESPONSIBILITIES OF STUDENT EMPLOYEES IN TECHNICAL SERVICES

Technical service operations are dependent on student employees to perform many tasks. Acquisitions departments depend on students with language skills for preorder searching for monographs and serials. Automated acquisitions systems are quickly learned by students who perform many of the same functions as staff. Routine receiving activities and serials check-in are usually assigned to student workers. In addition, there are many bindery and preparation operations that are handled by student workers. Cataloging departments utilize student assistants in many of the more routine cataloging activities such as catalog maintenance for automated and manual files. Student assistants with language abilities are indispensable to cataloging departments.

Clerical tasks in all departments have become the responsibility of student employees in most libraries. The dean/director's office staff is supplemented with student hours as are library personnel, facilities, and fiscal services offices. There are very few clerical or manual tasks that cannot be assigned to student assistants. Former student employees remember, with varying degrees of fondness, their experiences in dismantling and building shelves, shelfreading, shifting books, and moving whole library collections. Student employees bring to their library jobs a wide range of talents and skills, which if properly identified and matched with jobs, can provide meaningful employment for the students, valuable contributions to the operation of the library, and lifelong friendships among students and staff. Clearly, one of the most valuable benefits of student employee supervision is getting to know students and taking vicarious pleasure in their growth, development, and future successes. Reliance on students as employees in American academic libraries can be traced back to the 1800s.

HISTORY OF STUDENT EMPLOYMENT

In a report of the Librarian's Conference in 1853, G. B. Utley noted, regarding staffing, that some university librarians had student assistants only and others didn't have any help at all.[1] During the late 1800s, universities experienced rapid growth in science and technology programs, resulting in the need for research by faculty and students. Libraries expanded their collections, services, and staff to meet the demand. Brown University Librarian Harry Lyman Koopman reported that in 1893 that the staff consisted of himself, an assistant librarian, and one student helper. By 1930, the staff had grown to 25 and the student assistants to 17.[2] (Mr. Lyman might be surprised to discover that in 2004, Brown University employed 116 student employees.)

STUDENT EMPLOYMENT IN THE 1930S

Mary Elizabeth Downey in a paper delivered at ALA Midwinter in 1932 commented on the conflicting attitudes of librarians on student employees. She said that "so far as the attitude of college librarians is concerned, our problem naturally resolves itself into two sides: on the one hand are those who do not see how the library can be run without the aid of student assistants, and who feel that a greater amount of work can be done satisfactorily with them. This type of librarian gets a real kick out of seeing a boy come to college not knowing how to use his hands and legs, to say nothing of his head, to see him develop into a well-rounded adult, and from the feeling that his work in the library is somewhat responsible for the transformation. On the other hand are college librarians who do not know how to organize and manage such help, who do not have teaching ability, and so strenuously object to being bothered with student assistants. They feel that teaching and supervising the work of students has no part in their work as librarian and that none of it should be delegated to those not having come through a library school."

Ms. Downey, in addition to providing a long list of duties that may be performed by students, also reported that suitable work for students may include "emptying waste baskets; sweeping, dusting, and mopping floors; washing woodwork, shelves and windows; and even painting woodwork and floors in unsightly quarters to make them more sanitary and attractive. Sometimes men students, who cannot do clerical things well, are suited to this very necessary work." For their work, Ms. Downey suggests a rate of 25 to 30 cents an hour for Freshmen, 30 to 35 cents for Sophomores, 35 to 40 cents for Juniors, and 40 to 45 cents for Seniors.[3]

SOME STUDENT EMPLOYEES ARE POTENTIAL LIBRARIANS

In addition to being the source of inexpensive labor and expediters of library processes and procedures, student employees were sometimes viewed as potential librarians. Wilson and Tauber in 1956 noted in *The University Library*, "Through his activities in the library the student assistant sometimes discovers his interest in librarianship as a profession, and his training can be directed by the librarian to that end."[4]

The same is true today. More than 30 percent of professional librarians were at one time student employees in libraries. Many academic libraries provide encouragement and guidance to promising student employees who are interested in pursuing librarianship as a career. Special programs are in place in some academic libraries and library schools to encourage minority students to become librarians. There is also a demand for librarians with subject specialties. An example of a program to recruit students with science backgrounds to the profession is a project called PULS (Program for University Librarians in the Sciences). In late 2003, the University of Nebraska-Lincoln, Iowa State University, and The University of Iowa libraries acquired funding from the Institute of Museum and Library Services as part of a Recruiting & Educating Librarians for the 21st Century for a program designed to recruit and train individuals with science backgrounds in order to help address a shortage of academic librarians in the sciences. Nine individuals with a background in the sciences and an interest in academic librarianship became the first participants in the program in June 2004. Three of these students were placed at The University of Iowa, three at the University of Nebraska-Lincoln, and three at Iowa State University. Each student benefited from having a half-time academic assistantship, which not only helped to fund their studies in librarianship but also gave them real-world experience in an academic library. Students outside Iowa City attend courses in classrooms with live two-way interactive video capability. The program ended in December 2005 and the nine students sought employment in academic and research libraries.

STUDENT EMPLOYMENT IN RECENT YEARS

In recognition of student capabilities, libraries in recent years have treated student employees as coworkers, almost like colleagues. Keith M. Cottam, based on his work at Brigham Young University, in 1970 suggests, "It is doubtful that any library, as a major resource for teaching and learning can reach a maximum level of service without full utilization of the capabilities, opinions, talents, and background of capable, part-time student employees as well as of its full-time staff. Librarians are in the business of education and in developing people for the future of the profession . . . [and] should apply the widest possible latitude to their utilization of student assistants if they aspire successfully to accomplish their goals."[5]

The debate continues today about the cost effectiveness and efficiency of student employees in academic libraries and what kinds of responsibilities should be assigned to them. The title of Andrew Melnyk's 1976 article, "Student Aides in Our Library (Blessings and Headaches)," reflects that attitude. Emilie C. White suggests that "At the very least, students constitute a labor reserve for the monotonous and repetitious tasks that are necessary for successful library operation. Their willingness to perform largely time-consuming, routine chores in the midst of their own intellectual accomplishments has contributed significantly to the professional posture of academic librarianship."[6]

Student employees today are not required to mop floors or paint woodwork in the library for 30 cents an hour. Today's academic libraries employ a large number of their institutions' students to augment their permanent staff positions in order to accomplish their missions.

SIZE OF THE STUDENT WORKFORCE

Students are employed on all of America's college and university campuses by departments for all types of jobs. The employers of the largest number of students on most campuses are food services and libraries.

Student workers comprise a significant portion of academic libraries' staffing. An examination of Association of Research Libraries statistics for 1996–1997[7] shows that in the 110 university member libraries there are 8,470 FTE student employees. Generally, smaller college and university libraries have a larger student to staff ratio.

In ARL university libraries, librarians comprise 27 percent of all staff. Professional, technical, and clerical staff make up 49 percent, and students account for 24 percent. The median number of students employed in ARL university libraries is 69. Using an average of 17 hours per week or .425 FTE for each student, there are an estimated 19,929 students employed by ARL university libraries.

STUDENT WORKERS AND REGULAR STAFF

The contribution of student assistants to the successful operation of college and university libraries is extremely important. Student employees have much in common with regular staff. Working closely with regular full-time and part-time staff, students perform many of the same tasks and often work without staff supervision nights and weekends. Students are expected to abide by the policies of the library and follow its

ARL LIBRARY DATA TABLES, 2004–2005
SUMMARY DATA: PERSONNEL AND PUBLIC SERVICES

(Survey Question #)	Professional Staff (FTE) (26.a)	Support Staff (FTE) (26.b)	Student Assistants (FTE) (26.c)	Total Staff (FTE) (26)	Staffed Service Points (27)	Service Hours Per Week (28)
University Libraries						
Median	80	120	54	265	21	113
High	504	583	224	1,198	100	168
Low	32	29	2	120	6	86
Totals	10,744	16,276	7,242	34,262	2,732	
Number of Libraries Responding	113	113	113	113	110	110
Nonuniversity Libraries						
Median	174	128	14	303	10	46
Totals	3,188	4,118	241	7,547	242	
Number of Libraries Responding	10	10	9	10	10	10
Grand Total	13,932	20,394	7,483	41,809	2,974	

procedures. Student assistants often participate in departmental staff meetings and have the opportunity to make suggestions for improvements.

Student workers differ from regular staff in their work schedules, job duties, benefits, funding sources, and their planned impermanence. Some universities prohibit student employees from working more than 20 hours per week, partly because of the desire to provide employment for more students and partly because it is felt that full-time students should devote their attention to academic pursuits. Their work schedules must be arranged around classes which change each semester. Students applying for work are often selected because they can work the desired hours in a department's schedule.

Job duties for students are dependent on the department's needs and on available staff but are typically of the lowest level in the department. Student workers do not earn vacation or sick leave and are not eligible for the benefits provided to staff. The funding sources for student assistants are normally College Work-Study or a separate library student employment budget. It is known beforehand, when students are hired, that they are temporary employees. Freshmen students may stay with the library throughout their undergraduate careers but more often than not, they do not stay that long.

Not all regular staff are model employees and the same is true of student employees. Nearly all of the problems associated with regular staff are also found in the student employee workforce. Just as with regular staff, not all student assistants are productive employees. They often lack the commitment expected of other staff or are simply unable to work and also keep up their grades. Student employees are not immune to any of the potential problems in the workplace. We will discuss how to deal with problems in a later chapter.

WORK-STUDY VERSUS NON WORK-STUDY STUDENT EMPLOYEES

We should also dispel, once and for all, the myth that nonwork-study students are better employees than work-study students and therefore deserve better pay. It is true that fewer upperclassmen qualify for work-study awards because of grants, loans, or scholarships that reduce their financial need. Often students begin as work-study qualified students, become invaluable to the department, and then have their work-study awards reduced or eliminated. Those students are either lost to the library or must be paid from other funds.

Many nonwork-study students are more experienced than beginning work-study students and are viewed as better employees. In some libraries, nonwork-study students are permitted to work more hours than work-study students who must stay within their award amounts. Some supervisors prefer not to be bothered with tracking work-study students' awards and definitely do not want to lose needed help near the end of the year because awards have been exhausted. The most significant difference, however, between work-study and nonwork-study student employees is the account from which they are paid.

A salary scale that provides for work-study student employees and nonwork-study student employees to be paid at different hourly rates should be avoided if at all possible. We will discuss pay rates in the chapter on organizing for student employment.

WHY DO STUDENTS WORK?

Most people work first for the money with which to pay for the necessities of life and for the pleasure money can buy, and second for the satisfaction work can provide—being with other people or gaining satisfaction from accomplishment. The college student's first priority is to gain an education and a degree that will lead to a "real" job, a career. The money earned by student workers is generally used to stay in school by providing for food, shelter, and college expenses as well as for supporting families. Until their paychecks become sufficient to cover basic living expenses, job satisfaction and collegiality in the workplace will not be the primary reason students work. That is not to say the supervisors should not strive to provide for job satisfaction, only that it should be recognized that job satisfaction is not the reason students seek employment in the library.

How many people are truly happy with their jobs? A study published in 1974 showed that nearly 90 percent of all employees were satisfied, if not happy with their work ("Job Satisfaction: Is There a Trend?" Research Monograph no. 30, Manpower Administration, U.S. Dept. of Labor, 1974, p. 4). Studies show that blue-collar workers are more dissatisfied with their work than white-collar workers, and young people were more dissatisfied than older workers. Job satisfaction tends to increase with age.

Different people gain satisfaction from different things. Factory workers place the most importance on wages. Some workers feel that comfortable working conditions, good hours, or good transportation are most important. Generally speaking, the more education a person has, the greater the need for challenging and interesting work. Satisfaction in the workplace is also a function of how many hours a person works. A student working half time or less is most concerned with money but wants to be challenged by the work. Concerns about working conditions are more important to full-time staff members than to student employees who normally work half time or less.

WORK AS A UNIQUE ACTIVITY

Work is a unique activity in that it requires a degree of conformity through rules and procedures, one has to report to a supervisor, and one's performance becomes a matter of written record. Students may be working in this type of formal situation for the first time and adjustments must be made. Recognition by supervisors of these concepts will help new student employees. In addition, incoming freshmen will most likely be experiencing a whole new sensation of freedom and lack of structure in their lives. When students arrive on campus, there is no one to tell them when to go to class, when to go to work, or when to study. The real challenge for eighteen-year-old freshmen is not the coursework. The challenge is to manage all of the hours of the day and week. They must attend classes, study and do homework, maintain a work schedule, and remember to eat and sleep, all the while resisting a myriad of temptations to do everything else. Library employment can provide an anchor for students, a place where people care about them, and a constant amid the whirlwind of other activities. Recognition of the place of work in their students' lives is part of the information supervisors must possess in order to effectively supervise student employees.

LIBRARY EXPECTATIONS

Are libraries just providing a way for students to get spending money? No, libraries require that essential work be accomplished by students and in the process libraries provide positive work experiences for many students for whom this is their first job. No, there is no time to study on the job but the supervisor is humane, remembering what it was like to be a college student. Libraries must require that student assistants perform essential work but at the same time realize why students seek employment on campus in the first place. Allowances must be made to permit students to accomplish their first objective—the degree. We will discuss the seemingly perpetual problem of student employee requests for time off or rescheduled work time in the chapter on student employee problem resolution.

Academic libraries have a right to expect that student employees will perform their assigned duties, practice good work habits, and contribute to the library's mission. Student employees are expected to maintain a schedule, come to work on time, and adhere to the library's policy on reporting absences. Expectation is a two-way street. The employees have a right to expect fair treatment in return for their contributions to the library. The rights of the employee and the employer are detailed in Chapter 5.

The student employees' primary contact with the library organization is the student employees' supervisor. Much of what student employees learn and think about the library will be as a direct result of their relationships with the student employee supervisor.

WHO SUPERVISES STUDENT EMPLOYEES?

In academic library organizations it is most efficient to assign student employee supervision responsibilities to a staff member in the department. The department head often delegates student employee supervision to a position that does not have responsibility for "regular" staff supervision. In many cases, there are two or more student employee supervisors in a single department. For example, in Acquisitions, there may be separate units for searching, receiving, gifts, and serials. Each of these units has a group of student assistants reporting to a supervisor.

Job descriptions for many staff positions include the supervision of student assistants. Attrition in these staff positions, especially at the lower levels, sets the stage for a relatively high number of new supervisors each year, many without prior supervisory experience. Assuming there are 10 student assistants reporting to each supervisor, ARL libraries employ approximately 1,915 staff members with student supervisory responsibilities.[8] Generally, student supervisors work with fewer than 10 students each.

WHAT DOES A SUPERVISOR DO?

A supervisor plays many roles. Some are well defined but some are not. Supervision is without doubt a people-oriented activity. One study found that supervisors spend two-thirds of their time relating with other people. One of the roles of supervisors is that of a connecting bridge between management and operations. The supervisor has the responsibility of communicating and interpreting library policy and procedures to student employees, making recommendations, and communicating employee concerns to management. Supervisors serve as role models to workers in interpreting and carrying out those activities that help the library achieve its goals. A study performed in industry showed that supervisors spend much more time with those they supervise (55%) than with those with the same or higher level positions in the organization.

In addition to the bridging role of supervisors, they perform all of the managerial functions: planning, organizing, staffing, leading and motivating, and controlling. Planning includes determining the goals and objectives of the unit and strategies for achieving them. It includes such activities as examining alternative uses of staff, thinking, gathering data, and evaluating procedures. Organizing involves creating a structure for accomplishing unit objectives. The supervisor identifies the tasks to be performed, groups those tasks into jobs, and establishes relationships between people and jobs. Staffing is the process of selecting, training, evaluating, and rewarding employees. By leading and motivating, the supervisor directs the work of student employees so their tasks are performed correctly and efficiently. The final managerial function of supervisors is controlling. It is the process by which actual performance is compared to planned performance. Controlling involves monitoring the work being accomplished and taking corrective action if necessary.

Managerial functions are not discrete or independent activities. The objectives set in planning are used in controlling. Organizing, staffing, and leading and motivating are continuous activities. Although most supervisors of student workers don't think about the names of these functions, all supervisors perform the whole range of managerial functions. Supervisors of student employees plan and organize the work to be done by students; hire, train, evaluate, and reward workers; and monitor the results. Because supervisors of student employees have their own job responsibilities in addition to supervision, they lead and motivate by example.

WHY IS GOOD SUPERVISION IMPORTANT?

It is assumed, because most library staff members were at one time student employees or at least college students, that student employee supervision is not difficult. It is also assumed that there could be no problems, because, after all, they are only students. You hire them, you train them, and if they don't like it, they quit. Why worry? They are students who will inevitably quit anyway because college isn't supposed to be forever.

This assumption is simply not valid today. Libraries are so dependent on the work done by student employees, it is critical that supervision is taken seriously. Through careful selection, thorough training, and skillful supervision, libraries can maximize their investment in students while giving them meaningful work experiences. The need for proper training and support by student employee supervisors also makes good sense because pay rates for students are such that they can be expected to produce.

Are student employees worth the hassle? Absolutely. Are good supervisory techniques and skills needed to make the experience worthwhile? You bet! Should students expect to develop and practice good work habits through library employment? Yes. Should libraries expect their supervisors of student employees to practice sound supervision and management principles while giving students valuable work experiences? Yes, absolutely.

THE REWARDS OF STUDENT EMPLOYEE SUPERVISION

The effort exerted in student employee supervision is not without its rewards. Library staff members, whether they supervise or not, value their associations with students over the years. Supervisors see students mature and become self-confident and take pride in student accomplishments long after their departure from the library. The student supervisory experience translates well to staff supervision, permitting staff members to advance to higher level positions. How many librarians and professional, technical, and clerical staff members do you know who were library student employees? How many of those people will tell you that the primary reason they are in their present positions is because of positive student work experiences? The student employee position in a library is often the experience that starts people on the track to library careers. Good supervision gives students the correct message—library careers are viable options.

Student employee supervision is a skill that can be acquired, providing the supervisor has the desire to learn, the ability to get along with people, and knowledge of his or her job. It is an important responsibility that can be very rewarding. A poor supervisor will most certainly be remembered but a good one will be thought of fondly for providing a meaningful work experience. If successful supervision is your goal, the information in this handbook can be adapted to your own situation.

LOOKING AHEAD

You are, or have decided that you would like to be, a student employee supervisor. Remember that while not everyone has the aptitude for supervision and that while it is true that the skills come more naturally to some people than to others, many of the skills can be learned. Supervision is a difficult yet rewarding job that can be performed well by those who are willing to work at it. If you are willing, this book is designed for you. In the course of the next twelve chapters, we will review the basic principles of supervision and relate them to student employees in libraries. Suggestions and advice are offered throughout to help you improve your knowledge and skills in supervision and to help you apply what you know to your student supervisory responsibilities.

NOTES

1. Elizabeth W. Stone, *American Library Development, 1600–1899* (New York: H.W. Wilson Company, 1977), pp. 115–116.

2. Harry Lyman Koopman, "The Student Assistant and Library Training," *Libraries* 35 (March 1930): 87.

3. Mary Elizabeth Downey, "Work of Student Assistants in College Libraries," *Library Journal* 57 (May 1, 1932): 417–420.

4. Louis Round Wilson and Maurice F. Tauber, *The University Library*, 2nd ed. (New York: Columbia University Press, 1956), p. 57.

5. Keith M. Cottam, "Student Employees in Academic Libraries," *College & Research Libraries* 31 (July 1970): 248.

6. Emilie C. White, "Student Assistants in Academic Libraries: From Reluctance to Reliance," *The Journal of Academic Librarianship* 11 (May 1985): 97.

7. Association of Research Libraries, *ARL Statistics 1996–1997* (Washington, 1998), pp. 38–45.

8. Association of Research Libraries, pp. 38–45.

BIBLIOGRAPHY

Baird, Brian J. "Motivating Student Employees: Examples from Collections Conservation." *Library Resources & Technical Services (*October 1995): 410–416.

Boyer, Ernest L. *College: The Undergraduate Experience in America.* New York: Harper and Row, 1988.

Brown, Helen M. "Conditions Contributing to the Efficient Service of Student Assistants in a Selected Group of College Libraries." *College and Research Libraries* 5 (December 1943): 44–52.

Camp, Mildred. "Student Assistants and the College Library." *Library Journal* 59 (December 1, 1934): 923–925.

Cottam, Keith M. "Student Employees in Academic Libraries." *College and Research Libraries* 31 (July 1970): 246–248.

Crawford, Gregory Alan. "Training Student Employees by Videotape." *College & Research Libraries News* (March 1988): 149–150.

Downey, Mary Elizabeth. "Work of Student Assistants in College Libraries." *Library Journal* 57 (May 1, 1932): 417–420.

Downs, Robert B. "The Role of the Academic Librarian: 1876–1976." *College and Research Libraries* 37 (November 1976): 491–502.

Evans, Charles W. "The Evolution of Paraprofessional Library Employees." *Advances in Librarianship* 9 (1979): 64–102.

Floyd, Barbara L. and Richard W. Oram. "Learning by Doing: Undergraduates as Employees in Archives." *The American Archivist* (Summer 1992): 440–452.

Fuller, F. Jay. "Evaluating Student Assistants as Library Employees." *College & Research Libraries News* (January 1990): 11–13.

Gregory, David James. "The Evolving Role of Student Employees in Academic Libraries." *Journal of Library Administration* (Winter 1995): 3–27.

Heron, Alexander R. *Why Men Work.* Stanford, CA: Stanford University Press, 1948.

Holley, Edward G. *The Land–Grant Movement and the Development of Academic Libraries.* College Station: Texas A & M University Libraries, 1977.

Kathman, Michael D. and Jane McGurn Kathman. "Integrating Student Employees into the Management Structure of Academic Libraries." *Catholic Library World* (March 1985): 328–330.

———. *Managing Student Employees in College Libraries*. Chicago, IL: Association of College and Research Libraries, 1994.

Kaufman, Diane B. and Jeanne M. Drewes. *Using Student Employees to Focus Preservation Awareness Campaigns. Promoting Preservation Awareness in Libraries*. Westport, CT: Greenwood Press, 1997.

Kendrick, Curtis L. "Cavalry to the Rescue: The Use of Temporary Employees in Place of Student Assistants." *College & Research Libraries News* (April 1989): 273–274.

Koopman, Harry Lyman. "The Student Assistant and Library Training." *Libraries* 35 (March 1930): 87–89.

Lyle, Guy R. *The Administration of the College Library*, 4th ed. New York: H.W. Wilson Company, 1974.

McHale, Cecil J. "An Experiment in Hiring Student Part-Time Assistants." *Libraries* 36 (October 1931): 379–382.

Melnyk, Andrew. "Student Aides in our Library (Blessings and Headaches)." *Illinois Libraries* 58 (February 1976): 141–144.

Metz, T. John. *Student Employees Enhance Internet Expertise for a Liberal Arts College Library: The Internet Initiative*. Chicago, IL: American Library Association, 1995.

Riley, Cheryl and Barbara Wales. "Introducing the Academic Library to Student Employees: A Group Approach." *Technical Services Quarterly* (Winter 1997): 47–59.

Rosen, C. Martin, Mary G. Wrighten, Beverly Stearns, and R. Susan Goldstein. "Student Employees and the Academic Library's Multicultural Mission." *The Reference Librarian* (1994): 45–55.

Shores, Louis. *Origins of the American College Library, 1638–1800*. New York: Barnes & Noble, 1935.

Shores, Louis. "Staff Spirit among Student Assistants." *Libraries* 34 (July 1929): 346–348.

Smith, Jessie J. "Training of Student Assistants in Small College Libraries." *Library Journal* 34 (April 1, 1930): 306–309.

Stone, Elizabeth W. *American Library Development, 1600–1899*. New York: H.W. Wilson Company, 1977.

Student Assistants in ARL Libraries, SPEC Kit 91. Washington, DC: Association of Research Libraries, 1983.

White, Emilie C. "Student Assistants in Academic Libraries: From Reluctance to Reliance," *Journal of Academic Librarianship* 11(2) (May 1985): 93–97.

Wilson, Louis Round and Maurice F. Tauber. *The University Library*, 2nd ed. New York: Columbia University Press, 1956.

Worthy, John "A Graduate Assistant at the University of Florida." *Library Association Record* 67 (November 1965): 395–396.

Wright, Alice E. *Library Clerical Workers and Pages Including Student Assistants*. Hamden, CT: Linnet Books, 1973.

2

Supervisors of Student Employees

In any moment of decision the best thing you can do is the right thing, the next best thing is the wrong thing, and the worst thing you can do is nothing.
—Theodore Roosevelt (1858–1919)

THE ROLE OF STUDENT EMPLOYEE SUPERVISOR

The student employee supervisor in an academic library occupies a unique and important position. The supervisor of student employees' job description likely includes the line, "supervises student employees." In fact, the supervisor of student employees has responsibility for hiring, training, scheduling, assigning duties, disciplining, evaluating, counseling, and above all, assuring that student workers contribute to the accomplishment of the unit or department's objectives and the objectives of the library.

The supervisors of student workers have much in common with supervisors in industry. The same basic principles of supervision may be applied to the academic library situation. While it has much in common, the supervision of student employees is different in very important ways. The type of employees supervised is quite different from industry. Nearly all of the student employees are postsecondary students who typically work half time or less; seldom work all year; are not considered regular or permanent employees; and who usually aspire to a career different from the work they are asked to do in the library. Recognizing that there are differences between student employees and those employees in business and industry, let's examine the student employee supervisor's role.

DEFINITION OF SUPERVISOR

By definition, "anyone at the first level of management who has the responsibility for getting the 'hands-on-the-work' employees to carry out the plans and policies of higher level management is a supervisor." The Taft-Hartley Act of 1947 defines a supervisor as " . . . any individual having authority, in the interest of the employer, to hire, transfer, suspend, lay off, recall, promote, discharge, assign, reward, or discipline other employees, or responsibility to direct them, or to adjust their grievances, or effectively to recommend such action, if in connection with the foregoing the exercise of such authority is not of a merely routine or clerical nature, but requires the use of independent judgment."

The word supervisor derives from a Latin term which means "look over." Early on, the supervisor was the person in charge of a group of workers and was a foreman or "fore man" at the lead of a group, setting the pace for the rest. Today's supervisor is a leader, one who watches over the work, and a person with technical/professional skills.

GETTING THINGS DONE THROUGH OTHERS

The most common definition of management is "getting things done through other people." Unfortunately, the emphasis is placed on "through other people." The primary task of any employee is "getting things done." As a staff member, getting things done is the most important part of the job. Because it is clear that there is more work than one person can accomplish, it is necessary to utilize additional employees to do the work. Therefore, as a student employee supervisor, you must not only accomplish your own work but you must get things done through student workers.

Doing a job and getting someone else to do it are entirely different. Simply telling someone to do something right very seldom works. The employee must be motivated to do it right as well as having the prerequisite knowledge and skills. If the work is not done right, it is the supervisor's responsibility to teach and apply supervisory techniques that will allow the student worker to do things right.

Every student employee has different needs, skills, attitudes, and motivations. The student employee supervisor needs to deal with each employee differently while dealing with all employees fairly. There is no universal technique that will work with every student employee. What works today with one student may have no effect tomorrow and what works on one may have a completely negative effect on another student worker. The purpose of this handbook is to provide a foundation of supervisory principles and suggestions on how to get student workers to help you accomplish work.

WHO ARE THE STUDENT EMPLOYEE SUPERVISORS?

In most organizations, supervisors rise from the ranks and are usually employees with seniority who have worked at different jobs in the organization. These supervisors normally have more education than those they supervise.

The student employee supervisor either advances within the library to a position with student employee supervisory responsibilities or is hired into a position that has student supervision as a part of the job. It is not true in libraries that the most experienced employees become student employee supervisors. The most experienced staff become supervisors of other regular staff, not student employees. Student supervision is a valuable training ground for staff supervisors.

As a rule, most student employee supervisors are not senior members of a unit or department. Typically, the student employee supervisors report to senior staff in the department or to the unit or department head, usually a librarian. In libraries with clerical, technical, and professional staff classifications, student employee supervisors will be found in all classifications, with the majority at the technical level. Some student supervision is provided by librarians and occasionally senior student employees.

IDENTIFYING PROSPECTIVE STUDENT EMPLOYEE SUPERVISORS

Student employee supervisors may be chosen on the basis of seniority, proficiency, favoritism, demonstrated leadership, experience, or educational background. It is not unusual, and is often desirable, to select someone on the staff for a supervisory position. Making the transition to a student employee supervisory position requires a great deal of effort on the part of the employee as well as psychological, social, and educational support from management.

Persons who will become good supervisors of student employees can be identified quite easily from among existing staff. Those individuals must be very skilled at their jobs, have good communication skills, get along well with coworkers and management, and have a positive attitude. All of the attributes of a good staff member are needed to become a good supervisor. Above all, prospective supervisors must like their work, students, and themselves.

THE BEST WORKER MAY NOT BE THE BEST SUPERVISOR

The best worker, however, is not necessarily the best student employee supervisor. The skills required of an effective student employee supervisor are different from those required of a skilled worker. Selecting the best worker to be a student employee supervisor is a common and dangerous practice. Because of the money, prestige, or status, good workers often accept supervisory positions without realizing that the skills required of a good worker are not the same as those required of good supervisors. Because they do not have or develop the necessary supervisory skills, they perform poorly. If they don't enjoy the work, some quit, and others may receive poor evaluations, possibly leading to termination. Others may stay in student employee supervisory positions they dislike because they do not want to lose face.

People should aspire to or agree to assume supervisory positions because they want the challenge and satisfaction to be gained. If these are not your reasons for seeking student employee supervisory responsibility, no amount of pay, prestige, or status will compensate for the stress and other problems associated with work you dislike.

In selecting an applicant for a student employee supervisory position, you must look for someone who has good communication skills, likes people, has the aptitude for the work, and has energy and enthusiasm.

PERSONAL QUALITIES OF GOOD STUDENT EMPLOYEE SUPERVISORS

What are the personal qualities of good student employee supervisors?

1. Energy and good health. Supervision is a demanding activity and requires that individuals not only be able to handle a variety of activities but be physically and emotionally up to the task.
2. Leadership potential. Student employee supervisory responsibilities require the ability to get people to work for and with you to accomplish the objectives of your unit.

3. Ability to get along with people. One of the most important qualities management looks for in a student employee supervisor is the ability to get along with others. Getting others to carry out their responsibilities depends greatly on their feelings toward their supervisor.

4. Job know-how and technical competence. The supervisor must know the job in order to be effective in training and problem solving. Student employee supervisors usually have their own job duties and responsibilities in addition to supervision and must be proficient in those duties.

5. Initiative. The student employee supervisor needs to be able to recognize when adjustments must be made in the work flow or changes made in order to improve procedures. Initiative is required in order to be aware when potential problems loom and when problems occur.

6. Dedication and dependability. Workers who sense that their supervisor is not dedicated to the job/employer, will display the same attitude. The example set by the supervisor will be followed by the employees. For example, a supervisor who is regularly absent will find employees will also be absent often.

7. Positive attitude toward management. Workers will mirror the feelings of the student employee supervisor.

These characteristics are desirable in any employee but are most important in student employee supervisors. If your supervisors don't exhibit all of these positive attributes, training and staff development can be provided to enhance all of these characteristics.

DIFFERENCES BETWEEN SUPERVISORS AND LEADERS

Supervisors are also leaders. The following are examples of supervisor and leader characteristics. Do you lean toward one or the other or both?

- Supervisors tend to stress organization, coordination, and control of resources (e.g., plant, equipment, and people).
- Leaders tend to stress relationships with others, values and commitment—the emotional and spiritual aspects of the organization.
- Supervisors tend to focus on achieving short-term objectives and goals.
- Leaders tend to create and articulate a vision of what the organization could achieve in the long run.
- Supervisors tend to concentrate on maximizing results from existing functions and systems.
- Leaders tend to move the organization in new directions by being unsatisfied with maintaining the status quo.
- Supervisors tend to communicate directives, policies and procedures.
- Leaders tend to communicate the purpose of doing things.
- Supervisors tend to fear uncertainty and act cautiously.
- Leaders tend to favor taking risks and making changes.
- Supervisors tend to enforce fulfillment of agreements and contracts for work.
- Leaders tend to generate a feeling of meaning in work, including its value and importance.

TYPES OF PERSONS WHO SHOULD NOT BE SUPERVISORS

There are definitely types of persons to avoid when filling student employee supervisor positions. If selecting a person from your staff, avoid:

- the negative employee—The attitude of a negative employee will be contagious among student employees.
- the rigid employee—The rigid employee will be unable to effectively deal with student employees.
- the unproductive employee—The unproductive supervisory employee will find it difficult to get others to work hard if he/she does not.
- the disgruntled employee—The employee who is unhappy with the work, the supervisor, the organization, or life in general, will not be able to effectively deal with student employees who may mirror those feelings.

STUDENT EMPLOYEE SUPERVISOR ATTITUDES

Attitude is extremely important to good supervision. Student employee supervisors have the proper attitude if they agree with the following statements:

- Supervisors must manage with a high degree of integrity and lead by example.
- Supervisors must keep their word to employees.
- Supervisors must earn the respect, trust, and confidence of employees.
- Supervisors must strive to help employees develop to their full potential.
- Supervisors must give credit to employees who do a good job.
- Supervisors must accept higher level management decisions and directives and support them to employees.
- Supervisors must not discuss personal feelings about management with employees but should discuss disagreements privately with management.
- Supervisors must be responsible for the performance of their employees.
- Supervisors must be objective in judging the actions of employees.
- Supervisors must decide matters involving employees on the bases of facts and circumstances, not on personal sympathies.
- Supervisors must accept the responsibility for rehabilitating rather than punishing employees whenever possible.
- Supervisors must be prepared to support employees in cases where employees are in the right.
- Supervisors should attempt to allow employees to have as much control over their own work as possible.
- Supervisors must work to maintain a climate in the workplace that allows employees to express their feelings and concerns openly without fear of reprisal.

(Adapted from *The Effective Supervisor's Handbook*)

MOVING FROM A STAFF TO A SUPERVISORY POSITION

The transition from worker to supervisor is a difficult move for any staff member. The new student employee supervisor must realize that "doing" and "supervising" require entirely different skills. The supervisor has, in effect, a contractual arrangement with student workers. You, as the student employee supervisor, have a right to expect certain things from them and they have the right to expect certain things in return. You represent management and represent your student employees to management. It is a delicate balance that must be achieved if supervision is to be successful. Without question, supervision is one of the most difficult responsibilities any employee can assume.

DIFFERENCES BETWEEN WORKER AND SUPERVISOR

Because most new supervisors of student employees are selected from among present staff members in the department, it is important to remember that the move represents a significant change for everyone involved. Five major differences between being a subordinate and being a supervisor are:

1. Managing others' time—Supervisors must set time schedules for others to meet, as well as managing their own time.
2. Satisfaction becomes more abstract—A supervisor's satisfaction is often indirect. It comes from taking pride in helping others succeed, rather than from completing the job alone.
3. Shift in job evaluation—Performance is judged not just by one's boss, but by one's subordinates as well—top down and bottom up.
4. Long-term problems—A supervisor must deal with problems that may persist for weeks, months, or even years.
5. Key resources are people—Because a supervisor must get things done through others, people are a very important resource. Learning the capabilities of each person helps a supervisor make good use of this resource.

TRANSITION FROM WORKER TO SUPERVISOR

The step from employee to supervisor is a large and important one for both the individual and the organization. Much time and thought goes into selecting the right person for the job. The same careful attention is seldom given to helping this person develop into a productive member of management. All too often, new supervisors are left to "sink or swim" in their new positions. There are many changes which accompany a promotion from subordinate to supervisor.

- Perspective—Most employees are concerned primarily with doing a good job and planning how to get ahead. Supervisors, however, must keep the big picture in mind, considering the impact of decisions on the department and the library.
- Goals—A supervisor's primary concern is with meeting the organization's goals. This contrasts with the employee's focus on meeting personal goals, such as becoming more skilled at their jobs.
- Responsibilities—A supervisor must supervise and speak for a group of people in addition to completing technical and administrative tasks. A supervisor must also accept responsibility for decisions instead of criticizing others.
- Satisfaction—Because a supervisor does less of the actual work, satisfaction comes from watching other succeed rather than from the work itself.
- Job skills—Becoming technically competent is important but supervisors must also become proficient at communicating, delegating, planning, managing time, directing, motivating, and training others. Many of these are new skills which must be developed.
- Relationships—If one is promoted to a supervisory position, new relationships with former peers, other supervisors, and the new boss must be developed. People quickly change how

they act toward the new supervisor, whether or not the supervisor changes behavior toward them.

SEVEN TRANSITION STAGES

The new supervisor does not make an overnight transformation from thinking and behaving like a subordinate to thinking and behaving like a boss. Instead, the supervisor passes through several predictable stages. While people seldom move neatly from one stage to the next, they generally experience all seven stages.

1. First stage: Immobilization—The person feels overwhelmed by the changes. This may be typified by: "This job is a lot bigger than I thought. Everyone is making demands. How can I possibly do everything?"
2. Second stage: Denial of change—This phase allows the individual involved time to regroup and fully comprehend the change. "This job is not so different from your other job." "Let's see, first I'll take care of this and then I'll begin to work on that."
3. Third stage: Depression—Awareness sets in regarding the magnitude of the changes that must be made in one's habits, customs, relationships, etc. "Why did I ever leave my other job? I wish I could afford to quit. I hate my job!"
4. Fourth stage: Acceptance of reality—Feelings of optimism return and the person is ready to let go of the past. "Maybe this isn't so bad. Forget about that old job. I'm doing fine."
5. Fifth stage: Testing—This is a time of trying out new behaviors and ways of coping with the new situation. "If I meet with staff every Thursday and try this schedule, I think I can manage."
6. Sixth stage: Search for meanings—The person's concern shifts to trying to understand both how and why things are different now. "Now I feel comfortable in this job. It is different but not really that bad."
7. Seventh stage: Internalization—In this final stage, the person incorporates the new meanings into behavior. "I like my job and I'm good at what I do."

PROBLEMS FACED BY NEW STUDENT EMPLOYEE SUPERVISORS

One of the biggest problems facing new student employee supervisors is their lack of preparation for the job. An employee is often selected for promotion to a management position because of performance as a specialist. Those skills and abilities are often quite different than those needed by a supervisor. As a result, the new supervisor must develop new skills.

Organizations normally expect new supervisors to step into the job and function right away. This expectation exists even though statistics show that most organizations offer little help or support to them. Often, formal supervisory training is not provided to the new supervisor until after six to twelve months on the job. The "sink or swim" philosophy is prevalent.

Finally, the new student employee supervisor often lacks an immediate peer group. Former peers no longer regard the new supervisor as one of them. Other supervisors are hesitant to consider this person a part of their group until the new supervisor has demonstrated the ability to think and act like management. This leaves the new supervisor belonging to neither group at a time when support from others is badly needed.

The new supervisor of student employees must be willing to learn, change, adapt, and ask for help when needed. A person must have realistic expectations about what supervision is like. These newcomers can expect expertise from a previous job to be helpful in some, but not all, situations. They can expect to make mistakes, as this is an unavoidable part of learning a new job. It takes a lot of hard work to gain the loyalty and support of other people and new supervisors must recognize that. The new supervisor must realize that new behaviors are needed and that the change takes time. Practicing supervisors must also recognize that it takes time for the new supervisor to become effective and that they need help and support. The process of becoming a good supervisor is an ongoing process, and one never stops learning.

EXPECTATIONS FOR STUDENT EMPLOYEE SUPERVISORS

Supervising people is undoubtedly the most difficult and complex activity of managers. Student employee supervisors are the direct link between the managerial structure and the operational structure of an organization. To employees, the supervisor represents "the organization." Workers' feelings about the organization, management, and their jobs are directly affected by their relationship with their immediate supervisors. Management's assessment of a unit's effectiveness is based on the productivity of the employees reporting to supervisors. Student employee supervisors are in a unique position because their ability to accomplish work through others has a direct impact on the organization's accomplishing its mission.

Many people in technical and staff positions fail to recognize or appreciate the demands placed on student employee supervisors. Medical research has shown that supervisory positions carry with them tremendous stress. While it is true that some people work better under stress and channeling stress into productive activity can be satisfying, stress can also contribute to heart attacks, ulcers, and medical depression. To be able to successfully supervise other employees requires considerable training and skill development.

In the past, the role of supervisor was far less complex. Part of the reason is that supervisors of the past had far more authority. The controls and penalties imposed on employees for not following a supervisor's directives were much more severe. Today's student employee supervisor may still get cooperation through the use of indirect force but the supervisor is often frustrated by policies, rules, and regulations imposed by management. In some organizations, even though the supervisor has the power to discipline student employees, it is not unusual for decisions to be overruled by management, further frustrating supervisors.

Because student employee supervisors are the link between workers and management, they are sometimes called upon to represent both the employees' interests and those of management. If they were to represent only employee's views, they would find themselves at odds with management. If they represented only management, they would diminish their effectiveness in getting employee cooperation. Successful student employee supervisors must continually work to meet both organizational and individual needs. Is it any wonder that today's student employee supervisors feel confused, frustrated, and torn between two groups?

Libraries expect that student employee supervisors will recruit, hire, and train student employees in addition to performing other duties requiring technical expertise. Many supervisors are given the responsibility without training. The practice of hiring a new student employee supervisor to begin work after the incumbent has left further exacerbates the problem. Whether new to the library or taking on new responsibilities, the new student employee supervisor has to recognize that the development of supervisory skills takes time and effort.

COMMON MISTAKES NEW SUPERVISORS MAKE

We have all seen the mistakes supervisors can make. We've made them ourselves. Some of the most common are:

- Overcontrolling—The new supervisor, or experienced supervisor for that matter, may believe that it is necessary to show everyone who's boss.
- Undercontrolling—One who refuses to make decisions in an attempt to make everyone happy is headed for trouble.
- One-way communication—The supervisor may be guilty of just giving orders without listening or just listening and providing no leadership.
- Half-way delegation—Some supervisors are good at delegating responsibility without the authority to act. This too, leads to problems for all concerned.

These are only some of the mistakes that can be made by new supervisors (and by some experienced ones too). Mistakes will be made, but it is part of the responsibility of practicing supervisors to help new supervisors develop an effective management style.

WHAT EMPLOYEES DON'T LIKE ABOUT THEIR SUPERVISORS

One way to learn how to be a good supervisor is to think about all of the supervisors you have had and what it was about them that you would have changed if you could. By considering the traits, actions, and skills of supervisors you have known, you know what to avoid in your own supervisory style. The following are some of the things employees don't like about their supervisors:

Supervisor Traits

- Too sensitive—Employees don't like to tiptoe around their supervisors for fear of upsetting the boss or saying the wrong thing if the supervisor is in a bad mood or takes everything personally.
- Indecisive—Indecisive supervisors can survive in an organization but they will not win the support of employees.
- Opinionated—Supervisors who will not listen to any kind of reasoning but always have their minds made up will find that employees will soon stop making suggestions.
- Autocratic—Supervisors must understand that if they do not allow their employees to participate in decisions, a lot of good talent is wasted.
- Vulgar language—Crude language impresses no one and is to be avoided at all costs.
- Unstable personality—Employees shouldn't have to guess that supervisor came to work that day. Unpredictable changes in the supervisor's personality cause problems.
- Dishonest—Supervisors need to recognize the importance of honesty in the workplace and make it easy for employees to be honest.

Supervisor Actions

- Shows favoritism—Even if other employees are treated fairly, they resent it if another employee is given favorable treatment. Problems like this may lead to discrimination charges, even though in most cases prejudice is not involved.
- Does not listen—Good supervisors are anxious to hear what employees think about the job and try to get employees to talk. Nothing is more frustrating that to talk to a supervisor who does not listen.
- Can't accept bad news—Supervisors must be willing to listen to bad news and not punish the bearer. It won't take long for employees to realize that the supervisor wants to hear only good news and that the problems that need attention will be ignored.
- Ridicules employees—A supervisor who ridicules or makes sarcastic remarks to employees may not even realize it. Ridiculing an employee in front of peers is unforgivable. Supervisors must be aware of how their words affect employees. Supervisors must be tactful.
- Makes uninformed decisions—Employees respect supervisors who make decisions based on information.
- Does not trust employees—The supervisor must trust employees and the employees must be able to trust their supervisor.
- Makes impossible promises—Employees know when the supervisor makes promises that can not be kept. The supervisor's credibility is destroyed if this happens often.
- Breaks reasonable promises—Employees also know when the supervisor's promises can be kept and are not. Supervisors must keep to their word or be able to explain why a promise is not kept.

Supervisor Skills

- Poor time management—A supervisor with poor time management skills will waste their employees' time as well as their own.
- Disorganized—Employees want a supervisor who is organized and can get things done.
- Failure to exert authority—Employees respect supervisors who know how to use their authority. Employees want and need a leader.
- Poor planning—The supervisor who fails to plan anything in advance wastes employees' time. Poorly planned meetings for example are terrible time wasters.
- Poor communicator—Supervisors must develop good communication skills.

WHY STUDENT EMPLOYEE SUPERVISORS FAIL

Supervisory styles cover the full spectrum, from the laissez-faire supervisor to the authoritarian. The supervisor who lacks self-confidence or feels uncomfortable in the supervisory role tends to let the unit run itself. The dictatorial or authoritarian supervisor tends to oversupervise. Few good supervisors are found at either extreme but are most often found in the middle of the spectrum.

When a student employee supervisor doesn't succeed you must look at the specific situation to determine the exact reasons. It is possible that the failure can be traced to lack of support from the boss or lack of training or encouragement. Most failures, however, can be attributed to one of the following six supervisory pitfalls:

1. Poor personal relations with student employees, management, or other supervisors.
2. Lack of initiative or emotional stability on the part of the supervisor.

3. Unwillingness or inability to understand the management point of view.
4. Failure to spend the necessary effort or time to improve skills.
5. Lack of skill in planning and organizing the work of student employees.
6. Unwillingness or inability to adjust to changing conditions.

MOVING FROM CONTROL TO PARTNERSHIP

- Control: The supervisor is viewed as the boss who gives orders that others must follow.
- Partnership: The supervisor is seen as a facilitator of group efforts and ultimately responsible for the results of the group.
- Control: One-way, top-down communication is the norm.
- Partnership: Communication is a two-way process based on honesty.
- Control: The supervisor stands apart so as to not befriend the employees.
- Partnership: The supervisor relates to all members of the department as equals.
- Control: Information is kept close to the vest and not shared equally.
- Partnership: Information is shared equally so everyone knows the score.
- Control: The supervisor has to motivate employees to maximize performance and use discipline to get the job done.
- Partnership: The supervisor provides an environment for motivated employees in which all employees excel.

PREPARING TO BECOME A STUDENT EMPLOYEE SUPERVISOR

Many employees begin their careers in libraries in public service or technical service positions without supervisory responsibilities. The aspiring student employee supervisor would do well to begin with the first function of management: planning.

- Develop a career plan based on a realistic appraisal of your interests, aptitudes, and abilities.
- If you are in a library with a career development program, take advantage of it.
- Talk to student employee supervisors to learn more about what they do.
- Talk to your supervisor to learn about opportunities for supervisory responsibilities.
- Participate in supervisory and management training courses offered by the university.
- Complete your college education. Most supervisory positions require a bachelor's degree. Being a student will help you relate to those you will be supervising.
- Remember that advancement depends on successful performance. Although successful performance of your job will not guarantee advancement and will not guarantee that you will be a successful supervisor, good supervisors advance from the ranks of good workers, not bad ones.

THE STUDENT EMPLOYEE SUPERVISOR

The importance of the role of the student employee supervisor is underestimated in many libraries for a number of reasons. Librarians often do not receive the level of training in management in library school that is required to manage large organizations and usually develop their skills through postgraduate workshops or through on-the-job experience. Many supervisors have no formal training whatsoever. It is therefore not expected of the staff members who supervise student employees. Usually, student employees are on the bottom rung of the library staffing ladder.

By understanding the importance of student employee supervision and developing supervisory skills, the student employee supervisor can make a valuable contribution to the operation of the library and help students gain lifelong job skills. Yours is a critical role in the organization.

BIBLIOGRAPHY

Baldwin, David A. *Supervising Student Employees in Academic Libraries.* Englewood, CO: Libraries Unlimited, 1991.

Baldwin, David A., Frances C. Wilkinson, and Daniel C. Barkley. *Effective Management of Student Employment: Organizing for Student Employment in Academic Libraries.* Englewood, CO: Libraries Unlimited, 2000.

Belker, Loren B. and Gary S. Topchik. *The First-Time Manager.* New York: AMACOM, 2005.

Davis, Alberta, Emily Okada, and Rebecca Stinnett. "Managing Student Employees." *Indiana Libraries* 24(1) (2005): 47–51.

Dealy, M. David and Andrew R. Thomas. *Defining the Really Great Boss.* Westport, CT: Praeger, 2004.

Fournies, Ferdinand F. *Why Employees Don't Do What They're Supposed to Do and What to Do about It.* New York: McGraw-Hill, 1999.

Fox, Jeffrey J. *How to Become a Great Boss: The Rules for Getting and Keeping the Best Employees.* New York: Hyperion, 2002.

Giesecke, Joan and Beth McNeil. *Fundamentals of Library Supervision.* Chicago, IL: American Library Association, 2005

Harvard Business Essentials: Manager's Toolkit: The 13 Skills Managers Need to Succeed. Boston, MA: Harvard Business School Press, 2004.

Kathman, Jane McGurn and Michael D. Kathman. "What Difference Does Diversity Make in Managing Student Employees?" *College & Research Libraries* 59(4) (July 1998): 378–389.

Morgan, Steve. "Change in University Libraries: Don't Forget the People." *Library Management* 22(1/2) (2001): 58–60.

Suzaki, Kiyoshi. *Results from the Hear: How Mini-Company Management Captures Everyone's Talents and Helps Them Find Meaning and Purpose at Work.* New York: Free Press, 2002.

Trotta, Marcia. *Supervising Staff: A How-To-Do-It Manual for Librarians.* New York: Neal-Schuman Publishers, 2006.

Wiener, Jan Richard Mizen, and Jenny Duckham, eds. *Supervising and Being Supervised: A Practice in Search of a Theory.* New York: Palgrave Macmillan, 2003.

3

Job Descriptions for Student Employees in Today's Libraries

When your writing is filled with detail, it has a lot more impact

—Ivan Levison

ORGANIZING FUNCTION OF MANAGEMENT

The organizing function of library management involves the creation of a structure and system that provides stability and continuity for the student assistant supervisors as well as the student assistants hired. This system requires tasks that can be identified and grouped into jobs. In turn, these jobs should be designed in such a manner that they are fluid, dynamic, and flexible to accommodate internal and external pressures and changes (e.g., internal reorganization, technology). The primary goal is to define jobs that will meet the objectives of the unit or department, which in turn meet the objectives of the library. In the academic library, each unit or department supervisor must know what has to be accomplished and have a well-developed plan for getting the work done. This plan must include job descriptions and a system by which new student employees are matched to jobs.

Additionally, in today's digital environment user demands sometimes far exceed the capacity that full-time employees can fulfill. In the past student assistants were hired for a variety of mundane duties that did not require a professional degree or a number of years of experience (e.g., shelving, transmittal replacement, etc.). Today, however, student assistants bring more skills to their jobs including enhanced knowledge of computer hardware and software programs, communication skills among their peers, and other intangibles that are sometimes difficult to measure or think of including in a general job description. Therefore, hiring student assistants has become more critical because the jobs they fill will have an immediate and direct impact on technical and public service units or department as well as the library community served.

Student assistants may be the first face seen by those using the library; particularly those whose visit may be the first. Given that a public service unit is generally the first "face" a user interacts with, having well-trained student assistants is critically important in today's environment.

Finally, training student assistants should transcend simply filling a need or position. As educators, the responsibility lies in providing a well-rounded academic experience, including the work experience. Further, there should be a tenet that lies in enhancing the student assistant's library experience by providing each with fundamental library experiences and philosophies as adopted by the full-time library staff. A well-trained student assistant today may become a future library patron, donor, and as importantly, librarian.

ORGANIZING A SYSTEM FOR STUDENT EMPLOYEE POSITIONS

The recruitment, screening, and hiring of student employees for the library is described in more detail in Chapter 7. Before any of these activities can occur it is crucial that a solid foundation for student employment exist. On the basis of that foundation, the supervisor must be able to respond positively to the questions arising from those supervising as well as those being supervised. Some of the questions that may generally arise as student assistant job descriptions are being developed might include:

1. What tasks will student employees perform in each area of employment?
2. Are the specific duties of each position clearly documented in the form of approved job descriptions?
3. Is every task expected to be performed by each student employee included in the job description? Have you made a decision to whether or not to include the statement, "Other Duties as Assigned"?
4. Does each job description contain sufficient information to accurately describe the job? Is each job description concise, accurate, and complete? Are the terminologies used consistently and equally applied among each job description?
5. Can the tasks in every job description be evaluated?
6. Have you documented the required and desired experience and qualifications for each position?

JOB DESIGN

Every job must be specifically created and named before any student employee is selected for employment. Creating jobs is an organizational task called job design. The job design is a process by which tasks to be performed are identified, methods for performing the work are delineated, and the relationships of these tasks to other jobs are described.

In determining the work to be accomplished, the job designer groups together a manageable number of similar tasks. In designing a job, it is important to keep the student employees in mind. The following characteristics are important to student employees:

1. Jobs should provide for a variety of activities.
2. Completion of tasks should produce identifiable final results.

3. Jobs should be seen as significant to other workers. Other workers include full-time staff as well as other students employed in that department or area.
4. Student employees like to have freedom in determining their schedule and process for performing and completing their job assignments. It's important to understand that many student employees are working around their class schedules. Providing them flexibility with their work schedules will likely increase productivity.
5. Student assistants would like feedback on how well the assigned tasks have been performed and completed.

JOB ANALYSIS

Because student employees' jobs change with more frequency, it is vitally important to conduct continuing job analysis, which is the process of gathering and reviewing information about existing jobs and job descriptions. Such data can be gathered by observing the worker on the job, interviewing the worker, or having the worker keep a log of tasks performed over a period of time. The job analysis process is designed to answer the following questions about each job to be performed:

1. What are the major duties and responsibilities? Are the duties and responsibilities still commensurate with the actual job performed?
2. What tools and procedures are used? Do the tools and procedures require updating?
3. What knowledge, skills, and abilities are required? Are these still the requirements or do they need to be updated?
4. What are the physical requirements of the job?
5. What are the environmental conditions of the job?

The data gathered from job design and job analysis should used to prepare or revise job descriptions. The frequency of updating the job design and analysis are determined by a number of internal and external factors; many of which are exclusive to a particular institution. The aforementioned requirements are likely to change more often due to technology, full-time staff turnover (e.g., retirements), and other factors that each institutions undergoes.

PURPOSE OF JOB DESCRIPTIONS

A job description is a statement of the duties to be performed by the student employee(s) performing the described job. The purpose of a job description is two-fold:

1. For the student employee or prospective student employee, the job description details the exact duties and responsibilities of the position, as well as providing a written statement the evaluation process being utilized by the student employee's supervisor.
2. For the supervisor, the job description provides exact requirements and desired qualifications used in screening, interviewing, and hiring students for library positions and a method of evaluating the work performed.

The job description serves as the foundation for all organizing activities. It provides information on what the personnel in a given unit or department should be performing and assists supervisors in organizing student employees on the basis of experience and expertise. Job descriptions permit the library to establish career ladders for student employees and to establish a system for differentiated pay.

FEATURES OF A GOOD JOB DESCRIPTION

A job description is a list of activities for which the student employee is responsible. The following are some features of a good job description:

1. The job description contains factual statements about the job.
2. The job description is brief but concise.
3. The job description is easy to read and jargon-free.
4. The job description explains the environment in which the work is performed.
5. The job description lists the requirements for the position.
6. The job description explains the supervision to be received and given.
7. The job description contains the criteria for evaluation.

USES OF THE JOB DESCRIPTION

The job description must be useful to both the student employee and the supervisor. Information contained in the job description may be used in the following ways:

1. The job description should stimulate discussion between the supervisor and the student employee concerning the requirements and necessity of each job.
2. The job description should be used as part of a campus student employment recruitment program or job fair.
3. The job description should help the supervisor screen and hire the most skilled and experienced student employees.
4. The job description should help the new student employee become familiar with the nature and scope of the job quickly and easily.
5. The job description should be used as part of an orientation program.
6. The job description should serve as the basis for establishing performance standards.
7. The job description should serve as the basis for evaluating and comparing positions within a unit, department, or library.
8. The job description should serve as a communication device between supervisor and employee for the discussion of job expectations and objectives.

GUIDELINES FOR PREPARING JOB DESCRIPTIONS

Most of the following suggestions for preparing good job descriptions emphasize brevity and clarity:

1. The sentence structure for job duties and responsibilities should be verb, object, and explanatory phrase. The implied subject is always the incumbent occupying the job. For example, "respond to audio taping requests in a timely manner."
2. The present tense is to be used throughout.
3. Avoid using terminology that might be subject to varying interpretations, e.g., some, great, occasionally.

4. Avoid proprietary names, e.g., Word, Excel, Access. These references are subject to change and inclusion in the job description will necessitate change.
5. Avoid gender-specific terminology. Construct sentences in such a way that gender pronouns are not required.
6. Job descriptions should be kept to no more than two pages; one is preferred.
7. Describe the position as it is now and not as it will exist sometime in the future. (Not all anticipated changes take place.)

JOB DESCRIPTIONS FOR THE LIBRARY

Job descriptions can be very useful organizational tools for the student employee supervisors if they are carefully written and properly used. If you do not have them, you should. If you are writing or reviewing your student employee job descriptions, make certain the descriptions accurately reflect the jobs. If you have pay rates that differ per job, or that have different rates with a particular job (e.g., Grade 3, Step 2), make certain you can justify the pay differential. For example, you might wish to start a new student employee in a job at a lower grade and step that would reflect a lower hourly rate. However, a student employee who has some experience applicable to the job description might start at a higher grade and step, thus requiring a higher pay rate.

Job descriptions should be revised and updated every year. As well, job descriptions should be reviewed by the student employee supervisor periodically to ensure job duties reflect the continued need for that task to be performed. Remember, that job descriptions have no value if they cannot be understood or are too general. Inadequate descriptions can lead to serious complaints about inequitable compensation or poor managerial decisions.

STUDENT EMPLOYEE JOB DESCRIPTIONS

Recognizing that libraries require that student employees perform a wide variety of tasks of differing levels of complexity, it is necessary to differentiate between different jobs in terms of the knowledge, skills, abilities, and experience required—the substantive differences between jobs. Check with your campus student employment office to see if such a system already exists. If so, it can either be used as is or modified to fit the library's needs, generally with the approval of the campus office. If not, you should develop a classification system for library student positions. A system can be developed by library personnel or by a committee of library supervisors. This chapter does not attempt to prescribe a system for how student job descriptions must be designed, rather it provides one possible system for purposes of illustration. In this system, student positions are classed in one of four grades.

GRADE I STUDENT POSITIONS

These positions are generally entry-level positions, under general supervision, and with a low degree of responsibility. These positions are usually designed for those who have little if any library experience. In some instances the supervisor might be another student employee who has substantial library experience as well as being a veteran student employee within the department or unit. Most of these jobs will perform routine duties that may include, but not be limited to, answering phones, typing/keyboarding, photocopying, running errands, sorting incoming and outgoing mail, filing, internal recordkeeping, and shelving. Must have the ability to understand and execute basic procedural operations of the individual department and to understand the organizational structure of the library. These positions should have a low degree of responsibility and judgment.

GRADE II STUDENT POSITIONS

These positions are intermediate level position, under limited supervision, and with a moderate degree of responsibility. These positions generally provide specialized support to the individual department and, as appropriate, must be acquainted with the duties and responsibilities of Grade I. These positions will perform duties that may include, but not be limited to, positions heretofore mentioned as well as automated recordkeeping; receiving, sorting, and distributing library materials; initial processing of library materials; basic duplicate and bibliographic searching; limited reference and information services. May serve as a counter or desk attendant and provide basic referral and informational services. These positions should have moderate degree of responsibility and judgment.

GRADE III STUDENT POSITIONS

These positions are advanced level positions, under minimal supervision, and with a high degree of responsibility. The positions will provide highly technical/specialized support to the individual department and, as appropriate, must be acquainted with the duties and responsibilities of Grade II. Will perform duties that may include, but not be limited to, specialized instructional, operational, technical, security tasks, and/or involved in the training, monitoring, and supervision of other student employees. May handle cash and/or confidential records and may require knowledge of a second language.

GRADE IV STUDENT POSITIONS

These positions are very advanced level positions, under little if any direct supervision, and with a high degree or responsibility and judgment. These positions provide operational, administrative, technical, and public service support. The positions will perform a myriad of duties, many of which might also be provided by full-time staff. These positions require the most training, experience, and knowledge of library operations and procedures. Many of these positions might interact with the other faculty, staff, students and the general public.

SAMPLE STUDENT EMPLOYEE JOB DESCRIPTIONS

The following figures depict sample student employee job descriptions. They are divided into three broad categories—Administrative Services, Public Services, and Technical Services—and then further subdivided by department. Administrative Services includes the Director's Office, Budget (Fiscal), Human Resources, and other support services (mail, administrative secretaries, etc.); Public Services includes Access Services (Circulation, Interlibrary Loan, and Reserve), Reference Services includes Government Information, Maps and the Media Center (Photocopying, Digital Services), and Special

Collections (Manuscript or Photo Archives, Latin American Posters); Technical Services includes Acquisitions, Cataloging and Classification, Collection Development (Gifts), Serials (Bindery and the Exchange Program), and Technology Systems (that may also be a separate unit outside the library's preview).

Job descriptions may be used in more than one category due to similar duties or responsibilities, or pay. For example, a version of the Director's Office Assistant job description in Administrative Services could be used in almost any department that contains a job position. The Page job description in Circulation could also be used in Special Collections. The job descriptions are listed under a department name for illustration purposes only. Each library is organized differently and the actual department that a given job description is located, if it is used at all, will vary by library.

In some cases where there is clear progression, job descriptions are presented in families, one for each grade level, for example, Reference Assistant I (Grade I), Reference Assistant II (Grade II), and Reference Assistant III (Grade III). In other cases, a job description may be presented at a single grade level, for example Interlibrary Loan Assistant (Grade II) or Photo Archives Assistant (Grade III). The number of grade levels required in a given department will vary from library to library. Some grade levels within a single classification are used as incentives to induce students to stay longer, learn more, thus earning a higher wage over the course of these college careers.

The job descriptions are designed for libraries that have an Integrated Library System (ILS), which includes an online public catalog (OPAC); automated circulation, automated acquisitions, serials control, and fund accounting, a bibliographic utility (such as MARCIVE for government information), and the Library of Congress classification system. As well the job descriptions have been expanded to include libraries that have electronic reference resources (Web pages and Web links), supply staff with personal computer software and hardware packages, and may also offer patrons in-house or remote access to their electronic collections. However, they can be altered for libraries that use less automation and/or electronic resources, and other classification systems.

The format for the job descriptions includes the name of the department, section (if there is one), hiring supervisor (that is left blank in the sample descriptions), student job title, grade (I, II, or III), pay rate (that is left blank in the sample descriptions), degree of responsibility (low, moderate, or high), maximum supervision required (general, limited, or minimal), duties and responsibilities required (knowledge, skills, and abilities) and desired (knowledge, skills, and abilities). All the job descriptions are written to be as generic as possible while still serving as useful examples.

Administrative Services Job Descriptions
   Copy Center
   Director's Office
   Fiscal Services
   Human (Employee) Resources
   Mail Room

Library Student Job Description

Department: Administrative Services

Section: Media Center   **Hiring Supervisor:**_____

Student Job Title: Copy Assistant I

Grade (check one): √ I_II_III   **Pay Rate:**_____

Degree of Responsibility and Judgment (check one): √Low_Moderate_High

Maximum Supervision Required (check one): √ General_Limited_Minimal

Duties and Responsibilities:

Photocopying or scanning from books, microforms, and prepared original documents. Do velobinding and folding. Maintain coin-operated photocopiers with paper. General maintenance of copy center area and supply tables.

Required:

Good oral and written communication skills, reliability.

Desired:

Customer service skills.

Figure 3.1

Library Student Job Description

Department: Administrative Services

Section: Media Center   **Hiring Supervisor:**_____

Student Job Title: Copy Assistant II

Grade (check one): _I√II_III   **Pay Rate:** _____

Degree of Responsibility and Judgment (check one): _Low √ Moderate_High

Maximum Supervision Required (check one): _General√ Limited_Minimal

Duties and Responsibilities:

Photocopying or scanning from books, microforms, and prepared original documents. Operate cash register, make change, and handle money. Do velobinding and folding. Maintain coin-operated photocopiers with paper. Perform inventory procedures daily. Provide some assistance to public copy/scanning equipment when asked. General maintenance of copy center area and supply tables.

Required:

Cash register skills. Good math abilities. Mechanical aptitude for minor equipment maintenance and repair.

Desired:

Strong Customer service skills.

Figure 3.2

Library Student Job Description

Department: Administrative Services

Section: Media Center **Hiring Supervisor:**_____

Student Job Title: Copy Assistant III

Grade (check one): _I_II √ III   **Pay Rate:** _____

Degree of Responsibility and Judgment (check one):_Low_Moderate √ High

Maximum Supervision Required (check one):_General_Limited √Minimal

Duties and Responsibilities:

Photocopying or scanning from books, microforms, and prepared original documents. Operate cash register, make change, and handle large sums of money. Do velobinding and folding. Maintain coin-operated photocopiers with paper. Perform end-of-day closing procedures. Perform inventory procedures daily. General maintenance of copy center area and supply tables. Perform other special instructional, operational, technical, and security tasks as assigned. May work night shift without supervision. May train and/or coordinate and delegate photocopying assignments to lower graded student employees.

Required:

Cash register skills. Good math abilities. Mechanical aptitude for minor equipment maintenance and repair.

Desired:

Excellent customer service skills.

Figure 3.3

Library Student Job Description

Department: Administrative Services

Section: Director's Office   **Hiring Supervisor:** _____

Student Job Title: Office Assistant

Grade (check one):_I_II √ III   **Pay Rate:** _____

Degree of Responsibility and Judgment (check one):_Low_Moderate √ High

Maximum Supervision Required (check one):_General_Limited √ Minimal

Duties and Responsibilities:

Provide specialized support and handle confidential material. Perform data entry and word processing of draft versions of memorandums and reports. Maintain computer files. Assist in scheduling meetings via phone, e-mail, and mail. Coordinate meeting agendas, distribution, and room reservations. Answer phones, keyboard, photocopy, run errands, and sort incoming and outgoing mail. May perform literature search on identified topics.

Required:

Typing skills of a minimum 40 words per minute. Computer literacy. Knowledge of computer word processing, spreadsheet, and database software. Complex problem-solving ability. Ability to interact tactfully and efficiently with students, staff, and faculty members. Must be able to handle confidential matters with tact and good judgment.

Desired:

Knowledge of computer desktop publishing and presentation software. Proofreading skills. Research and computerized literature searching skills.

Figure 3.4

Library Student Job Description

Department: Administrative Services

Section: Fiscal Services **Hiring Supervisor:**_____

Student Job Title: Fiscal Services Assistant

Grade (check one):_I_II √ III   **Pay Rate:**_____

Degree of Responsibility and Judgment (check one):_Low_Moderate √ High

Maximum Supervision Required (check one):_General_Limited √ Minimal

Duties and Responsibilities:

Process and file confidential information, including payroll and budget information. Prepare book bills for payment. Sort invoices for mailing to customers. Receive, sort, and distribute some library supplies. Answer phones, keyboard, photocopy, run errands, and sort incoming and outgoing mail. In the absence of supervisor, staff public desk.

Required:

Typing for accuracy more than speed. Computer literacy. Ability to use a calculator. Ability to interact tactfully and efficiently with students, staff, and faculty members.

Desired:

Knowledge of accounting principles. Knowledge of computer spreadsheet software.

Figure 3.5

Library Student Job Description

Department: Administrative Services

Section: Employee Resources   **Hiring Supervisor:**_____

Student Job Title: Personnel Assistant

Grade (check one):_I_II √ III   **Pay Rate:** _____

Degree of Responsibility and Judgment (check one):_Low_Moderate √ High

Maximum Supervision Required (check one):_General_Limited √ Minimal

Duties and Responsibilities:

Prepare, process, and file confidential employee records. Update records on personal computer and compute student pay rates. Answer phones, keyboard, photocopy, run errands, and sort incoming and outgoing mail. In the absence of supervisor, staff public desk.

Required:

Typing skill, accuracy more important than speed. Computer literacy. Ability to interact tactfully and efficiently with students, staff, and faculty members. Must be able to handle confidential matters with tact and good judgment.

Desired:

Knowledge of computer word processing software. Ability to use calculator.

Figure 3.6

Library Student Job Description

Department: Administrative Services

Section: Mail/Delivery Room Services   **Hiring Supervisor:**_____

Supervisor:_____

Student Job Title: Mail Room Assistant

Grade (check one):_I_ II √ III   **Pay Rate:** _____

Degree of Responsibility and Judgment (check one):_Low_Moderate √ High

Maximum Supervision Required (check one):_General_Limited √ Minimal

Duties and Responsibilities:

Monitor security of the loading dock during daytime hours. Receive, sign for, and deliver

library and book shipments and supplies. Prepare and package materials for shipment.

Required:

Manual dexterity. Ability to lift up to 40 lbs.

Desired:

Knowledge of procedures used by campus mail office, US Postal Service, Federal Express,

and/or United Parcel Service.

Figure 3.7

Public Services Job Descriptions

    Access Services

        Circulation

        Interlibrary Loan

        Reserve

    Reference

        Government Information

        Map Room

        Media Center

    Special Collections

        Manuscript Archives

        Photo Archives

Library Student Job Description

Department: Access Services

Section: Circulation   **Hiring Supervisor:** _____

Student Job Title: Circulation Desk Assistant I

Grade (check one): √ I_II_III   **Pay Rate:** _____

Degree of Responsibility and Judgment (check one): √Low_Moderate_High

Maximum Supervision Required (check one): √ General_Limited_Minimal

Duties and Responsibilities:

Responsible for security and care of library materials and equipment. Perform basic circulation activities including check-out and discharge of books and process renewals on automated circulation system. File books in call number order in to-be-shelved area. Answer basic directional questions and make referrals. Answer phone.

Required:

Customer service skills. Manual dexterity. Reliability.

Desired:

Computer literacy.

Figure 3.8

Library Student Job Description

Department: Access Services

Section: Circulation   **Hiring Supervisor:** _____

Student Job Title: Library Aide/Counter/Reserve/Shelver II

Grade (check one): _I √ II_III   **Pay Rate:**_____

Degree of Responsibility and Judgment (check one):_Low_Moderate √ High

Maximum Supervision Required (check one):_General √ Limited_Minimal

Duties and Responsibilities:

Under general supervision, works in public service duties at the circulation and reserve counters throughout the library. Shelves books, coordinates stack maintenance, searches for books, and performs a variety of library tasks as needed. Functions are normally governed by established procedures, but independent judgment will be sometimes required. Job duties may require night and/or weekend hours.

Required:

Customer service skills. Computer literacy. Ability to lift up to 40 lbs. Ability to interact tactfully and efficiently with students, staff, and faculty members.

Desired:

Knowledge of Library of Congress classification system. Familiarity with library collection and borrowing policies.

Figure 3.9

Library Student Job Description

Department: Access Services

Section: Circulation   **Hiring Supervisor:**_____

Student Job Title: Library Aide/Counter/Reserve/Shelver III

Grade (check one):_I_II √ III   **Pay Rate:**_____

Degree of Responsibility and Judgment (check one):_Low_Moderate √ High

Maximum Supervision Required (check one):_General_Limited √ Minimal_

Duties and Responsibilities:

Responsible for security and care of library materials and equipment. Perform circulation activities including check-out and discharge of books and process renewals on automated circulation system. Place holds and call-ins on books, initiate requests for return of books from patrons, and contact patrons concerning the availability of recalled books. Search for missing books. Register patrons on automated circulation system. File books in call number order in to-be-shelved area. Answer patron questions regarding library fines and fees and make referrals. Answer phone. Perform other operational, technical, and security tasks as assigned. May assist with end-of-day building closing procedures. May train and/or coordinate and delegate circulation assignments to lower graded student employees.

Required:

Customer service skills. Computer literacy. Ability to interact tactfully and efficiently with students, staff, and faculty members. Knowledge of Library of Congress classification system. Familiarity with library collection and borrowing policies. Ability to work independently.

Desired:

Knowledge of Superintendent of Documents classification system. Minimum knowledge of reference collections and services.

Figure 3.10

Library Student Job Description

Department: Access Services

Section: Circulation   **Hiring Supervisor:** _____

Student Job Title: Page

Grade (check one): √ I_II_III   **Pay Rate:** _____

Degree of Responsibility and Judgment (check one): √ Low_Moderate_High

Maximum Supervision Required (check one): √ General_Limited_Minimal

Duties and Responsibilities:

Locate and retrieve books from closed stacks. Shelve returned books and perform stack

maintenance as required or directed

Required:

Manual dexterity. Reliability. Ability to maneuver fully loaded book trucks. Ability to work

independently.

Desired:

Knowledge of Library of Congress classification system.

Figure 3.11

Library Student Job Description

Department: Access Services

Section: Circulation   **Hiring Supervisor:** _____

Student Job Title: Shelver I

Grade (check one): √ I_II_III   **Pay Rate:** _____

Degree of Responsibility and Judgment (check one): √ Low_Moderate_High

Maximum Supervision Required (check one): √ General_Limited_Minimal

Duties and Responsibilities:

Responsible for maintenance of stacks including shelfreading and shifting as assigned. Retrieve and reshelve books from study areas and photocopying areas.

Required:

Manual dexterity. Reliability. Ability to maneuver fully loaded book trucks. Ability to work independently.

Desired:

Knowledge of Library of Congress classification system.

Figure 3.12

Library Student Job Description

Department: Access Services

Section: Circulation　　**Hiring Supervisor:**_____

Student Job Title: Shelver II

Grade (check one):_I √ II_III　　　　**Pay Rate:**_____

Degree of Responsibility and Judgment (check one):_Low √Moderate_High

Maximum Supervision Required (check one):_General √ Limited_Minimal

Duties and Responsibilities:

Responsible for maintenance of stacks including shelfreading and shifting assigned. Interfile loose-leaf updated pages and remove old ones. Retrieve and reshelve books from study areas and photocopying areas. Assist with the closing of the building as assigned. Ability to maneuver fully loaded book trucks. Ability to work independently.

Required:

Manual dexterity. Reliability. Knowledge of Library of Congress classification system.

Desired:

Figure 3.13

Library Student Job Description

Department: Access Services

Section: Circulation   **Hiring Supervisor:**_____

Student Job Title: Library Aide/Counter/Reserve/Shelver Supervisor

Grade (check one):_I_II √ III   **Pay Rate:**_____

Degree of Responsibility and Judgment (check one):_Low_Moderate √ High

Maximum Supervision Required (check one):_General_Limited √ Minimal

Duties and Responsibilities:

Responsible for maintenance, security, and end-of-day closing procedures for one or more library stacks on one or more nights per week or weekends. Train and supervise lower graded student employees; ascertain where shelfreading and shifting may be required and assigned lower grader student employees. May substitute for staff supervisor. Job may require nights and weekends.

Required:

Manual dexterity. Reliability. Knowledge of Library of Congress classification system. Ability to maneuver fully loaded book trucks. Ability to work independently.

Desired:

Supervisory experience.

Figure 3.14

Library Student Job Description

Department: All Branches

Section: Circulation   **Hiring Supervisor:**_____

Student Job Title: Senior Circulation Assistant/Senior Student Supervisor, Library Assistant IV

Grade (check one):_I_II_III_IV√   **Pay Rate:**_____

Degree of Responsibility and Judgment (check one):_Low_Moderate √ High

Maximum Supervision Required (check one): √General_Limited_Minimal

Duties and Responsibilities:

Under limited direction, is responsible for library operations as needed in the absence of a

library staff person. Performs duties of Circulation I, II, and III group employees as needed.

Supervises and trains student employees. Exercises independent judgment to make decisions

necessary for maintenance of positive public relations with library patrons. May perform a

variety of routine and specialized tasks necessary for library operations.

Required:

May require nights and weekends. Strong customer service skills. 1.5 years of directly related

experience. Ability to work independently in a fast-paced environment. Demonstrated ability

to perform a variety of specialized technical and supervisory skills

Desired:

Computer literacy. Knowledge of Library of Congress classification system.

Figure 3.15

Library Student Job Description

Department: Access Services

Section: Interlibrary Loan   **Hiring Supervisor:** _____

Student Job Title: Interlibrary Loan Aide III

Grade (check one):_I√ II_III   **Pay Rate:** _____

Degree of Responsibility and Judgment (check one):_Low_Moderate √ High

Maximum Supervision Required (check one):_General_Limited √ Minimal

Duties and Responsibilities:

Under limited supervision, assists the ILL staff as necessary. The student must have a thorough knowledge of ILL procedures, OPAC records, OCLC, and the ILLiad software system. Works independently retrieving materials from other campus branch locations, maintains ILL and other records, answers questions posed via electronic mail or on-site visits, and performs other duties as assigned by the ILL supervisor.

Required:

Strong customer service skills. Computer literacy. Knowledge of Library of Congress classification system.

Desired:

Knowledge of photocopying, scanning, and faxing procedures.

Figure 3.16

Library Student Job Description

Department: Access Services

Section: Reserve Desk   **Hiring Supervisor:**_____

Student Job Title: Reserve Desk Assistant

Grade (check one):_I √ II_III   **Pay Rate:**_____

Degree of Responsibility and Judgment (check one):_Low √ Moderate_High

Maximum Supervision Required (check one):_General √ Limited_Minimal

Duties and Responsibilities:

Provides public service assistance at the Reserve desk by circulating reserve materials for specific amounts of time. Articulates Reserve policies to patrons. Assists faculty in placing paper and electronic reserves in area. Performs all functions related to processing reserve materials including physical and digital processing and entering records onto the reserve database. May staff Circulation Desk as assigned.

Required:

Strong customer service skills. Computer literacy. Ability to interact tactfully and efficiently with students, staff, and faculty members.

Desired:

Familiarity with library collection and borrowing policies.

Figure 3.17

Library Student Job Description

Department: Government Information

Section:_____   **Hiring Supervisor:** _____

Student Job Title: Government Information Assistant I

Grade (check one):√ I_II_III   **Pay Rate:** _____

Degree of Responsibility and Judgment (check one): √ Low_Moderate_High

Maximum Supervision Required (check one): √ General_Limited_Minimal

Duties and Responsibilities:

Shelve materials housed in the Government Information shelving area using the
Superintendent of Documents (SuDoc) classification system. Perform shelfreading as directed.
Shift in areas of the collection as assigned. Answer phones, type/keyboard, photocopy, run
errands, and sort incoming and outgoing mail.

Required:

Manual dexterity. Ability to listen and follow directions. Typing accuracy rather than speed.
Ability to maneuver fully loaded book trucks. Ability to work independently.

Desired:

Computer literacy.

Figure 3.18

Library Student Job Description

Department: Government Documents

Section:_____   **Hiring Supervisor:**_____

Student Job Title: Government Information Assistant II

Grade (check one):_I√ II_III   **Pay Rate:**_____

Degree of Responsibility and Judgment (check one):_Low √Moderate_High

Maximum Supervision Required (check one):_General √Limited_Minimal

Duties and Responsibilities:

Under general supervision performs duties that include shelving materials of various formats

and multiple call number classifications, performs stack maintenance including shelfreading,

assists in the processing of materials received from the Federal Depository Library Program

(FDLP), and other duties as assigned by the supervisor. Duties are performed under

established guidelines and procedures but independent judgment may sometimes be required.

Required:

Similar skills required for Government Information Assistant I but at a higher degree of

expertise and knowledge.

Desired:

Knowledge of Library of Congress and SuDoc classification systems.

Figure 3.19

Library Student Job Description

Department: Government Documents

Section:_____   **Hiring Supervisor:**_____

Student Job Title: Government Information Assistant III

Minimal Grade (check one): _I_II √ III   **Pay Rate:**_____

Degree of Responsibility and Judgment (check one): _Low_Moderate √ High

Maximum Supervision Required (check one): _General_Limited √ Minimal

Duties and Responsibilities:

Under limited supervision provides Library Assistants I and II with appropriate training in process and shelving. Supervises new student assistants. Assists library staff with public service duties including assisting library patrons, retrieving materials, and in locating materials through online and traditional bibliographic resources. Performs complex processing that requires in-depth knowledge of materials received from the FDLP.

Required:

Strong microcomputer skills. Customer service skills. Computer literacy.

Desired:

Knowledge of Library of Congress and SuDoc classification systems. Supervisory experience.

Figure 3.20

Library Student Job Description

Department: Government Information

Section: _____   **Hiring Supervisor:** _____

Student Job Title: Government Information Assistant IV

Grade (check one): I_II_III   **Pay Rate:** _____

Degree of Responsibility and Judgment (check one): Low_Moderate_High

Maximum Supervision Required (check one): General_Limited_Minimal

Duties and Responsibilities:

Under direction, performs the duties of a Library Assistant III but at a higher level of knowledge and expertise. Supervises Library Assistants I, II, and III, performs complex processing of materials received from the FDLP. Performs public service duties, sometimes alone.

Required:

Strong oral and written communication skills. Strong knowledge of library processes and procedures including the use of online and traditional bibliographic resources. Knowledge of Library of Congress and SuDoc classifications systems. Strong computer skills.

Desired:

Computer skills including web page design and editing.

Figure 3.21

Library Student Job Description

Department: <u>Reference</u>

Section:_____   Hiring Supervisor: _____

Student Job Title: <u>Reference Assistant I</u>

Grade (check one): √ I_II_III Pay Rate:_____

Degree of Responsibility and Judgment (check one): √ Low_ Moderate_High

Maximum Supervision Required (check one):√ General_Limited_Minimal

Duties and Responsibilities:

Staffs information desk. Answers basic directional questions and make referrals to para- and professional staff. Answers phones, assists in data entry and photocopying when necessary, and sorts incoming and outgoing mail. Shelves new and returned reference materials. Performs stack maintenance as required.

Required:

Good oral and written communication skills.

Desired:

Computer literacy. Knowledge of Library of Congress classification system.

Figure 3.22

Library Student Job Description

Department: Reference

Section: _____   **Hiring Supervisor:** _____

Student Job Title: Reference Assistant II

Grade (check one):_I √ II_III   **Pay Rate:**_____

Degree of Responsibility and Judgment (check one):_Low √ Moderate_High

Maximum Supervision Required (check one):_General √ Limited_Minimal

Duties and Responsibilities:

Staffs information desk. Answers questions and make referrals to para- and professional staff.

Answers phones, photocopies, performs data entry, and sorts incoming and outgoing mail.

Performs word processing in correcting user guides and pathfinders. Processes new materials.

Pulls materials for binding. Shelves reference materials. Performs stack maintenance.

Required:

Strong written and oral communication skills. Computer literacy.

Desired:

Knowledge of Library of Congress classification system.

Figure 3.23

Library Student Job Description

Department: Reference

Section:_____   **Hiring Supervisor:**_____

Student Job Title: Reference Assistant III

Grade (check one):_I_II √ III   **Pay Rate:**_____

Degree of Responsibility and Judgment (check one):_Low_ Moderate √High

Maximum Supervision Required (check one):_General_Limited √ Minimal

Duties and Responsibilities:

Under limited supervision, performs administrative support to the Department Head. Duties include word processing, research, data gathering, statistic and status reports, and other special projects. Maintains reference room area, orders and distributes supplies, maintains bulletin boards and display cases. Performs other duties as assigned.

Required:

Word processing and data entry skills. Strong communication and organizational skills. Ability to maintain confidentiality of personal records and information. May require heavy physical work including lifting, pushing, or pulling of objects.

Desired:

Previous reference assistant. Supervisory experience.

Figure 3.24

Library Student Job Description

Department: Reference

Section: Map Room   **Hiring Supervisor:** _____

Student Job Title: Map Room Assistant

Grade (check one): _I √ II_III   **Pay Rate:** _____

Degree of Responsibility and Judgment (check one): _Low √ Moderate_High

Maximum Supervision Required (check one): _General √ Limited_Minimal

Duties and Responsibilities:

Staff Maps Desk. Answer questions and make referrals as appropriate. Assist patrons and circulates maps. File maps according to Library of Congress G-Schedule call numbering system. Preliminary processing of maps.

Required:

Customer service skills. Computer literacy. Good oral and written communication skills.

Desired:

Geography or geology major.

Figure 3.25

Library Student Job Description

Department : <u>Media Center</u>

Section:_____ **Hiring Supervisor:**_____

Student Job Title: <u>Media Center Assistant</u>

Grade (check one):_ I √ II_III   **Pay Rate:**_____

Degree of Responsibility and Judgment (check one):_Low √ Moderate_High

Maximum Supervision Required (check one):_General √ Limited_Minimal

Duties and Responsibilities:

Staff Media Center Desk. Answer questions and make referrals to other staff and faculty. Assist patrons, and check-in and out media. Monitor patrons using materials. Assist patrons with use of audio, video, and other equipment. Research items requested by patrons. Fill recording requests as described by requester. Minor equipment maintenance and repair, clean and exercise tapes, sort and categorize materials, and label collections.

Required:

Customer service skills. Strong oral and written communication skills. Experience with audio and video taping equipment.

Desired:

Knowledge of music and films. Ability to read music scores.

Figure 3.26

Library Student Job Description

Department: Special Collections

Section: _____   **Hiring Supervisor:** _____

Student Job Title: Special Collections Assistant II

Grade (check one): _I_II √ III   **Pay Rate:** _____

Degree of Responsibility and Judgment (check one):_Low_Moderate √ High

Maximum Supervision Required (check one):_General_Limited √ Minimal

Duties and Responsibilities:

Under general supervision, performs moderately complex processing, clerical or public service functions requiring training in one or more general areas of library procedures and policies. Functions are normally governed by established procedures, but independent judgment may be required. Retrieves and shelves a variety of special collections materials, may process copy orders by a variety of means including photo prints, scanning, or other electronic copying. May assist staff with processing of new materials, work on limited preservation and conservation materials, conduct searches for materials deemed missing and assist staff at the public access desk. Works without direct supervision on nights and weekends. Answers routine and directional reference questions in person, by phone or by e-mail.

Required:

Familiarity with materials in Special Collections and library OPAC. Strong written and oral communication skills. Strong organizational skills. Ability to work independently after training. Ability to identify and apply appropriate security measures. Ability to lift boxes of up to 40 pounds.

Desired:

Previous library experience.

Figure 3.27

Library Student Job Description

Department: Special Collections

Section: Manuscript Archives   **Hiring Supervisor:** _____

Student Job Title: Manuscript Archives/Reference Assistant III

Grade (check one): _I_II √III   **Pay Rate:** _____

Degree of Responsibility and Judgment (check one): _Low_Moderate √High

Maximum Supervision Required (check one): _General_Limited √Minimal

Duties and Responsibilities:

Under limited supervision performs complex processing, clerical or public service functions requiring in-depth knowledge of specialized areas or comprehensive understanding of a broad area of library operations. Works independently after training. May supervise and help train student employees in lower classifications. Assists library staff and faculty in processing new materials received. Assists staff and faculty on preservation and conservations of materials received including mending, boxing fragile and rare materials, and correcting minor errors in the spines of bound volumes. Conducts searches for missing items. May process copy orders by a variety of means including photo prints, scanning, or other electronic copying. Provides input in the development, evaluation, and revision of procedures to improve efficiency and accuracy of department works. Works without supervision on nights and weekends. Answers routine and directional reference questions, in person, by phone or by e-mail. Shelves books, micro materials, pictorial archives, and manuscripts. Retrieves materials requested by patrons.

Required:

Minimum one year experience in library special collections and archives. Basic office skills. Organizational skills. Ability to carry out detailed tasks. Strong written and oral communication skills. Ability to work independently. Ability to identify and apply appropriate security measures.

Desired:

Some knowledge of the special collections contained in the department. Knowledge of Library of Congress call number order. One year of library, archival, or conservation experience.

Figure 3.28

Library Student Job Description

Department: Special Collections

Section: Photo Archives/Conservation Assistant IV   **Hiring Supervisor:** _____

Student Job Title: Photo Archives Assistant

Grade (check one): _I_II_III √ IV   **Pay Rate:** _____

Degree of Responsibility and Judgment (check one): _Low_ Moderate_High

Maximum Supervision Required (check one): _General_Limited_Minimal

Duties and Responsibilities:

Under direction, utilizes similar skills required of Assistant III, but at a higher level of expertise. Duties necessitate independent judgment and may include planning and independent execution. Performs highly skilled, independent and technical work, including preservation treatments for one or more of the collections maintained in the Department. Preparation and installation of exhibition materials; cataloging archival materials according to national standards, and entering same information on electronic databases. May process copy orders by a variety of means including photo prints, scanning, or other electronic copying. Answers complex reference questions about the particular collection area. Opens and closes the area when a staff member is unavailable. May supervise student employees at a lower classification. Will work with staff on ensuring adequate and appropriate security measures are in place.

Required:

Minimum of 1.5 years experience in library special collections and archives. The ability to exercise independent judgment. Good office skills. Strong oral and written communication skills. Strong organizational skills. Ability to work independently. Experience with computers and scanners.

Desired:

Photography, art, or art history major. Experience in a visual resource collection, library, or archive.

Figure 3.29

TECHNICAL SERVICES JOB DESCRIPTIONS

        Acquisitions

        Cataloging and Classification

        Collection Development

            Gifts

    Serials

            Bindery

            Exchange Program

        Library Technology Department

Library Student Job Description

Department: Acquisitions

Section: _____   **Hiring Supervisor:** _____

Student Job Title: Acquisitions Assistant I

Grade (check one): √ I_II_III   **Pay Rate:** _____

Degree of Responsibility and Judgment (check one): √ Low_Moderate_ High

Maximum Supervision Required (check one): √ General_Limited_Minimal

Duties and Responsibilities:

Under general supervision performs basic duplicate and bibliographic checking and searching for books to be ordered using conventional and online acquisition resources. Performs other duties such as answering the phone, data entry, photocopying, and sorting of mail received.

Required:

Ability to understand and follow directions. Basic knowledge of library operations.

Desired:

Computer literacy.

Figure 3.30

Library Student Job Description

Department: Acquisitions

Section:_____ **Hiring Supervisor:**_____

Student Job Title: Acquisitions Assistant II

Grade (check one):_I√_II_III   **Pay Rate:**_____

Degree of Responsibility and Judgment (check one):_Low √ Moderate_High

Maximum Supervision Required (check one):_General √ Limited_Minimal

Duties and Responsibilities:

Under general supervision performs moderately complex processing and clerical duties involving a high degree of responsibility and independent judgment. Duties include marking, bindery processing, receiving, processing and routing materials and checking for accuracy of records in database management systems.

Required:

Computer literacy. Accurate typing rather than speed. Good organizational skills. Ability to lift up to 50 pounds and move fully loaded book trucks. Able to work independently.

Desired:

Knowledge of library's integrated library system.

Figure 3.31

Library Student Job Description

Department: Acquisitions

Section:_____ **Hiring Supervisor:**_____

Student Job Title: Resource Acquisitions Assistant III

Grade (check one): _I_II √ III   **Pay Rate:**_____

Degree of Responsibility and Judgment (check one):_Low_Moderate √ High

Maximum Supervision Required (check one):_General_Limited √ Minimal

Duties and Responsibilities:

Under limited supervision perform advanced bibliographic checking and searching for books and electronic materials to be ordered through vendors via conventional and online databases. Verify citations. Perform specialized technical tasks including the use of bibliographic utilities in searching routines and the creation of bibliographic/order records in the library's integrated library system. Answer phones. May train and/or coordinate and delegate assignments to lower graded student employees.

Required:

Computer literacy in a Web environment. Keyboarding for accuracy rather than speed. Ability to lift 50 pounds and move fully loaded book trucks.

Desired:

Complex problem-solving skills. Knowledge of bibliographic utility databases.

Figure 3.32

Library Student Job Description

Department: Cataloging and Classification

Section:_____ **Hiring Supervisor:**_____

Student Job Title: Cataloging and Classification Assistant I

Grade (check one): √ I_II_III **Pay Rate:**_____

Degree of Responsibility and Judgment (check one): √ Low_ Moderate_ High

Maximum Supervision Required (check one): √ General_Limited_Minimal

Duties and Responsibilities:

Under general supervision search and verify bibliographic records in library's integrated library system. Type, cut, and apply spine labels to books. Attach barcodes to books. Check books for errors in physical processing. Mark withdrawn items. File cards in withdrawn file and shelf list. Pull books from stacks as assigned. Answer phones, type/keyboard, photocopy, and sort incoming mail.

Required:

Keyboarding for accuracy rather than speed. Ability to understand and follow directions

Desired:

Knowledge of Library of Congress classification system.

Figure 3.33

Library Student Job Description

Department: Cataloging and Classification

Section:_____   Hiring Supervisor:_____

Student Job Title: Cataloging and Classification Assistant II

Grade (check one): _I √ II_III   Pay Rate:_____

Degree of Responsibility and Judgment (check one):_Low √ Moderate_High

Maximum Supervision Required (check one):_General √ Limited_Minimal

Duties and Responsibilities:

Under general supervision perform bibliographic searching for books and serials in bibliographic utility online databases. Search and verify name/series in bibliographic utility database authority files. Perform withdrawal and transfer procedures. Perform special projects relating to the maintenance of the library's integrated library system involving searching, updating, correcting, and deleting records. Answer phones, type/keyboard, photocopy, run errands, and sort incoming and outgoing mail.

Required:

Computer literacy. Keyboarding for accuracy rather than speed. Knowledge of Library of Congress classification system.

Desired:

Knowledge of OCLC online database.

Figure 3.34

Department: Cataloging and Classification

Section:____ **Hiring Supervisor:**_____

Student Job Title: Cataloging and Classification Assistant III

Grade (check one):_ I_II √ III   **Pay Rate:**_____

Degree of Responsibility and Judgment (check one):_Low_Moderate √ High

Maximum Supervision Required (check one):_General_Limited √ Minimal

Duties and Responsibilities:

Under limited responsibility supervision performs varied and complex duties involving a high degree of responsibility and independent judgment including receiving, processing, and routing materials, updating or creating bibliographic records in the library's integrated library system, database searching and exporting for bibliographic records, and ensuring accuracy of database input.

Required:

Requires considerable computer training in online bibliographic utilities. Knowledge of Library of Congress classification system. Keyboarding for accuracy rather than speed. Requires attention to detail and good organizational skills.

Desired:

Knowledge of MARC format. Reading knowledge of one or more foreign language.

Figure 3.35

Library Student Job Description

Department: Cataloging and Classification

Section:_____ **Hiring Supervisor:**_____

Student Job Title: Cataloging and Classification Assistant IV

Grade (check one):_I_II_III √ IV **Pay Rate:**_____

Degree of Responsibility and Judgment (check one):_Low_Moderate √ High

Maximum Supervision Required (check one):_General√ Limited_Minimal

Duties and Responsibilities:

Under limited supervision, utilizes similar skills required for the Cataloging and Classification Assistant III, only at a higher level of expertise. Duties necessitate independent judgment and include planning and organization skills. Duties include marking, bindery processing, receiving, processing and routing materials, checking for accuracy of records and quality of materials, updating and creating records in multiple databases and training and supervising lower graded student employees.

Required:

Must possess a high degree of computer skills and knowledge. A high degree of independent judgment, strong organizational skills, strong oral and written communication skills and the ability to work independently are necessary. A minimum of 1.5 years of library experience is necessary.

Desired:

Strong computer skills. A knowledge of one or more foreign languages is desirable.

Figure 3.36

Library Student Job Description

Department: Collection Development

Section: Gifts   **Hiring Supervisor:**_____

Student Job Title: Gifts Assistant

Grade (check one): _I √ II_III   **Pay Rate:**_____

Degree of Responsibility and Judgment (check one):_Low √ Moderate_High

Maximum Supervision Required (check one):_General√ Limited_Minimal

Duties and Responsibilities:

Under limited supervision, receive, count, and sort gift books by subject and alert the

appropriate selector/bibliographer. Perform searching of gift monographs or serials on library's

integrated library system to eliminate duplicated materials. Type and install gift donor plates

in books. Prepare lists of duplicated gift materials that will be made available to other libraries.

May perform serials shelf check to verify holdings. Answer phones, type/keyboard, photocopy,

and sort incoming/outgoing mail. Assist with special projects as assigned.

Required:

Computer literacy. Keyboarding for accuracy rather than speed. Ability to lift up to 40 lbs.

Desired:

Knowledge of library classification systems. Knowledge of library's integrated library system.

Word processing skills.

Figure 3.37

Library Student Job Description

Department: Serials

Section:____ **Hiring Supervisor:** _____

Student Job Title: Serials Assistant I

Grade (check one): √ I_II_III **Pay Rate:** _____

Degree of Responsibility and Judgment

(check one): √ Low_Moderate_High

Maximum Supervision Required (check one): √ General_Limited_Minimal

Duties and Responsibilities:

Assist staff in the sorting, and distribution of materials received through mail or other shipping services. Prepare serials invoices for payment including date stamping and photocopying as needed. Process superseded serials. Perform basic duplicate and bibliographic checking/searching for serials to be ordered in manual files and online databases. Answer phones, type/keyboard, photocopy, and sort incoming/outgoing mail.

Required:

Knowledge of the Library of Congress classification system. Keyboarding for accuracy rather than speed. Ability to lift up to 40 lbs.

Desired:

Computer literacy.

Figure 3.38

Department: Serials

Section:_____ **Hiring Supervisor:**_____

Student Job Title: Serials Assistant II

Grade (check one):_I √ II_III   **Pay Rate:**_____

Degree of Responsibility and Judgment (check one):_Low √ Moderate_High

Maximum Supervision Required (check one):_General √ Limited_Minimal

Duties and Responsibilities:

Under general supervision process serials and newspapers utilizing the library's integrated library system, property stamp, security strip, and label. Place serials in to-be-shelved area. Route serials as assigned. Pull older newspapers from shelves for storage or recycling. Perform basic bibliographic checking/searching for serials to be ordered in manual files and online databases. Answer phones, type/keyboard, photocopy, and sort incoming/outgoing mail.

Required:

Knowledge of the Library of Congress classification system. Keyboarding for accuracy rather than speed. Computer literacy. Ability to lift up to 40 lbs.

Desired:

Knowledge of library's integrated library system.

Figure 3.39

Library Student Job Description

Department: Serials

Section:_____ **Hiring Supervisor:**_____

Student Job Title: Serials Assistant III

Grade (check one):_I_II √ III   **Pay Rate:**_____

Degree of Responsibility and Judgment (check one):_Low_ Moderate √ High

Maximum Supervision Required (check one):_General_Limited √ Minimal

Duties and Responsibilities:

Under limited supervision process serials utilizing the library's integrated library system, property stamp, security strip, and label. Place serials in to-be-shelved area. Route serials as assigned. Process serials that are classed separately and analyzed. Perform advanced bibliographic checking/searching for serials to be ordered in online databases. Verify series. Perform specialized technical tasks including the use of online bibliographic utility database in searching routines and the creation of bibliographic/order records in the library's integrated library system. Answer phones. May train and/or coordinate and delegate assignments to lower graded student employees.

Required:

Knowledge of the Library of Congress classification system. Keyboarding for accuracy rather than speed. Computer literacy. Knowledge of library's integrated library system.

Desired:

Complex problem-solving skills. Knowledge of online bibliographic utility databases.

Figure 3.40

Library Student Job Description

Department: Serials

Section: Bindery   **Hiring Supervisor:** _____

Student Job Title: Bindery Assistant

Grade (check one):_ I √ II_III   **Pay Rate:**_____

Degree of Responsibility and Judgment (check one):_Low √ Moderate_High

Maximum Supervision Required (check one):_General √ Limited_Minimal

Duties and Responsibilities:

Under general supervision pull material to be bound consisting mostly of periodicals. Update records on library's integrated library system when books and serials are shipped or received for binding. Pack and unpack bound items and process paperwork. Perform in-house mending procedures including pamphlet binding, making boxes for brittle books, etc. Correct minor errors in the spine labels of bound materials. Order missing pages, verify material received, and tips-in pages. Verify completeness of theses and dissertations and send to be bound and/or microfilmed. Answer phones, type/keyboard, photocopy, and sort incoming/outgoing mail.

Required:

Knowledge of the Library of Congress classification system. Keyboarding for accuracy rather than speed. Computer literacy. Ability to lift up to 40 lbs.

Desired:

Knowledge of library's integrated library system.

Figure 3.41

Library Student Job Description

Department: Serials

Section: Exchange Program   **Hiring Supervisor:**_____

Student Job Title: Exchange Program Assistant

Grade (check one): _I_II √ III   **Pay Rate:**_____

Degree of Responsibility and Judgment(check one): _Low_Moderate √ High

Maximum Supervision Required (check one): _General_Limited √ Minimal

Duties and Responsibilities:

Under general supervision be responsible for the maintenance activities related to the materials exchange program. Compose correspondence to institutions proposing, modifying, and terminating exchange agreements (frequently in foreign languages, especially Spanish). Prepare and mail exchange material. Receive exchange material from other institutions and route it for processing. May act as a liaison with library subject selectors/bibliographers and other departments. Search manual and online library files and databases. Special projects as assigned. Answer phones, type/keyboard, photocopy, and sort incoming and outgoing mail.

Required:

Computer literacy. Keyboarding for accuracy rather than speed. Reading and writing knowledge of one foreign language, preferably Spanish. Ability to interact tactfully and efficiently with students, staff, and faculty members.

Desired:

Library experience. Additional foreign language reading ability.

Figure 3.42

Department: <u>Library Information Technology Department</u>

Section:_____ **Hiring Supervisor:**_____

Student Job Title: <u>Library Systems Assistant I</u>

Grade (check one): √ I_II_III   **Pay Rate:** _____

Degree of Responsibility (check one): √ Low_Moderate_High

Maximum Supervision Required (check one): √ General_Limited_Minimal

Duties and Responsibilities:

Under general supervision clean personal computers, printers, and terminals on a periodic basis. Assist in set-up of personal computers and peripheral devices. Answer phones and provide other limited services as required by library staff.

Required:

Customer service skills.

Desired:

Computer literacy.

Figure 3.43

Library Student Job Description

Department: Library Information Technology Department

Section:_____ Hiring Supervisor:_____

Student Job Title: Library Systems Assistant II

Grade (check one):_ I √ II_III   **Pay Rate:_____**

Degree of Responsibility (check one):_ Low √ Moderate_High

Maximum Supervision Required (check one):_ General √ Limited_Minimal

Duties and Responsibilities:

Under general supervision receive, unpack, and inspect personal computers, printers, terminals as new equipment is ordered and received. Assist in set-up of personal computers and peripheral devices. Install software upgrades on personal computers in public and staff environments. Provide assistance and do basic trouble shooting for computer hardware problems in public and staff environments. Maintain an inventory database of personal computers, printers, and terminals owned by the library. Special projects as assigned.

Required:

Knowledge with personal computer software and hardware. Mechanical aptitude for minor computer equipment maintenance and repair. Ability to interact tactfully and efficiently with students, staff, and faculty members. Ability to troubleshoot problems in computer hardware and software.

Desired:

Knowledge of computer programming and software design.

Figure 3.44

Library Student Job Description

Department: Library Information Technology Department

Section:_____ **Hiring Supervisor:**_____

Student Job Title: Library Systems Assistant III

Grade (check one):_ I_ II √ III   **Pay Rate:**_____

Degree of Responsibility (check one):_Low_ Moderate √ High

Maximum Supervision Required (check one):_General √ Limited_Minimal

Duties and Responsibilities:

Under limited supervision set-up personal computers and peripheral devices. Install software upgrades on personal computers. Provide assistance and do trouble shooting for personal computer hardware and software problems. Assist in the maintenance of the library's Web site. May act as a liaison with staff and faculty. May work on the assistance line.

Required:

Advanced knowledge of computer software, hardware, and peripherals. Ability to troubleshoot personal computer hardware and software problems. Mechanical aptitude for minor computer equipment maintenance and repair. Ability to interact tactfully and efficiently with students, staff, and faculty members.

Desired:

Knowledge of computer server operating systems. Knowledge of programming languages, Web-to-database programming tools, and server database environments.

Figure 3.45

JOB MATCHING

Job matching is simply the process of bringing together the work and the people in such a way that the requirements of the work are matched with the skills and abilities of the persons available to do that work. Some student employees are extremely good at detailed work such as those tasks required in academic library public service, technology, acquisitions, and cataloging departments. Others are extremely well organized and can coordinate the activities of other student workers, while still other prefer the routine or physical work of shelving, while others like the challenges and diversity of a service desk. No one is good at everything but most people have one or two skills or abilities which are higher than average. If the right student is matched with the right job, the library will function more efficiently and each student employee will have an opportunity to excel. Job matching is a necessity that academic libraries must perform well in order to meet growing demand from the clients coupled with the continued reliance on technology and dwindling or shrinking library personnel.

STUDENT EMPLOYMENT APPLICATION FORM

In order to effectively match student applicant to student jobs, it is necessary to have an application form that solicits the kind of information you need to screen applicants. A generic example of such a form can be seen in Figure 3.46.

LIBRARY STUDENT EMPLOYMENT APPLICATION

Application will remain on file for the current year only. Please PRINT clearly.

Date of Application: _____ Date Available to Begin Work: _____

_____

Last Name First Name Middle Initial Social Security Number

Current Address: _____ Daytime Phone No.: _____

_____ Best Time To Call: _____

E-mail address: _____ Cell Phone No./Pager: _____

Academic Major: _____ Minor: _____

Year in School (check one) FR ____ SO ____ JR ____ SR ____ Grad ____

Anticipated Graduation Date: _____ Amount of Financial Award:
_____

How Many Hours Per Week Do You Want To Work? _____

Please list the times when you will be available to work. Notify this office of any changes.

Monday: _____

Tuesday: _____

Wednesday: _____

Thursday: _____

Friday: _____

Saturday: _____

Sunday: _____

Library Experience: _____

_____

_____

_____

Other Experience: _____

_____

_____

_____

Skills (such as computer, language, office, etc.): _____

_____

_____

Preferred Position(s) at the Library: 1. _____

2. _____

3. _____

References (name, address, phone number(s)):
1. _____

2. _____

3. _____

Thank you.

Figure 3.46

CONCLUSION

The organizing function is extremely important to supervision. You must know what you expect of the employees, just as they must know what you expect of them. The job description provides structure and lays the groundwork for everything that follows—compensation, training, and evaluation. Continual reevaluation of the tasks performed and the work distribution is critical and should be done annually to keep job descriptions accurate and up-to-date.

BIBLIOGRAPHY

Avila, Antionette, Collette Ford, and Rayna Hamre. "Library Training Day: Developing an Effective Academic Library Student Training Program." *Library Mosaics* 16(1) (January/February 2005): 18–19.

Baird, Lynn N. "Student Employees in Academic Libraries: Training for Work, Education for Life." *PNLA Quarterly.* 67(2) (2003): 13–23.

Boone, Morell D., Sandra G. Yee, and Rita Bullard. *Training Student Library Assistants.* Chicago, IL: ALA, 1991.

Borin, Jacqueline. "Training, Supervising, and Evaluating Student Information Assistants." *The Reference Librarian* 72 (2001): 195–206.

Creth, Sheila. "Personnel Planning, Job Analysis, and Job Evaluation with special reference to Academic Libraries." *Advances in Librarianship* 12 (1982): 47–97.

Gael, S. *Job Analysis: A Guide to Assessing Work Activities.* San Francisco, CA: Jossey-Bass, 1983.

Hill, Virginia S. and Tom G. Watson. "Job Analysis: Process and Benefits." *Advances in Library Administration and Organization* 3 (1984): 209–219.

———. *Job Analysis in ARL Libraries.* Washington, DC: ARL/OMS, 1987.

Holtze, Terri L. and Rebecca E. Maddos. "Student Assistant Training in a Multi-library System." *Technical Services Quarterly* 19(2) (2001): 27–41.

Kathman, Jane M. and Michael D Kathman. "Training Student Employees for Quality Service." *The Journal of Academic Librarianship* 26(3) (2000): 176–182.

Kathman, Michael D. and Jane McGurn Kathman, comp. *Managing Student Employees in College Libraries.* Chicago, IL: ALA, 1994 (Clip Note #20).

Klingner, Donald E. "When the Traditional Job Description Is Not Enough." *Personnel Journal* 58 (April 1979): 243–248.

Marks, Susan and David James Gregory. "Student Employment in Academic Libraries: Recommended Readings and Resources." *Journal of Library Administration* 21(3/4) (1995): 161–176.

McCormick, Ernest J. *Job Analysis: Methods and Applications.* New York: AMACOM, 1979.

Mussman, K. "Socio-technical Theory and Job Design in Libraries." *College & Research Libraries* 39 (January 1978): 20–28.

———. *Personnel Classification Schemes.* Washington, DC: ARL/OMS, 1978.

Neuhaus, Chris. "Flexibility and Feedback: A New Approach to Ongoing Training for Reference Student Assistants." *Reference Services Review* 29(1) (2001): 53–64.

Rapp, Karla M. and Millini R. Skuba. "An Interactive Library Classification Systems Module: A Viable Solution for Training Student Workers at Bloomsburg University." *Technical Services Quarterly.* 18(3) (2001): 11–19.

Russell, Thyra Kaye. "Student Employment Manuals." *Journal of Library Administration* 21 (1995): 95–108.

————. *Student Employment Programs in ARL Libraries*. Washington, DC: ARL/OMS, 1990. (SPEC Kit #168).

Wu, Qi (Kerry). "Win-win Strategy for the Employment of Reference Graduate Assistants in Academic Libraries." *Reference Services Review* 31(2) (2003): 141–153.

Van Rijn, Paul. *Job Analysis for Selection: An Overview*. Washington, DC: U.S. Office of Personnel Management, Staffing Services Group, 1979.

4

Understanding Financial Aid for Student Employees

I ain't ever had a job. I just always played baseball.

—Satchel Paige (1906–1982)

FEDERAL AID FOR STUDENT EMPLOYMENT

As Table 4.1 indicates, the majority of students attending an academic institution will receive some type of financial assistance. Within this context the majority of students employed in academic libraries will also be the beneficiaries of financial assistance. The predominant source of funding is provided by the United States Department of Education (USDE) although there are other federal and state agencies that may also provide financial aid to eligible students.[1] While the USDE provides the financial resources to public and private institutions, it is solely up to each institution under broad guidelines to mete out the financial aid. There are still many private programs geared toward students who qualify for academic or special scholarship programs. The focus of this chapter will be on federal assistance and the various programs that fall under this umbrella. Currently, more than 9,800[2] colleges and universities participate in one or more of the programs offered by the USDE; however, there are still many colleges and universities who do not participate at all.

Academic libraries generally vie for the distinction of being the largest undergraduate and graduate student employers on campus. Therefore it is essential that supervisors of student employees possess a fundamental understanding of the student financial aid system administered by their respective college or university. It is especially necessary that supervisors understand some of the major financial aid programs, particularly those sponsored by the federal government, and how their students qualify for and receive their financial assistance.

Table 4.1 Percentage of full-time and part-time undergraduates receiving aid, by federal aid program and control and type of institution: 2003–2004

Control and Type of Institution	Number of Undergraduates \1\, in Thousands	Any Federal Aid	Any Title IV Aid	Percent Receiving Federal Aid in 2003–04, by Type					
				Selected Title IV Programs \2\					
				Pell	SEOG\3\	CWS\4\	Perkins\5\	Stafford\6\	PLUS\7\
1	2	3	4	5	6	7	8	9	10
Full-time, full-year students All institutions	7,824 (93.5)	61.7 (0.42)	60.6 (0.44)	32.1 (0.34)	10.0 (0.37)	10.3 (0.36)	7.0 (0.31)	47.1 (0.44)	6.3 (0.22)
Public	5,662 (78.1)	56.1 (0.47)	54.9 (0.49)	30.6 (0.33)	7.9 (0.33)	7.3 (0.31)	5.3 (0.25)	39.9 (0.46)	4.9 (0.23)
4-year doctoral	2,411 (33.2)	58.2 (0.71)	57.1 (0.75)	26.5 (0.77)	8.0 (0.49)	7.9 (0.34)	8.5 (0.34)	48.2 (0.77)	7.7 (0.33)
Other 4-year	1,198 (42.8)	64.0 (1.20)	63.2 (1.22)	34.0 (1.40)	8.1 (0.67)	9.9 (0.87)	6.3 (0.98)	49.6 (1.37)	5.7 (0.82)
2-year	2,026 (59.1)	48.9 (1.15)	47.4 (1.16)	33.5 (0.88)	7.7 (0.51)	5.3 (0.50)	1.1 (0.16)	24.4 (1.03)	1.2 (0.15)
Less than 2-year	27 (2.1)	48.7 (2.75)	47.8 (2.70)	35.9 (1.73)	2.3 (0.88)	1.1 (0.57)	‡ (†)	24.1 (2.56)	0.3 (0.28)
Private, not-for-profit	1,635 (38.9)	73.1 (0.81)	72.5 (0.82)	30.4 (0.77)	14.6 (0.92)	23.0 (1.17)	14.0 (0.95)	62.2 (1.05)	11.0 (0.51)
4-year doctoral	668 (27.5)	66.2 (1.69)	65.3 (1.72)	22.9 (3.07)	11.7 (1.78)	22.5 (1.53)	18.1 (1.24)	55.6 (2.22)	11.5 (0.87)
Other 4-year	921 (36.8)	77.9 (1.25)	77.5 (1.26)	35.0 (2.30)	16.9 (1.31)	24.2 (1.93)	11.6 (1.57)	67.4 (2.38)	10.8 (0.90)
Less than 4-year	47 (4.4)	76.8 (4.76)	75.5 (4.30)	48.0 (3.70)	12.2 (3.24)	8.6 (2.71)	1.3 (0.88)	53.5 (5.17)	8.1 (2.92)
Private, for-profit	527 (21.6)	86.9 (0.92)	86.1 (0.98)	53.2 (1.74)	17.5 (2.05)	3.1 (0.62)	2.6 (0.79)	78.0 (1.17)	6.7 (0.88)
2-year and above	393 (21.0)	90.6 (1.14)	89.6 (1.24)	52.7 (2.24)	16.2 (2.63)	3.7 (0.82)	3.3 (1.07)	85.8 (1.46)	6.8 (1.10)
Less than 2-year	134 (3.0)	76.0 (1.31)	75.8 (1.33)	54.7 (1.59)	21.4 (2.14)	1.5 (0.22)	0.8 (0.63)	55.0 (1.55)	6.5 (0.89)

Part-time or part-year students All institutions	11,230 (93.5)	38.5 (0.44)	36.3 (0.43)	23.0 (0.34)	4.4 (0.20)	2.2 (0.09)	1.2 (0.08)	23.5 (0.31)	1.2 (0.07)
Public	9,015 (74.6)	32.0 (0.52)	29.8 (0.51)	19.9 (0.38)	2.9 (0.19)	1.9 (0.10)	1.0 (0.08)	16.2 (0.36)	0.7 (0.05)
4-year doctoral	1,516 (33.3)	42.9 (0.92)	41.6 (0.91)	19.8 (0.70)	3.4 (0.36)	2.8 (0.27)	3.3 (0.31)	34.7 (0.84)	2.5 (0.22)
Other 4-year	984 (47.7)	42.0 (2.03)	40.2 (2.07)	22.5 (1.77)	3.4 (0.42)	2.1 (0.41)	2.0 (0.41)	29.3 (1.48)	0.7 (0.18)
2-year	6,449 (59.1)	28.0 (0.66)	25.5 (0.63)	19.6 (0.52)	2.8 (0.22)	1.7 (0.12)	0.3 (0.05)	9.9 (0.37)	0.3 (0.04)
Less than 2-year	66 (2.1)	19.6 (1.80)	18.4 (1.75)	14.9 (1.61)	2.1 (0.70)	1.0 (0.56)	0.2 (0.24)	5.6 (1.21)	# (†)
Private, not-for-profit	1,204 (37.4)	52.4 (1.42)	49.2 (1.37)	24.0 (0.99)	6.3 (0.44)	5.9 (0.64)	3.4 (0.45)	40.5 (1.28)	3.2 (0.44)
4-year doctoral	356 (17.6)	45.8 (2.20)	44.8 (2.24)	18.3 (2.01)	6.2 (0.84)	8.4 (1.16)	4.9 (0.67)	37.7 (2.30)	3.4 (0.64)
Other 4-year	786 (37.2)	54.2 (2.21)	49.8 (2.18)	24.8 (1.83)	6.0 (0.66)	5.0 (0.78)	3.0 (0.60)	41.9 (2.08)	3.0 (0.64)
Less than 4-year	62 (4.4)	66.9 (3.72)	66.3 (3.79)	45.9 (3.05)	9.9 (2.31)	2.9 (0.83)	0.6 (0.62)	39.2 (4.40)	3.6 (1.35)
Private, for-profit	1,011 (19.5)	79.8 (0.85)	78.6 (0.96)	49.8 (1.34)	14.7 (1.37)	1.1 (0.21)	0.9 (0.26)	68.2 (1.02)	4.0 (0.35)
2-year and above	636 (19.2)	83.3 (1.26)	81.9 (1.40)	49.3 (2.10)	14.3 (2.17)	1.0 (0.31)	1.3 (0.41)	76.1 (1.43)	2.8 (0.50)
Less than 2-year	375 (3.0)	73.8 (0.91)	73.0 (0.90)	50.7 (0.58)	15.5 (0.77)	1.2 (0.15)	0.2 (0.03)	54.7 (0.81)	5.9 (0.38)

†Not applicable.

#Rounds to zero.

‡Reporting standards not met.

\1\Numbers of undergraduates may not equal figures reported in other tables, since these data are based on a sample survey of students who enrolled at any point during the year.

\2\Title IV of the Higher Education Act.

\4\College Work Study (CWS). Prior to October 17, 1986, private, for-profit institutions were prohibited by law from spending CWS funds for on-campus work. Includes persons who participated in the program, but had no earnings.

\5\Formerly National Direct Student Loans (NDSL).

\6\Formerly Guaranteed Student Loans (GSL).

\7\Parent Loans for Undergraduate Students (PLUS).

Note: Excludes students whose attendance status was not reported. Detail may not sum to totals because of rounding and because some students receive multiple types of aid and aid from different sources. The numbers in column 2 do not add to totals because of rounding. Standard errors appear in parentheses. Data include Puerto Rico.

Source: U.S. Department of Education, National Center for Education Statistics, 2003–04 National Postsecondary Student Aid Study (NPSAS:04). (This table was prepared August 2005.)

In this chapter, many of the federal student financial aid programs offered by the USDE will be described. Although the basic provisions of each program have remained intact since the Higher Education Act of 1965 (HEA) created them, the reader is advised that frequent revisions regarding funding, expected family contributions (EFC) and other eligibility factors are made by the USDE and Congress regularly. Before one advises student employees on federal student aid programs, it would be best to consult with your on-campus student employment office and its chief Financial Aid Advisor (FAA).

As well, over the course of the past decade Congress has made attempts to limit the amount of money appropriated toward the College Work-Study Program. Additionally, it is essential that one reviews the latest *FSA Handbook* (http://www. ifap.ed.gov/IFAPWebApp/currentSFAHandbooksYearPag.jsp?p1=2006-2007&p2=c) due to the number of changes that have taken place regarding distance education, home-schooling, and citizenship requirements. Also, as administrative changes to each program are proposed, a regular search of the *Federal Register* is strongly encouraged. Because student employee supervisors have direct contact with those impacted by any proposal, scanning the *Federal Register* regularly ensures your ability to input and perhaps influence proposed changes to the financial aid programs administered by the USDE.

It should be noted at this juncture that there are also a number of financial aid services that advertise themselves as "the source" to aid students and their parents in locating financial aid resources. While many of these services are legitimate and can be of some value and assistance, particularly in locating private, corporate, and endowment funds, caution should be used. Those services found exclusively on the Internet should be carefully scrutinized because they may provide information for a fee that, in some cases, can be found for free at other Internet sites. As well, providing personal information via the Internet may lead to the loss of said information thus resulting in severe financial losses. The motto when utilizing any financial aid service, especially one available only on the Internet, is "caveat emptor."

FEDERAL STUDENT AID PROGRAMS

The United States Congress built the foundation of the current student financial aid program by enacting the Higher Education Act of 1965 (P.L. 89-329, 79 STAT 1219); specifically Title IV of the Act. Throughout the past forty plus years, numerous changes have been made through amendments to the Act.[3] Currently, the Office of Federal Student Aid (FSA) of the USDE administers the Federal Pell Grant Program, campus-based programs such as the Federal Perkins Loan (Perkins Loan) Program, the Federal Work-Study (FWS) Program, the Federal Supplemental Educational Opportunity Grant (FSEOG) Program, the William D. Ford Federal Direct Loan (Direct Loan) Program that also includes the Federal Parent Loans to Undergraduate (PLUS) Program, the Federal Direct Stafford Loans Program, the Federal Family Education Loans (FFEL's) that includes the Federal Stafford Loans and the Federal PLUS Loans, the State Grant and Scholarship Program, and beginning January 1, 2006, the Academic Competitiveness Grant, and the PLUS Loans for graduate or professional students For the 2005 fiscal year, the FSA distributed approximately $73.02 billion in aid to over 21 million students.[4]

Grants (Pell Grants and FSEOG's) do not have to be repaid. Loans (Perkins, Direct, PLUS, Stafford, and FFEL's) must be repaid, with some exceptions that will be noted later in the chapter. The FWS program provides eligible students with income from part-time jobs.

Each of these programs is described in this chapter. With the exception of the Loan Programs, a student must demonstrate financial need in order to receive assistance from a FSA program.

The following is a summary of the U.S. Department of Education's Federal Student Aid (FSA) programs that will help you pay for school. Check with your school to find out which programs your school participates in.

Federal Student Aid Program	Types of Aid	Program Details	Annual Award Amounts
Federal Pell Grant	Grant: does not have to be repaid	Available almost exclusively to undergraduates; all eligible students will receive the Federal Pell Grant amounts they qualify for	$400 to $4,050 for 2005–2006
Federal Supplemental Educational Opportunity Grant (FSEOG)	Grant: does not have to be repaid	For undergraduates with exceptional financial need; priority is given to Federal Pell Grant recipients; funds depend on availability at school	$100 to $4,000
Federal Work-Study	Money is earned while attending school; does not have to be repaid	For undergraduate and graduate students; jobs can be on campus or off campus; students are paid at least minimum wage	No annual minimum or maximum award amounts
Federal Perkins Loan	Loan: must be repaid	5% loans for both undergraduate and graduate students; payment is owed to the school that made the loan	$4,000 maximum for undergraduate students; $6,000 maximum for graduate students; no minimum award amount
Subsidized FFEL[1] or Direct[2] Stafford Loan	Loan: must be repaid; you must be at least a **half-time** student	Subsidized: U.S. Department of Education pays interest while borrower is in school and during grace and deferment periods	$2,625 to $8,500, depending on grade level
Unsubsidized FFEL[1] or Direct[2] Stafford Loan	Loan: must be repaid; you must be at least a **half-time** student	Unsubsidized: Borrower is responsible for interest during life of the loan; financial need not a requirement	$2,625 to $18,500, depending on grade level (includes any subsidized amounts received for the same period)
FFEL or Direct PLUS Loan	Loan: must be repaid	Available to parents of dependent undergraduate students enrolled at least **half time**	Maximum amount is **cost of attendance** minus any other financial aid the student receives; no minimum award amount

[1] This type of Stafford Loan is from the Federal Family Education Loan (FFEL) Program. The loan is known as a FFEL (or Federal) Stafford Loan.

[2] This type of Stafford Loan is from the William D. Ford Federal Direct Loan Program. The loan is known as a Direct Loan.

Source: Federal Student Aid at a Glance

(http://studentaid.ed.gov/students/publications/student_guide/2005–2006/english/glance.htm)

STUDENT AID ELIGIBILITY

For federal financial assistance a student's aid is based almost solely on the financial need of that student. However, there are several other criteria a student must meet in order to be eligible. A student must:

- Qualify for financial need (with the except of certain loans);
- Possess a high school diploma or a GED, pass a test approved by the U.S. Department of Education, meet other standards established by the state in which the student resides, or complete a high school education in a home school setting that is recognized and treated under state law;
- Either be working toward a degree or certificate in an eligible program;
- Be a U.S. citizen or eligible noncitizen;
- Possess a valid Social Security Number (unless the student is from the Republic of the Marshall Islands, the Federated States of Micronesia, or the Republic of Palau);
- Be registered with the Selective Service, if required;
- Maintain satisfactory academic progress once enrolled in classes;
- Certify that the student is not in default on a federal student loan nor owe money on a federal student grant; and
- Certify that the financial assistance will only be used for education purposes.

INDEPENDENT/DEPENDENT STUDENT DEFINITION
FOR ELIGIBILITY DETERMINATION

In determining financial need for the dependent student, the needs analysis has assumed that a certain amount of financial assistance will be forthcoming from the student's parents. Naturally, there are exceptions, such as an older, nontraditional student or those no longer in contact with their parents. The *Higher Education Act Amendments of 1986 and 1992* (P.L. 96-49 and P.L. 102-325, respectively) redefined the concept of a dependent student as well as providing student aid counselors and administrators with criteria to allow for exceptions for students who have individual circumstances that cause them to be independent even though they do not meet the definition of the law.

Independent students fall into a separate category for financial assistance. Independent students report only their own income and assets (and those of a spouse, if married). Independent students cannot live with a parent or parents or be claimed by them on the tax form. Dependent students must report on the FAFSA their parents' income and assets as well as their own.

Many of the loan programs are based on the concept that a dependent student's parents have the primary responsibility for the student's education. Your parents' information will be used to calculate your Expected Family Contribution (EFC)

- You were born before January 1, 1984.
- You will be enrolled in a master's or doctorate program (beyond a bachelor's degree) at the beginning of the 2007–2008 school year.
- You're married as of the day you apply (or you're separated but not divorced).
- You have children who receive more than half their support from you.
- You have dependents (other than your children or spouse) who live with you and who receive more than half their support from you at the time you apply and through June 30, 2008.

- Both your parents are deceased, or you are (or were until age 18) a ward or dependent of the court.
- You're a veteran of the U.S. Armed Forces. (A "veteran" includes students who attended a U.S. service academy, engaged in active duty in the U.S. Armed Forces, is a National Guard or Reserve enlistee who was called to duty for purposes other than for training or was released from the military with an honorable discharge. This definition also includes someone who is not now a veteran but will by prior to June 30, 2008.)
- You are an orphan or ward of the court or you were a ward of the court until age 18.

If none of these criteria applies to you, you're considered dependent.[5]

A student may also be considered to be independent if the school can document that:

- A legal restraining order has been issued against both parents of the student because of abusive behavior.
- Both parents of the student have been incarcerated or are believed to be dead.
- Parents can not be located.
- Student legally adopted by their current guardian.
- The student's parents live in another country and the student has been, or is in the process of being, granted refugee status by the U.S. Immigration and Naturalization Service.
- Both parents of the student live in a country where they cannot easily leave or get money out.
- The student can provide adequate documentation to satisfy the financial aid administer that the student is truly self-supporting for the financial aid administrator to override the student's dependency status.[6]

Some financial aid administrators may require proof of annual income of $10,000 or more. Naturally, it is best to check with your school's chief financial aid administrator to ascertain the school's requirements.

Additionally, a student will not qualify for independent status simply because the student's parents have decided not to claim the student as an exemption on their tax returns or refuse to provide the student financial support. In the past, an income of $4,000 or two successive years of not being claimed as a tax exemption sufficed. If you are reviewing several financial aid guidebooks, these old criteria may still be referenced but they are no longer valid. Regardless of the situation between students and their parents (remember, there are always two sides to every story), it's always best to check with your local Financial Aid Advisor (FAA).

Terms used in the independent student definition:

- CUSTODIAL PARENT: If a student's parents are divorced or separated, the custodial parent is the one whom the student has lived with the most during the past twelve months. The student's need analysis is based primarily on information supplied by the custodial parent.
- LEGAL DEPENDENT: Any person who lives with the student, receives more than half-support from the student, and will continue to receive more than half-support from the student during the award year. Also, the natural or adopted child of the student, or a child for whom the student is the legal guardian, if the child receives more than half-support from the student (the child does not have to live with the student).

- OVER 23 YEARS OF AGE: A student who is at least 24 years old on December 31.
- PARENT: A natural, adoptive, foster, or step-parent or legal guardian who has been appointed by a court and directed to use his or her financial resources to support the student.
- PROFESSIONAL JUDGMENT: For need-based federal aid programs, the financial aid administrator (FAA) can adjust the Expected Family Contribution (EFC) adjust the Cost of Attendance or change the dependency status (with appropriate documentation) when extenuating circumstances exist.
- PROFESSIONAL STUDENT: A student in pursuit of an advanced degree in law or medicine.
- RESOURCES: Includes not only traditional sources of income (such as wages, salaries, tips, interest and dividend income, untaxed income and benefits, fellowships and veteran's cash benefits) but also any student financial aid (except PLUS loans), and personal long-term cash loans used for education purposes. These resources, of course, do not include any support from the student's parents.

CITIZENSHIP REQUIREMENTS FOR FINANCIAL AID

The FSA programs are intended to provide student financial aid to financially challenged students who are in one of the following categories:[7]

- A U.S. citizen or national. The term national includes citizens of American Samoa and Swain's Island.
- A U.S. permanent resident. A permanent resident's citizenship status should be evidenced by a comment on output documents noting that the Immigration and Naturalization Service (INS) match has been successful. If no such evidence is available, the permanent residence must provide the school with verifying INS documentation.
- Citizens of the Freely Associated States: the Federated States of Micronesia and the Republics of Palau and the Marshall Islands.

If a student does not meet the following criteria they may still qualify for financial assistance if they possess an *Arrival-Departure Record (I-94)* from the U.S. Citizenship and Immigration Services (USCIS) showing one of the flowing designations:

- Refugee;
- Asylum Granted;
- Cuban-Haitian Entrant, Status Pending;
- Conditional Entrant (valid only if issued before April 1, 1980); and
- Parolee (must be paroled into the United States for at least one year and provide evidence from the USCIS that you are in the United States for other than a temporary purpose and your intent is to become a U.S. citizen or permanent resident).

If a student has a *Notice of Approval to Apply for Permanent Resident* (I-171 or I-464), that student is not eligible for financial assistance. If a student has entered the United States under a certain type of visa (e.g., F1, F2, J1, or J2) that student is not eligible for financial assistance. As well, students with a "G" series visa are ineligible for financial assistance. Again, if in doubt have the student check with your school's financial aid office.

Citizens and eligible noncitizens may receive loans from the *FFEL Program* at participating foreign schools. Citizens from the Federated States of Micronesia, the

Table 4.2 Eligibility requirements for federal student financial aid

REQUIREMENTS	PELL	FFELP	FSEOG	FWS	PERKINS	DIRECT	PLUS
Undergraduate	YES	YES	YES	YES	YES	YES	YES
Graduate	NO	YES	NO	YES	YES	YES	NO
At least 1/2 time	NO	YES	YES	YES	YES	YES	YES
Must pay back	NO	YES	NO	NO	YES	YES	YES
U.S. citizen or eligible non-citizen	YES	YES	YES	YES	YES	YES	YES
Registered with Selective Service (if applicable)	YES	YES	YES	YES	YES	YES	YES
Have financial need	YES	YES	YES	YES	YES	NO	
Attend participating school	YES	YES	YES	YES	YES	NO*	YES
Working toward a degree or certificate	YES	YES	YES	YES	YES	YES	YES
Making satisfactory academic progress	YES	YES	YES	YES	YES	YES	YES
Not in default or owe a refund on a federal grant or loan	YES	YES	YES	YES	YES	YES	YES
Having a bachelor's degree makes student ineligible	YES	NO	YES	NO	NO	NO	YES
Conviction of drug distribution or possession may make student ineligible	YES	YES	YES	YES	YES	YES	YES

PELL—Pell Grants
FWS—Federal Work-Study Program
FSEOG—Federal Supplemental Educational Opportunity Grants [NDSL] Program
FFELP—Federal Family Education Loans (FFELs) Program (authorized under Title IV Higher Education Act in conjunction with Student Loan Reform Act of 1993–PL 103 66, 312, 107 Stat)
*—Must be taking coursework for enrollment in an eligible program

Republic of the Marshall Islands, and the Republic of Palau are eligible ONLY for *Federal Pell Grants*, *Federal Supplemental Education Opportunity Grants*, or *Federal Work-Study*.

ELIGIBILITY REQUIREMENTS

Table 4.2 describes the eligibility requirements for the seven federal student financial aid programs.[8]

COST OF ATTENDANCE

Each school is responsible for determining the Cost of Attendance (COA) as established by the *Higher Education Act* (as amended), Section 472. The law specifies the types of costs that are included in the COA. However, each student must also determine the appropriate amount to include in each category at the school attended. By definition, except as noted below, a student's COA is the sum of the following based on the minimum of half-time attendance:

- Actual tuition and fees normally assessed a student carrying the same academic workload, including costs for rental or purchase of equipment, materials, or supplies required of all students in the same course of study;

- Cost of room and board (or living expenses for students who do not contract the school for room and board);
- An allowance for books, supplies, transportation, loan fees, and miscellaneous personal expenses (including a reasonable amount for the documented cost of a personal computer);
- For a student without dependents living at home with their parents, an allowance for room and board is determined by the school; or, for a student without dependents living in institutionally owned or operated housing, a standard allowance for room and board based on the amount normally assessed most residents. For students living off campus but not with their parents, the allowance is based on what the school determines are "reasonable expenses" for that school and area;
- For students with dependents, an allowance based on expected expenses incurred for dependent care (during periods including but not limited to class time, study time, fieldwork, internships, and commuting time for students) based on the number and age of each dependent, not to exceed the reasonable cost in the community in which the student resides;
- For study abroad programs that are approved by the student's home institution, reasonable costs associated with such study;
- For a student with a disability, an allowance for expenses related to the student's disability including special services, personal assistance, transportation, equipment, and supplies that are reasonably incurred and not provided for by other agencies;
- For students placed in work experience under a cooperative education program, an allowance for reasonable costs associated with such employment; and
- For student receiving loans, the fees required to receive them. The issuing school may also include the fees required for nonfederal student loans as well. In all cases, the school can either use the exact loan fees charged to the student or an average of fees charged to borrowers of the same type of loan at that school. To be included in the COA any loan fee for a private loan must be charged to the borrower during the period of enrollment for which that loan is intended.

Exceptions:

- Less than half-time student's COA can include only tuition and fees, an allowance for books, supplies, and transportation, and an allowance for dependent care expenses in accordance with the fourth item above;
- The COA for correspondence study is restricted to tuition and fees, which include books and supplies. If the costs of books and supplies are separate those costs must then be factored into the COA. If the student is fulfilling a residential training requirement, the COA can include the required books and supplies, an allowance for travel, and room and board costs specific to the period of residential training.
- Incarcerated students may have an allowance for tuition and fees and, if required, books and supplies. No other expenses can be included. An incarcerated student is ineligible to receive an FSA loan. If the student is incarcerated in a federal or state penal institution, he or she is ineligible to receive a Pell Grant;
- Students receiving instruction by telecommunications receive no distinction regarding the mode of instruction in determining costs, except the cost of rental or the purchase of equipment cannot be included as an element of the cost of attendance. The costs of equipment, such as a computer can be included in the COA, if it's part of the requirement to take that course. However, if the financial aid administrator determines using his or her professional judgment under section 479A of the Higher Education Act of 1965, as amended, that a course

of instruction offered results in a substantially reduced COA to the student, the financial aid administrator must reduce the student's eligibility for grants, loans, or work-study assistance.

EXPECTED FAMILY CONTRIBUTION (EFC)

The Expected Family Contribution (EFC) is the amount of financial assistance that a family is expected to contribute toward a student's educational costs. By comparing the EFC to the student's actual COA, the financial aid advisor can determine the student's financial need for federal assistance from the USDE and other available sources. The EFC formula is used to determine need for assistance for the following Student Financial Assistance Programs:

- Federal Pell Grant
- Subsidized Stafford Loan (under the Direct Loan Program and the Federal Family Education Loan Program)
- Campus-based programs
  - Federal Supplemental Educational Opportunity Grants
  - Federal Perkins Loans
  - Federal Work-Study programs

The methodology for determining the EFC is contained in Part F, Title IV, Higher Education Act of 1965, as amended. Updated tables for each award year are also published in the *Federal Register*, usually at the end of May, with any corrections appearing in late August. EFC worksheets can be obtained at http://www.studentaid.ed. gov/pubs. Worksheets can also be obtained by calling 1-800-4-FED-AID (1-800-433-3243).

The EFC calculation includes:

- The family's income (taxable and untaxed);
- Assets and benefits (e.g., Social Security, unemployment);
- The family's size; and
- The number of students from the family that are enrolled in either a college or career school.

529 College Savings Plans are unlike scholarships and most other resources. 529 College Savings Plans will not affect other financial aid awards. These funds are considered part of the expected family contribution (EFC) and do not reduce demonstrated financial need. Therefore, students who receive assistance from any 529 College Plan should not see a reduction or cancellation of other financial aid awards.

529 Pre-Paid Tuition Plans are treated like scholarships and most other resources, and therefore, may affect other financial aid awards. These funds should not be reported on the FAFSA as an asset for either the parent or the student, since they are not considered part of the expected family contribution (EFC). Because funds from a prepaid tuition plan will reduce demonstrated financial need, students who receive assistance from any 529 Pre-Paid Tuition Plan may see a reduction or cancellation of other federal financial aid awards.

All data used to calculate a student's EFC comes from the information provided on the USDE's *Free Application for Federal Student Aid (FAFSA)*. The student can submit the FAFSA through the Web (see: http://www.fafsa.ed.gov/), filing an application electronically at schools who participate in the USDE's Electronic Data Exchange (EDE), or by mailing a paper copy of the FAFSA to the USDE (for an example of a paper copy see: http://ifap.ed.gov/fafsa/attachments/0607FAFSAApplication(eng) 100605.pdf) A student who applied for federal student aid the previous award year may be eligible to apply by filing a *Renewal FAFSA* either by using a paper renewal application mailed to the student's permanent home address or via the Internet (see: http://www.fafsa.ed.gov/FOTWWebApp/complete004). Applying for federal student aid is free. However, if one is to be considered for nonfederal aid such as institutional aid, a student may have to fill out additional forms and pay a processing fee.

Although the student's FAFSA can be filed in paper, the USDE strongly encourages students to use the electronic FAFSA. Upon completion of the FAFSA, the information is sent to a central processing system and using the information provided on the form, the EFC is computed. Upon completion, each student will receive a Student Aid Report (SAR) that reports the information from the student's application, and if the information provided was correct and the form completely filled out, the student's EFC. The student is advised to check the FAFSA completely prior to submission as well as to check the accuracy of the data contained on the SAR. If corrections to the SAR are necessary, a student's school may submit corrections electronically (only if the school participates in the EDE program). If the corrections are submitted by mail, using the FAFSA Express, or by using FAFSA on the Web, the student may make the necessary corrections on Part 2 of the SAR and file it electronically.

It is extremely important to read the FAFSA instructions completely and carefully. While many questions may seem straightforward, like one's Social Security Number, there are many questions posed on the form for the purpose of determining a student's financial need. Common words such as "household," "investments," and "parent" all hold careful meaning and might be subject to misinterpretation.

Apply early. State and school deadlines vary and due tend to be early. It's best to check with each school to ascertain their deadlines. If your application, or renewal, is received on or before the deadline, the USDE will process the FAFSA. Because the FAFSA requires parent and student tax information, ensure that this information is completed. While a student may file the FAFSA without the current tax year information on file, having that information already completed will make the entire process go easier and much more smoothly.

FINANCIAL AID ADMINISTRATOR

The Financial Aid Administrator (FAA) is a college or university employee who is involved in the administration of financial aid. Sometimes referred to as a Financial Aid Advisor or a Financial Aid Counselor, he or she is responsible for ensuring the consistency of information submitted at the federal level at that institution regarding a student's eligibility. That individual must also be aware of all sources of aid at that institution and must be able to coordinate with all financial aid programs an institution offers to ensure that a student's aid does not exceed his or her need. The FAA can make individual judgments based on his or her professional judgment, to override a student's dependency status (from dependent to independent), to adjust the components of a student's cost of attendance (COA), and to adjust the data elements used to calculate the student's EFC.

FEDERAL PELL GRANTS

The Federal Pell Grants (FPG) Program is a unique type of federal assistance in that a student's eligibility for a FPG is not based on the availability of funds at the student's respective school. The USDE provides funds to each participating school to pay eligible students and can increase a school's initial authorization when necessary. Because the USDE pays the award, the school has no responsibility in determining or selecting eligible students. However, the school must ensure that each student meets the FPG eligibility requirements.[9] The student must be an undergraduate and the award is based on the student's EFC and cost of attendance. The 2006–2007 award maximum is $4,050. The maximum can change each award year and is dependent on program funding from Congress. The amount will also vary depending on your student status (e.g., full or part time).

Two new grant programs became effective on July 1, 2006. The *Academic Competitiveness Grant* and the *National Science & Mathematics Access to Retain Talent Grant (National Smart Grant)* are two grants aimed specifically at recent or soon to be high-school graduates. Each program provides money that would be in additional to any money received via a Pell Grant. Each grant was a result of the passage of the *Higher Education Reconciliation Act of 2005 (HERA)*.

The Academic Competitiveness Grant

This grant is available to first year students who have graduated from high school after January 1, 2005. The grant provides up to $750 for the first year of undergraduate study and up to $1,300 for the second year of undergraduate study to full-time students who are also eligible for a Pell Grant. The award requires a student to have completed an intensive high-school program as determined by the state or local education agency and is also recognized by the U.S. Secretary of Education. Second year students are required to maintain a 3.0 GPA.

There are some additional requirements for this grant:

- Be a U.S. citizen;
- Be a Federal Pell Grant recipient;
- Be enrolled in a full-time degree program;
- Be enrolled in the first or second academic year of their program of a 2- or 4-year degree granting institution;
- Completed an intensive secondary school program (after January 1, 2006 if a first year college student; January 1, 2005 if a second year student);
- If a first year student, not be previously enrolled in an undergraduate program;
- If a second year student have a minimum GPA of 3.0 on a 4.0 scale for the first academic year.

It should be noted that this grant combined with a Pell Grant may not exceed the student's COA. As well, if the number of eligible students exceeds the amount of appropriate to each institution in any fiscal year, the amount of each grant may be reduced. For further information on this grant and its requirements for both first and second year students see http://www.ed.gov/admins/finaid/about/ac-smart/state-programs06.html.

The National Science & Mathematics Access to Retain Talent Grant (National Smart Grant)

This grant is available to third and fourth-year undergraduate students who are also eligible for a Pell Grant. These students must be full time and have a declared major in the physical, life or computer sciences, mathematics, technology or engineering or in a foreign language determined critical to national security. The student must also have maintained a 3.0 GPA in coursework related to the declared major.

The grant will provide up to $4,000 for each of the third and fourth years of undergraduate study for full-time students. A recipient of the Smart Grant must be eligible for a Pell Grant, be a U.S. citizen, and enrolled in a full-time degree program in a four-year degree granting institution. As well, the Smart Grant combined with the Pell Grant can not exceed the student's COA. As well, if the number of eligible students exceeds the appropriation to that institution in a given fiscal year, the amount of each grant may be reduced. For additional information including fields of study see http://www.ifap.ed.gov/dpcletters/attachments/GEN0606A.pdf.

STUDENT FEDERAL LOANS

There are a number of federal student loans currently available. Each loan provides for differing amounts, interest rates, and repayment schedules. Each loan available is highlighted below. Where possible Internet URLs are provided for further information.

FEDERAL FAMILY EDUCATION LOAN (FFEL) PROGRAM

Part B of Title IV of the Higher Education Act (HEA) of 1965, as amended, established the guaranteed student loan programs. PL. 102-325 (HEA Amendments of 1992) brought together the various loan programs and renamed them the "*Federal Family Education Loan Program.*" The FFEL is now comprised of:

- Federal Stafford Loans (formerly the Guaranteed Student Loans Program)
- Federal Unsubsidized Stafford Loans
- Federal PLUS Loans
- Federal Consolidated Loans

The FFEL provides long-term loans to students attending colleges, universities, vocational, technical, business, and trade schools along with some foreign school attendance. Stafford Loans do not require a financial need. If you do demonstrate financial need, the USDE will pay the interest that accrues on this loan during certain periods.

Bank, Credit Unions, or other participating private nonprofit lenders provide the loan principle for FFEL's. The federal government guarantees these loans and if the loan is defaulted, the guaranty agency is reimbursed by the federal government. The federal guaranty replaces the collateral (security) usually required to secure a loan of this nature.

Schools certify student eligibility that is then forwarded to the lender for loan approval. Once approved, the lender sends the loan amount to the borrower's school that distributes the loan in two equal parts. Loans come in the form of "subsidized" or "unsubsidized." A subsidized loan is one where the federal government pays the accruing interest on the loan while the borrower is in school, or during certain grace or deferment periods.

Unsubsidized loans, on the other hand, accrue interest from the date of origination and the repayment of the interest is the borrower's responsibility.

Federal Stafford Loans provide low-interest, variable rate (changes yearly; for the 2005–2006 year the interest was 5.3% for loans in repayment) loans to borrowers proving a financial need. Federal Unsubsidized Stafford Loans are available to undergraduate or graduate students regardless of financial need. Interest accrues from the date or origination, during in-school, grace or deferment periods, and is the responsibility of the borrower to repay. The interest accrued on the loan can be repaid while the student is enrolled in school or during a period of deferment or forbearance.

Federal PLUS (Parent Loan for Undergraduate Students) Loans are designed for parents without adverse credit history. These loans enable parents to pay for educational expenses for each child, regardless of financial need. The PLUS loans are to help pay for a dependent undergraduate student who is enrolled in an eligible program.

Federal Consolidated Loans enable a borrower (parent or independent student) with loans from various lenders or loan programs to consolidate their loans into one. The lender repays the existing loans and establishes a new loan that has one interest rate and repayment schedule. Loans eligible for consolidation include all FFEL's, Perkins and selected Public Health loans.

WILLIAM D. FORD FEDERAL DIRECT LOAN PROGRAM

The William D. Ford Federal Direct Loan (DL) Program completes the loan programs funded and administrated by the federal government. There are four types of loans found in the DL Program:

- Federal Direct Plus Loan Program
- Federal Direct Consolidated Loan Program
- Federal Direct Stafford/Ford Loan Program
- Federal Direct Unsubsidized Stafford/Ford Loan Program

The DL Programs were authorized under Title IV of the Higher Education Act of 1965, as amended, with the enactment of the *Student Loan Reform Act of 1993*. The DL is a primary source of federal assistance providing loans to eligible borrowers to help defray the expense of postsecondary education. Federal Pell Grant awardees usually get top priority for the Perkin's Loan. The program uses loan capital that is provided by the federal government, requires only one aid application, and makes loans available directly through participating institutions rather than through private lenders or guaranty agencies (such is the case with the FFELs).

Like the FFEL Program, the DL Program provides eligible borrowers who have an outstanding balance on either DL's or FFEL loans and are unable to obtain an FFEL Consolidation Loan. The individuals must be currently enrolled in school or in a repayment status. Individuals in default may also qualify if they have made satisfactory arrangements to repay existing loans or agree to pay or repay loans under the income contingent repayment plan (ICRP).[10]

The Federal Direct Plus Loan Program is similar to the FDPL administered in the FFEL Program. Parents without an adverse credit history may borrow on behalf of a dependent postsecondary student. The borrower is responsible for the accruing interest and parents may borrow regardless of need. Loans are originated at the participating institution with funds provided by the federal government; in this particular case the sole lender is the USDE. Borrowers repay the USDE directly and the same terms and conditions apply here as they do with loans originating in the FFEL Program.

The Federal Direct Consolidated Loan Program is for individual borrowers who have an outstanding balance on either a DL or FFEL and are unable to obtain a FFEL Consolidated Loan. The individual borrower must be enrolled in school or in a repayment status. Borrowers in default may also qualify if they have made satisfactory arrangements to repay those loans or agree to repay them under the terms described in the ICRP. This loan combines one or more federal education loans into a single loan. Loans eligible for consolidation include those originating with the FFEL Program, the DL Program, the Federal Perkins Loan Program, and Select Public Health Loans.

The Federal Direct Stafford/Ford Loan Program is designed for individuals who are undergraduate, vocational, or graduate students and have been accepted and are enrolled at least part-time at a participating institution. These loans differ from others within the DL Program in that the federal government pays the accruing interest on the loan(s) while the borrower is in school or during a grace or deferment period. Borrowers must demonstrate a financial need. The loans originate from the participating institution with funds appropriated by the federal government. The USDE is the sole lender and the borrower repays them directly. Many of the same terms and conditions which exist in the FFEL Program are applicable to this program.

The Federal Direct Unsubsidized Stafford/Ford Loan Program is designed for undergraduate, vocational, or graduate students who have been accepted at a participating institution and are enrolled at least part-time. These loans require the borrower to pay all accruing interest including in-school, grace, and deferment periods. However, these loans are available regardless of the borrower's financial need. Loans originate at the participating institution with funds appropriated by the federal government. The USDE is the sole lender and borrowers repay them directly. Many of the same terms and conditions which exist in the FFEL Program are applicable to this program.

CAMPUS-BASED STUDENT FINANCIAL AID PROGRAMS

Campus-based aid programs include the Federal Supplemental Opportunity Grants (FSEOG) Program, the Federal Work-Study (FWS) Program, and the Perkins Loan Program (a.k.a. the National Direct Student Loan [NDSL] Program). They are considered "campus-based" because each participating school or university is responsible for the administration of these programs on its campus. The FAA ensures that funds are furnished to eligible students in accordance with the provisions of the laws and regulations and in cooperation with the Secretary of Education and the USDE. Unlike the Pell Grants, the FFEL, and the DL Programs, student eligibility does depend on the availability of funds at each participating institution.

Participating institutions apply for and receive funds directly from the USDE. Each institution must file a "Fiscal Operations Report and Application to Participate" form for each award year. Participants receive funding based on statutory formulas established each year by Congress. The institution's FAA is responsible for ensuring that eligible students receive program funds. For more detailed information on these programs and the requirements participating institutions must follow see http://www.ifap.ed.gov/sfahandbooks/attachments/0607Vol6Master.pdf.

FEDERAL SUPPLEMENTAL EDUCATIONAL OPPORTUNITIES GRANT PROGRAM

The Federal Supplemental Educational Opportunities Grant (FSEOG) Program was one of the first major federal student aid programs authorized under Title IV of the Higher Education Act of 1965, as amended. The purpose of the FSEOG Program is to encourage schools to provide grants, not loans, to eligible undergraduate applicants with exceptional financial need. A school must make FSEOG Program funds reasonably available to all eligible students although those who have the lowest EFC will be given first priority. The grant award can range from $100 to $4000 per year. Each participating school receives a certain amount of FSEOG funds for the academic year; once those funds are exhausted no more awards can be given. This program demonstrates quite aptly why it's important to file as early as possible. Not everyone eligible for an FSEOG may receive one.

Along with the other eligibility requirements outlined earlier in this chapter, FSEOG eligible students:

- must be enrolled in an undergraduate or vocational course of study at an institution of higher education;
- have not earned a bachelor's or first professional degree;
- will be considered eligible for only the first four academic years, regardless of length of program;
- must have a demonstrated financial need.

For more information on the FSEOG loan see http://www.ifap.ed.gov/sfahandbooks/attachments/0607Vol3Ch5.pdf.

FSEOG allocations are based on the institutional request for program funding first on the basis of the institution's 1999–2000 fiscal year program allocation. Each institution is then awarded additional funds on the basis of the aggregate need of eligible students in attendance.

THE FEDERAL WORK-STUDY (FWS) PROGRAM

One of the most commonly known sources of funding for student employees in academic libraries is the Federal Work-Study (FWS) Program. Although Congress has debated recently about the need to continue to appropriate funds at current levels for this program, academic libraries still rely heavily on FWS eligible students to perform a myriad of duties and tasks essential to the daily operations of an academic library.

The FWS program was originally established as a part of the *Economic Opportunity Act of 1964* (P.L. 88-452, 78 Stat 508). The intent of the FWS was to "stimulate and promote the part-time employment of students in institutions of higher education who are from low-income families and are in need of the earnings from such employment to pursue courses of study at such institutions." The HEA of 1965 provided the vehicle for which the FWS was transferred to in order to continue the original mission of the FWS program. The 1972 amendments to the HEA of 1965 created the Community Service Learning Program. The 1992 amendments to the HEA provided a 5 percent mandate for community service work for eligible FWS students. In 1998 President Clinton signed the *Higher Education Act of 1965* reauthorization which included a 7 percent mandate for community service, which included providing funds for a children's or family literacy projects. As well, eligible students can be compensated for the time spent in training or traveling to their community service projects.

The FWS program provides funds that are earned by eligible undergraduate or graduate students through part-time employment. Employment can be on or off campus. However, if it's off campus it must be in a federal, state, or local agency or a private nonprofit that serves the public's interests. FAA's at participating institutions have considerable flexibility in determining the amount of work-study awards given to eligible students. The hourly wage rate can not be less than the established federal minimal wage rate but it can be higher.

Institutional allocations are based on institutional requests for program funding under statutory formula. Like the FSEOG Program, funds are distributed to institutions on the basis of the institution's 1999–2000 Fiscal Year allocation and then on the basis of the aggregate need of the number of eligible students in attendance. Employers of work-study recipients must match a 30 percent funding formula, the remaining 70 percent is provided though federal funding. The exception to this 3:1 ratio is in the case of private, for-profit organizations that must provide 50 percent of the funding and in "community service" (for a definition of community service see 34 CFR 675.2[b]) types of positions for which the matching requirement is waived.

Financial need is determined by a USDE standard formula that has been established by Congress. Along with the EFC, the fundamental elements in the standard formula are the student's, and in the case of dependent students, the parent's income and assets, the family's household size and the number of family members attending postsecondary institutions. Different assessment rates and allowances are established for dependent students, independent students without dependents, and independent students with dependents. To qualify for FWS a student must be either a U.S. citizen or a permanent resident.

As noted earlier the FWS employer must meet federal minimum wage guidelines as well as all federal, state, and local employment laws. While the Small Business Job Protection Act of 1996 establishes a subminimum or training wage, the FWS program is exempt from this law and therefore must adhere to the current federal minimum wage. If a state or local law requires a higher minimum wage, the school must pay the FWS student that higher wage. Conversely, if a state or local law's wages are lower than the federal minimum wage, the FWS student must be paid at the currently established federal minimum wage rate.

ASSIGNING FWS JOBS

A participating institution must make FWS jobs reasonably available to all eligible participants. Also, to the extent possible, the institution must also make "equivalent employment"[11] available to all students at the institution who wish to work. To the extent possible and practical, each participating institution must provide FWS jobs that will complement and reinforce each recipient's education or career goals.

FWS jobs may be on or off campus. Off-campus jobs must be in the public interest if the work involved is for a federal, state, or local public agency or for a private, nonprofit organization. An institution may wish to allocate part of its FWS award to provide jobs in private for-profit organizations. Also, FWS employment may be used for community service programs. Some of these programs include:

- fields such as health care, child care, literacy training, education (including tutorial services), welfare, social services, transportation, housing and neighborhood improvement, public safety, crime prevention and control, recreation, rural development, and community improvement;
- work in service opportunities or youth corps as defined in Section 101 of the National and Community Service Act of 1990, and service in the agencies, institutions and activities designated Section 124(a) of that act;
- support for students (other than for an institution's own students) with disabilities; and,
- activities in which an FWS student serves as mentor for such purposes as:
  - tutoring;
  - supporting educational and recreational activities; and
  - counseling, including career counseling.

In assigning FWS jobs, each institution must consider the student's financial need, the number of hours per week the student can work, the period of employment, the anticipated wage rate, and the amount of other assistance available to each eligible participant. Although no minimum or maximum award limits are established, the amount for each student is determined based on the above mentioned factors.

JOB DESCRIPTIONS

Each FWS position should have a job description that includes the following:

- the name and address of the student's employer (department, public agency, nonprofit organization);
- the purpose of the student's job;
- the student's duties and responsibilities;
- the job qualifications;
- the job's wage rate or range;
- the length of the student's employment (beginning and ending dates); and
- the name of the student's supervisor.

The job description has several purposes:

- It clearly defines whether the job qualifies under the FWS Program;
- It provides the information needed to explain the position to a student and to help him or her select the type of employment most closely related to his or her educational or career objectives;
- It helps the financial aid administrator, the student, and the supervisor determine the number of hours of work required at the specified wage rate to meet a student's financial need; and,
- It establishes a written record, for both student and employer, of the job's duties and responsibilities so that there will be no misunderstanding.

EMPLOYMENT CONDITIONS AND LIMITATIONS

The provisions discussed below apply to all work under FWS, whether on or off campus.

- FWS employment must be governed by employment conditions, including pay, that are reasonable according to the type of work performed, the geographic region, the employee's proficiency, and any applicable federal, state, or local law;
- FWS employers must pay students at least the current federal minimum wage;
- FWS employment must not displace employees (including those on strike) or impair existing service contracts. If the school has an employment agreement with an organization in the private sector, the organization's employees must not be replaced with FWS students. Replacement is interpreted as displacement;
- FWS positions must not involve constructing, operating, or maintaining any part of a building used for religious worship or sectarian instruction;
- Neither a school nor an outside employer that has an agreement with the school to hire FWS students may solicit, accept, or permit soliciting any fee, commission, contribution, or gift as a condition for student's FWS employment. A student may pay union dues to an employer if they are a condition of employment and the employer's non-FWS employees also pay dues;
- The Fair Labor Standards Act of 1938, as amended, prohibits employers (including schools) from accepting voluntary services from any paid employee; any FWS student must be paid for all hours worked;
- An FWS student may not be paid for receiving instruction in a classroom, laboratory, or other academic setting. However, the fact that a FWS student may receive academic credit from the work performed does not disqualify the job under FWS; and,
- An FWS student's wages may be garnished only to pay any costs of attendance that the student owes the school or that will become due and payable during the period of the award.

ESTABLISHING WAGE RATES

Undergraduate students are paid FWS wages on an hourly basis only. Graduate students may be paid by the hour or may be paid a salary. Regardless of who employs the student, the school is responsible for making sure the student is paid for the work performed.

The school should determine the number of hours a student works based on the student's financial need and on how the combination of work and study hours will impact the student's health and academic progress. There are no statutory or regulatory limits on the number of hours per week or pay period a FWS student may work although they are not permitted to work more than 40 hours per week. The only factor one needs to keep in mind is that a FWS may not work more hours than the award for which he or she has been given.

An FWS student must be paid at least the current federal minimum wage. While there is no maximum wage rate, it is not permissible to pay a lower subminimum or training wage to FWS students. A school may not include fringe benefits as part of the compensation package and may not pay an FWS student commissions or fees. In determining an appropriate rate, the school must consider the following:

- The skills needed to perform the job;
- How much persons with those skills are paid in the local area for performing similar types of work;
- Rates the school would normally pay similar non-FWS employees; and,
- Any applicable federal, state, or local laws that require a specific wage rate.

An FWS student's need places a ceiling on the total earnings allowable but has no bearing on his or her wage rate. It is not permissible to base the wage rate on need or on any other factor not related to the student's skills or job description. If an FWS student's skill level depends on his or her academic advancement, the school may pay a student on that basis. However, students who perform jobs that are comparable to those of other employees should be paid comparable wages, whether the other employees are students at different class levels or are regular employees.

WORK-STUDY EMPLOYMENT DURING NONENROLLMENT PERIODS

FWS students may be employed during summer, or equivalent vacation periods, if the student is planning to enroll for the next regular session. Some universities require that FWS students enroll for at least a minimum number of hours in the summer to maintain their eligibility. Additionally, some schools may require a student pre-enroll for a minimum number of hours in the Fall semester in order to maintain summer eligibility. During the regular academic year, FWS students must be at least half-time students in order to qualify for FWS jobs.

WORK-COLLEGES PROGRAM

The *Higher Education Act Amendments of 1992* authorized the Work-Colleges Program. Schools that satisfy the definition of "work college" may apply with the USDE to participate in the program. An eligible institution may transfer funds from its allocation for the FWS Program and/or the Federal Perkins Loan Program to provide funding for this Program.

The Work-College Program views and values the use of comprehensive work-learning programs as a valuable educational approach. When used as a part of a school's educational program or as a financial plan that decreases the institutions reliance on grants and loans, the institution may also qualify for this program. This program also encourages student participation in community service activities.

Work College is defined as an eligible institution that:

- is a public or private nonprofit school with a commitment to community service;
- has operated a comprehensive work-learning program for at least two years;
- provides students participating in the comprehensive work-learning program with the opportunity to contribute to their education as well as to the welfare of the community;
- requires all students who reside on campus to participate in a comprehensive work-learning program; and,
- requires providing services as a integral part of the school's education program and as part of the school's educational philosophy.

A comprehensive student work-learning program is defined as a student work/service program that:

- is an integral and stated part of the institution's educational philosophy and program;
- requires participation of all resident students for enrollment, participation, and graduation;

- includes learning objectives, evaluation, and a record of work performance as part of the student's college record;
- provides programmatic leadership by college personnel at levels comparable to traditional academic programs;
- recognizes the educational role of work-learning supervisors; and,
- includes consequences for nonperformance or failure in the work-learning program similar to the consequences for failure in the regular academic program.

The Higher Education Act Amendments of 1998 provide for additional flexibility for work colleges in the use of federal funds allocated. To that extent program funds may be used to:

- support the educational costs of students through self-help provided under the work-learning program within the limits of their demonstrated financial need;
- promote the work-learning service experience as a tool of education and community service;
- carry out FWS and JLD (Job Location & Development Program) activities;
- administer, develop, and assess comprehensive work-learning programs;
- coordinate and carry out joint projects and activities to promote work-service learning; and
- conduct a comprehensive longitudinal study of academic progress and academic and career outcomes.

Additional requirements for the Work-Colleges program are updated regularly in 34 CRF 675, Subpart C. As well more details and information about the Work-Colleges Program can also be found at http://ifap.ed.gov/sfahandbooks/attachments/0607Vol6Master. pdf.

FEDERAL PERKINS LOAN PROGRAM

The Federal Perkins Loan Program allocations are made to eligible institutions for the purpose of providing low-interest loans to needy undergraduate and graduate students attending that institution. Loans under this program include the Federal Perkins Loan, the National Direct Student Loans, and the National Defense Student Loans. Named to honor the late Carl D. Perkins (D-KY), the former Chairman of the House Education and Labor Committee, the Federal Perkins Loan Program replaced the National Direct Student Loan program in the 1987–1988 award year.

To be eligible, undergraduate or graduate students must demonstrate exceptional financial need. The loan is provided from government funds plus a shared contribution by the institution. The institution must also take into consideration evidence related to the student's willingness to repay the loan. A default on previous loans or a history of unpaid debt may render a student ineligible. The fundamental difference between a Federal Perkins Loan and other federal loan programs is that the institution acts as the lender and the loan must be repaid directly to the institution.

Currently the interest rate on the loan is 5 percent; however that is subject to change and the borrower should check the appropriate sources to ascertain current interest rates. Undergraduates are eligible for loans up to $4,000 per academic year; graduate or professional students are eligible for a maximum amount of $6,000 per academic year.

LEVERAGING EDUCATION ASSISTANCE PARTNERSHIP PROGRAM (LEAP)

The Leveraging Education Assistance Partnership Program (LEAP, a.k.a State Student Incentive Grants [SSIG] Program) provides grants to states to assist them in providing need-based grant and work-study assistance to eligible postsecondary students. States must administer the LEAP Program under a single state agency and adhere to maintenance of effort criteria. Undergraduate and graduate students demonstrating substantial financial need may apply to the states in which they are permanent residents. The LEAP Program provides funds to the 50 states, the District of Columbia, Puerto Rico, the Virgin Islands, American Samoa, Guam, the Northern Mariana Islands, and the Republic of Palau.

Each state's allocation is based on the state's eligible postsecondary education enrollment. The federal allotments must be matched by funds appropriated by the state and this matching must represent an increase in the state appropriated grant and work-study expenditure over the amount spent during an established base year, usually defined as the second year before the state began its participation in the SSIG Program. The state must maintain its matching expenditure at a level not less than the average for the preceding three fiscal years, or at the level of the average of the full-time equivalent student enrollment levels for those three years. If a state does not utilize its entire allotment, the excess funds are distributed to other states in a similar proportion as the original distribution.

A state may use up to 20 percent of its allocation for community service-learning job programs. The eligible student must receive compensation for work but not in a grant form. The job program or community service must be administered by the appropriate postsecondary school in each state, and each student employed must perform work that is in the community's or public interest.

Student eligibility may differ among the states depending on constitutional, statutory, or policy restrictions. Some states actually have a legislative formula used to determine student eligibility and the amount of assistance that can be provided. Regardless, every student must be the prevailing eligibility requirements as detailed in 34 CFR 668.31–39 as well as demonstrate substantial financial need.

The LEAP Program in various states is known by a variety of names and may not contain the words "student incentive grants" in their program titles. A student who wishes to apply for LEAP Program funding or has questions regarding eligibility or award procedures should contact the appropriate education assistance agency in his or her state.[12]

THE ROBERT C. BYRD HONORS SCHOLARSHIP PROGRAM

The Robert C. Byrd Honors Scholarship Program is authorized until Title IV of the Higher Education Act of 1965, as amended. Under this Program, the secretary of education makes available, through grants to states, scholarships to exceptionally gifted students for study at postsecondary schools. This program recognizes and promotes student excellence and achievement.

Eligible students follow the application procedures established by the State Education Agency (SEA) in the state in which he or she legally resides. The SEA is a state board of education (or the equivalent state agency) that is primarily responsible for the supervision of public elementary and secondary schools. The SEA establishes criteria and procedures for selecting the scholars after consulting with school administrators, school boards, teachers, counselors, and parents. Prior to those procedures being implemented, the state's selection criteria and application procedures are reviewed and approved by the USDE.

Eligible students receive a scholarship for one academic year. Awards can be renewed for up to three additional years, provided that funds are appropriated and the awardee remains eligible. Students are selected on the basis of demonstrated outstanding academic achievement and promise of continued achievement and in a way that each state, the District of Columbia and Puerto Rico are fairly represented. An awardee may attend any public or private nonprofit postsecondary institution, proprietary institution of higher education, or postsecondary vocational institution.

COUNSELING THE STUDENT ON FINANCIAL AID

By periodically reviewing pertinent information found in this chapter as well as sources cited in the notes and bibliography, you should gain a valuable understanding of how each Student Financial Aid Program operates. For example, if one of your student employees receives a grant, any work-study award they also qualify for will most likely be reduced, thus changing the number of hours that student can work and requiring you to seek, perhaps, additional student employees.

Student employee supervisors are often surprised or caught off guard by circumstances of the individual and their interconnected financial aid package. A supervisor who has a basic knowledge and understanding of each program can avoid many unpleasant experiences and work-related situations. Supervisors are strongly urged to contact their FAA should questions arise. Supervisors should also help students:

- Explore all sources of aid;
- Stress constraints on aid;
- Urge each student employee to read and save all of their loan and grant documents and related materials;
- Review requirements for satisfactory academic progress;
- Remind students to keep their lenders, private and public, informed;
- Review loan terms and conditions;
- Describe consequences of multiple borrowing;
- Review student rights and responsibilities;
- Review deferment and forbearance conditions;
- Review loan repayment obligations;
- Provide general information on average indebtedness of students;
- Provide data on average, anticipated monthly repayment;
- Provide information on debt management strategies;
- Counsel on personal financial planning.

WHAT YOU CAN DO

As the supervisor of student employees in an academic library, you have the most frequent contact with students who are receiving some type of federal financial assistance. Understanding the procedures, rules, and regulations of, for example, the Federal

Work-Study Program, helps you deal with and understand awards and allotments and also helps you abide by the program's regulations and requirements. As supervisors, we often forget that many of our student employees may also be paying off loans. In recognition of their financial obligations, we as supervisors should do what we can to allow student employees to make up missed work time and attempt to provide long term employment. If the workload eases, we may think we are helping our student employees by giving them time off, forgetting that those students may have financial obligations that can not be met without a regular paycheck.

Again, before you advise any of your student employees on federal financial aid programs, check with your Financial Aid Administrator to be certain you know each program's rules and regulations as well as those applicable to your University.

INTERNET SITES OF INTEREST

It should be noted that the Internet is now the primary resource tool not only to find the latest information regarding student financial aid programs but also for submission of financial aid information to the USDE. The use of the electronic *FAFSA* form enhances and expedites the chances of a successful award for an eligible student. As always, when utilizing any type of Internet form to submit confidential information, be sure that you and the receiver are using the latest in encryption software to guard against the transmission of sensitive data to those who might use it for illegal means or purposes. In the case of the USDE, they utilize the best software possible.

There are numerous sites currently in existence on the Internet. The list below is by no means comprehensive or inclusive but should be used as a good starting point for information residing in an electronic format. One can search the Web through an appropriate search engine (i.e.—Google, FirstGov.) to find additional or new sites that have recently appeared.

The Catalog of Federal Domestic Assistance (CFDA)

http://12.46.245.173/pls/portal30/CATALOG.FUNCTIONAL_AREA_RPT2 .SHOW?p_arg_names=func_cat_cd&p_arg_values=G.

The CFDA, published by the U.S. government, contains information on all federal agencies that provide oversight to the myriad of domestic aid programs, including those that fall outside the USDE. The CFDA should be used as a resource for grants that are not administered by the USDE. In most cases the grants available are for very specific types of educational research and may or may not be useful for those who fall into the general undergraduate definitions.

Compilation of Student Financial Aid Regulations: 34 CFR

http://www.access.gpo.gov/nara/cfr/waisidx_05/34cfrv3_05.html#600.

A link to the *Code of Federal Regulations (CFR), Chapter 34* contains the latest rules and regulations as promulgated by the federal government on student financial aid.

FAFSA on the Web

http://www.fafsa.ed.gov.

The *Free Application for Student Aid (FAFSA)* site that allows an applicant to apply for financial aid, find the necessary school codes for the form, and other valuable information needed to complete the application form. This is the recommended site to use for federal financial assistance. This site is free and sponsored by the USDE. If you are requested to provide a bank account or credit card number, you are not at the correct site.

Federal School Code Search

http://www.fafsa.ed.gov/fotw0607/fslookup.htm.
This is the site used to find the school code needed to complete the FAFSA. Very easy searchable Web site.

FinAid: The SmartStudent™ Guide to Financial Aid

http://www.finaid.org/.
Established in 1994 as a public service FinAid has grown into one of the most comprehensive resources available on the Internet today. Created by Mark Kantrowitz, a noted financial aid and college planning author, this site provides an independent, objective guide to student financial aid resources, federal or private.

Financial Aid for College—A Guide to Financial Aid Information on the WEB

http://web.lwc.edu/administrative/library/finaid.htm.
An Internet guide produced by the Longwood College Library. Provides many links that will take one to additional Internet sites containing financial aid information.

Funding Education Beyond High School: The Guide to Student Aid, 2006–2007

http://studentaid.ed.gov/students/attachments/siteresources/StudentGuide.pdf.
Now available exclusively online, this resource should be the first consulted when researching the various types of student aid available from the U.S. Department of Education. Included in this 60-page document are frequently used Web sites, telephone numbers, and detailed explanations of the various loan programs available.

High School Counselor's Handbook, 2004–2005 Federal Student Aid

http://www.ifap.ed.gov/chandbooks/attachments/0405HSCHB.pdf.
Available exclusively online, this resource is a valuable tool for those counseling high-school students who aim to attend college and require some type of federal financial assistance. Included in this 93-page resource is information on each type of federal financial assistance, eligibility requirements, and other useful information. Phone number, Web sites, and other general information can also be located in this resource.

Grant Information

http://www.vcu.edu/mdcweb/new/resource/grant.html#fund.
The Virginia Commonwealth University (VCU) has gathered and compiled a unique page in that it provides links to a variety of financial aid resources from federal, state, business, foundations, and other pertinent resources. Updated regularly this site is one that should be reviewed for nonfederal sources of financial aid.

National Association of Student Financial Aid Administrators

http://www.teachermag.org/context/orgs/nasfaa.htm.
Provides a link to the National Association of Student Financial Aid Administrators, a national organization that helps to coordinate information exchange between FAAs.

Other Financial Aid Information

http://www.consortium.org/otheraid.htm.
Compiled by the *Consortium of Universities*, provides links to a variety of sources that provide information on student financial aid. Included is information about the Consortium, which members participate in which federal student aid programs, pending federal legislation on financial aid programs, and the *Chronicle of Higher Education*.

PIN Web Site

http://www.pin.ed.gov.
This site allows an applicant to apply for a USDE pin number in order to expedite the application form and process.

SallieMae

http://www.salliemae.com/salliemae_home.htm.
Now the leading provider of student loans as well as a major administrator of college saving plans. Provides federal and private student loans, including consolidation loans, for undergraduate and graduate students and their parents. Also offers comprehensive information and resources to assist students, parents, and guidance professionals with the financial aid process.

Student Aid on the Web

http://studentaid.ed.gov/students/attachments/siteresources/54.pdf.
Information about student aid and preparing for college.

The Student Guide—Financial Aid, 2003–2004

http://wwwed.gov/prog_info/SFA/StudentGuide/.
The most comprehensive guide on student financial aid available from the USDE. Provides a wealth of information on grants, loans, and work-study programs available

from the USDE. Updated each award year, this guide provides excellent information and includes a link to the *FAFSA* electronic application form.

StudentLoanNetwork

http://www.studentloannetwork.com/resources/.
Provides a wealth of information on student loans. Included are PowerPoint™ presentations, loan calculators, federal loan glossary, and information sheets on the application process, the COA, and other pertinent information.

Students.gov

http://www.students.gov/STUGOVWebApp/Public.
This is an official government Web site designed for students and their families. This Web site was designed as a one-stop site providing access to information resources from the U.S. government. Included are links to scholarship and grant sites, and state aid information.

Studentjobs.gov

http://studentaid.ed.gov/PORTALSWebApp/students/english/othersources.jsp?tab=funding.
Although this site is primarily aimed at assisting in finding employment opportunities within the U.S. government, this site does have a link to *E-Scholar* (http://www.studentjobs.gov/e-scholar.asp) that provides information on educational opportunities offered by Federal Government departments and agencies, or partnering organizations.

Welcome to AFSA's Education Financing Overview

http://www.acs-education.com
A compilation of information, mostly on the various federal loans available, produced by a private enterprise. AFSA, founded in 1967 to provide student loan billing and collections to higher education institutions, is part of the Fleet Financial Group. The information contained is useful to help both eligible students and parents determine that federal loan program is best for them plus provides answers on obtaining and repayment of federal loans.

NOTES

1. *Digest of Educational Statistics, 2004,* United States Department of Education, Office of Educational Research and Improvement, Washington, DC: United States Government Printing Office, 2004. See also http://nces.ed.gov/programs/digest/d05/tables/dt05_322.asp.

2. *1997 Directory of Post Secondary Institutions, Volume 1, Degree Granting Institutions,* United States Department of Education, Office of Educational Research and Improvement. Washington, DC: United States Government Printing Office, 1998, p. XXI

3. The Higher Education Act of 1965, as amended, includes the following:
   Higher Education Act of 1965 (P.L. 89-329, 79 STAT 1219);

Higher Education Act of 1965 Amendments (P.L. 108-98, 117 Stat 1174);

Higher Education Act Amendments of 1966 (P.L. 89-752, 80 STAT 1240);

Higher Education Act Amendments of 1968 (P.L. 90-575, 82 STAT 1014);

Higher Education Act Amendments of 1986 (P.L. 99-498, 100 STAT 1268);

Higher Education Act Amendments of 1992 (P.L. 102-325, 106 STAT 448);

Higher Education Act Amendments of 1995 (P.L. 104-19, 109 STAT 219, Title 1, Ch.4);

Higher Education Act Amendments of 1995 (P.L. 104-66, 109 STAT 715, Title 1, Subtitle D);

Higher Education Amendments of 1998 (P.L. 105-244, 112 Stat. 1581);

Higher Education Act Amendments of 1998 (P.L. 109-162, 119Stat 2960);

Higher Education Extension Act of 2006 (P.L. 109-212, 120 Stat. 321);

Higher Education Hurricane Relief Act of 2005 (P.L. 109-148, 119 Stat 2809);

Natural Disaster Student Aid Fairness Act (P.L. 109-86, 119 Stat. 2056);

Emergency Supplemental Appropriations Act for Defense, the Global War on Terror, and Hurricane Recovery Act of 2006 (P.L. 109- 234; 120 Stat. 418);

Pell Grant Hurricane and Disaster Relief Act (P.L. 109-66, 119 Stat 1999);

Second Higher Education Extension Act of 2005 (P.L. 109-150, 119 Stat 2884);

Student Grant Hurricane and Disaster Relief Act (P.L. 109-67, 119 Stat 2001);

Student Loan Rates and Lender Allowances (P.L. 107-139, 116 Stat 8);

Higher Education Review Act (Cost of) (P.L. 105-17, 111 STAT 211, Title 4, Sections 40001 to 40007);

Higher Education Reconciliation Act of 2005 (P.L. 109-171, 120 Stat 4);

Higher Education Technical Amendments Act of 1979 (P.L. 96-49, 93 STAT 351);

Higher Education Technical Amendments Act of 1991 (P.L. 100-50, 101 STAT 335);

Higher Education Technical Amendments of 1991 (P.L. 102-26, 105 STAT 123);

Higher Education Technical Amendments of 1993 (P.L. 103-208, 107 STAT 2457).

4. *U.S. Statistical Abstract*, Table 277, p. 182 Federal Student Financial Assistance: 1995 to 2005.

5. *The Federal Student Financial Aid Handbook, 2006–2007*, United States Department of Education, Washington, DC: United States Government Printing Office. See: http://www.ifap. ed.gov/IFAPWebApp/currentSFAHandbooksPag.jsp. Also check this Web site for updated information on independent vs. dependent status: http://studentaid.ed.gov/students/publications/ student_guide/2005-2006/english/general-dependency.htm.

6. *Fin-Aid: The Financial Aid Information Page*, http://www.finaid.org/otheraid/parentsrefuse. phtml.

7. *FSA Handbooks, 2006—2007*, U.S. Department of Education, Federal Student Aid Library, http://www.ifap.ed.gov/IFAPWebApp/currentSFAHandbooksYearPag.jsp?p1=2006-2007p2=c. See specifically http://www.ifap.ed.gov/sfahandbooks/attachments/ 0607FSAHBkVol1Ch2.pdf.

8. Ibid. See specifically http://www.ifap.ed.gov/sfahandbooks/attachments/ 0607FSAHBkVol1.pdf.

9. Ibid. See specifically http://www.ifap.ed.gov/sfahandbooks/attachments/ 0607FSAHBkVol2Ch4.pdf.

10. Under an income contingent repayment schedule, the size of the monthly payments depends on the income earned by the borrower. As the borrower's income increases, so do the payments. The income contingent repayment plan is not available for PLUS Loans. For more information on all loan repayment plans see http://studentaid.ed.gov/students/attachments/siteresources/ StudentGuide.pdf.

11. Equivalent Employment jobs are similar nonfederal work-study jobs offered or arranged by a school or university.

12. *State Grants*, http://www.edonline.com/collegecompass/state.htm.

BIBLIOGRAPHY

Andersen, Charles J. *Financial Aid for Full-Time Undergraduates*. Washington, DC: American Council on Education, 1984.

Blum, Laurie. *Free Money for College from the Government*. New York: Henry Holt and Co., 1993.

Choy, Susan P. and Mark D. Premo. *How Low Income Undergraduates Financed Postsecondary Education, 1992–93*. Washington, DC: U.S. Department of Education, Office of Educational Research and Improvement, National Center for Education Statistics, 1996.

College Student's Guide to Merit and Other No-need Funding. San Carlos, CA: Reference Service Press, 1996.

The Condition of Education, 2006; Indicator 50: Federal Grants and Loans to Undergraduate Students. Washington, DC: U.S. Department of Education, Institute of Education Sciences, 2006. See also http://nces.ed.gov/programs/coe/2006/pdf/50_2006.pdf.

Cronin, Joseph Marr and Sylvia Quarles Simmons, eds. *Student Loans: Risks and Realities*. Dover, MA: Auburn House, 1987.

Cuccaro-Alamin, Stephanie and Susan P. Choy. *Postsecondary Financing Strategies: How Undergraduates Combine Work, Borrowing, and Attendance*. Washington, DC: U.S. Department of Education, Office of Educational Research and Improvement, National Center for Education Statistics, 1998.

Dennis, Marguerite J. *Mortgaged Futures: How to Graduate from School without Going Broke*. Washington, DC: Hope Press, 1986.

Digest of Education Statistics List of Tables and Figures, 2005. http://www.nces.ed.gov/programs/digest/d05_tf.asp.

Directory of Financial Aids for Minorities. San Carlos, CA: ABC-Clio Information Services, Reference Service Press, 1997.

Federal Student Aid: The Blue Book: Accounting, Recordkeeping and Reporting by Postsecondary Educational Institutions Participating in the Federal Student Aid Programs. Washington, DC: U.S. Department of Education, 2005. See also http://www.edupubs.org/webstore/EdSearch/.

Financial Aid for African Americans. El Dorado Hills, CA: Reference Service Press, 2006.

Financial Aid for Asian Americans. El Dorado Hills, CA: Reference Service Press, 2006.

Financial Aid for Hispanic Americans. El Dorado Hills, CA: Reference Service Press, 2006.

Financial Aid for Minorities: Awards to Students with Any Major. Garrett Park, MD: Garrett Park Press, 1994.

Financial Aid for Native Americans. El Dorado Hills, CA: Reference Service Press, 2006.

Financial Aid for Veterans, Military Personnel, and Their Dependents. Redwood City, CA: Reference Service Press, 2006.

Fossey, Richard and Mark Bateman, eds. *Condemning Students to Debt: College Loans and Public Policy*. New York: Teachers College Press, 1998.

Gladieux, Lawrence E. and Arthur M. Hauptman. *The College Aid Quandary: Access, Quality, and the Federal Role*. Washington, DC: Brookings Institution, 1995.

McPherson, Michael S. and Morton Owen Schapiro. *The Student Aid Game: Meeting Need and Rewarding Talent in American Higher Education*. Princeton, NJ: Princeton University Press, 1998.

Merrill, Edward and Michael McCanna. *Financial Aid Resource Guide*, 5th ed. Corvallis, OR: Oregon State University, Indian Education Office, 1996.

Miskelly, Matthew, project editor. *Scholarships, Fellowships and Loans: A Guide to Education-Related Financial Aid Programs for Students and Professionals*. Farmington Hills, MI: Gale, 2004.

O'Sullivan, Marie and Sara J. Steen. *Financial Resources for International Study: A Guide for US Nationals*. New York: Institute of International Education, 1996.

Statistical Abstract of the United States. Washington, DC: U.S. Department of Commerce, 2005.

St. John, Edward P., ed. *Rethinking Tuition and Student Aid Strategies*. San Francisco, CA: Jossey-Bass Publishers, 1995.

Sutterlin, Rebecca and Robert A. Kominski. *Dollars for Scholars: Postsecondary Costs and Financing, 1990–1991*. Washington, DC: U.S. Department of Commerce, USGPO, 1994.

U.S. Department of Education. *The Student Guide: Five Federal Financial Aid Programs*. Washington, DC: USGPO, 1995.

———. *Direct Loans: A Better Way to Borrow*. Washington, DC: USGPO, 1997.

———. *Direct Loans: William D. Ford Federal Direct Loan Program: PLUS Loan Basics*. Washington, DC: USGPO, 1997.

———. *FAFSA on the Web: the Wave of the Future*. Washington, DC: USGPO, 1997.

———. *The Federal Student Aid Information Center*. Washington, DC: USGPO, 1997.

———. *The Counselor's Handbook for Postsecondary Schools*. Washington, DC: USGPO, 1998.

U.S. Department of Education, National Center for Educational Statistics. *Federal Support for Education, Fiscal Years 1980 to 1997*. Washington, DC: USGPO, 1998.

U.S. Department of Education, Office of Educational Research and Improvement, Educational Resources Information Center. *Financing Postsecondary Education: The Federal Role: Proceedings of the National Conference on the Best Ways for the Federal Government to Help Students and Families Finance Postsecondary Education: College of Charleston, Charleston, South Carolina, October 8–9, 1995*. Washington, DC: USGPO, 1996.

U.S. Department of Education, Office of Student Financial Assistance. *1992–93 Congressional Methodology*. Washington, DC: USGPO, 1992.

———. *The EFC Formula Book: The Expected Family Contribution for Federal Student Aid*. Washington, DC: USGPO, 1997.

———. *The Federal Student Financial Aid Handbook, 1998–1999*. Washington, DC: USGPO, 1997.

U.S. Department of Education, Student Financial Assistance Programs. *The Student Guide: Financial Aid from the U.S. Department of Education, 1995–96*. Washington, DC: USGPO, 1995.

———. *Compilation of Student Aid Regulations: Through 12/31/97: 34 CFR*. Washington, DC: USGPO, 1998.

U.S. General Accounting Office. *Supplemental Student Loans: Who Borrows and Who Defaults: Fact Sheet for Congressional Requesters*. Washington, DC: U.S. General Accounting Office, 1989.

———. *Supplemental Student Loans: Legislative Changes Have Sharply Reduced Loan Volume: Fact Sheet for the Chairman, Committee on Labor and Human Resources, U.S. Senate*. Washington, DC: U.S. General Accounting Office, 1990.

———. *Supplemental Student Loans: Who Are the Largest Lenders?: Fact Sheet for Congressional Requesters*. Washington, DC: U.S. General Accounting Office, 1990.

U.S. General Services Administration. *Catalog of Federal Domestic Assistance*. Washington, DC: 1997.

5

Employee/Employer Rights and Responsibilities

No man was ever endowed with a right without being at the same time saddled with a responsibility.

—Gerald W. Johnson

EMPLOYEE/EMPLOYER RIGHTS

It is not uncommon to hear comments by employees such as, "You can't do that—I know my rights!" It would seem that rights are a one-way proposition. In fact, employees do have rights, but so do employers. Supervisors of student employees must understand employee rights and clearly communicate them to the employees. By the same token, it is important that the student employee supervisor have a basic understanding of the law as it relates to employment. Employee's rights may be legally guaranteed or granted by the library or university.

LEGAL RIGHTS

Employees are protected by certain inalienable rights. Those rights include the right to a safe work environment and a nondiscriminatory and harassment-free workplace. Employees also have last-resort termination rights, privacy rights, and where applicable, the right to participate in unions.

RIGHT TO A SAFE WORK ENVIRONMENT

The Occupational Safety and Health Act of 1970 (OSHA) guarantees employees a safe work environment. Under the terms of the law, all employees have the right to request a department of labor inspection of any perceived safety or health problem. The request must identify specific violations and be sent to the department of labor with a copy to the employer. The employee requesting an inspection must sign the department of labor request but need not sign the employer copy. Employees may refuse to work or perform a task if the work itself or the work environment is felt to be unsafe. The following conditions must be met before an employee can refuse to work:

1) Normal procedures to resolve the problem have not been successful.
2) The employee has notified the appropriate management officials and tried to correct the problem, but the unsafe conditions remain.
3) The worker's fears of unsafe conditions are supported by evidence and the worker believes that conditions are unsafe.

Occupational Safety and Health Act. Enacted to ensure safe and healthy working conditions for every worker in the United States. Provisions of the act are to create public safety and health standards; to conduct inspections and investigations; to issue citations and propose penalties; and to require employers to keep records of job-related injuries and illnesses.

Safety laws that are approved by OSHA.

REFERENCE: Title 29, *U.S. Code*, Sec. 651 et seq.

RIGHT TO A NONDISCRIMINATORY WORKPLACE

As a supervisor, it is your responsibility to assure that discrimination does not occur in hiring, promotion, transfer, or termination of student employees. It is also your responsibility to report any instances of discrimination to the appropriate person. Even the perception of discrimination based on race, creed, sex, age, sexual preference, national origin, or handicap in the library must be avoided. Among the laws designed to protect individuals from employment discrimination are the Civil Rights Act of 1991; Title VII of the Civil Rights Act of 1964; Title 42 of the United States Code, Section 1981; the Americans with Disabilities Act (ADA) of 1990; the Age Discrimination in Employment Act; the Equal Pay Act of 1963; and the First Amendment to the U.S. Constitution. The following are brief descriptions of major U.S. law relating to employment discrimination.

Title VII of the Civil Rights Act of 1964 (Title VII). As Amended by the Equal Employment Opportunity Act of 1972. Simply stated, Title VII of the Civil Rights Act of 1964 prohibits an employer from refusing to hire or from discriminating against an employee on the job because of the employee's race, color, religion, sex, or national origin. Enacted in 1964 with major amendments in 1972 and 1991.

REFERENCE: Title 42, *U.S. Code*, Sec. 2000e.

Civil Rights Act of 1991. An amendment to Title VII of the Civil Rights Act of 1964, it makes employment discrimination laws applicable to all aspects of the employment relationship and allows women, disabled individuals, and members of religious minorities to sue for damages for intentional discrimination and to choose trial by jury.

REFERENCE: Title 42, *U.S. Code*, Sec. 12101 et seq.

Executive Order 11246 (E.O. 11246). Prohibits discrimination by federal contractors and subcontractors and requires that they have written affirmative action plans outlining the action they will take to hire and promote women and minorities. Employers found in violation of E.O. 11246 may have their federal contracts canceled and future contracts denied. Enacted in 1978.

REFERENCE: E.O. 11246

SEX DISCRIMINATION

Discrimination based on sex occurs when an individual is treated differently because of his or her gender. Federal and state laws prohibit discrimination against anyone because of sex. An individual who is refused a job, a promotion, fired, or discriminated against in any terms or conditions of employment based on sex may have a discrimination claim.

Additional protections are provided by the Equal Pay Act of 1963, which makes it unlawful to pay females less than males who do similar work; the Vietnam Era Veterans' Readjustment Assistance Act of 1974 requires federal contractors and subcontractors to take affirmative action to employ and advance in employment, qualified disabled veterans, and veterans of the Vietnam era; and the Pregnancy Discrimination Act of 1978 protects against discrimination in employment because of pregnancy. Pregnancy should be treated as any other temporary disability and an employer may not refuse to hire a qualified female because she is pregnant.

SEXUAL ORIENTATION

Federal court decisions have served to declare that Title VII of the Civil Rights Act of 1964 protects job applicants and employees from discrimination based on sexual orientation, but there is no federal law specifically addressing the issue. Sexual orientation relates to an individual's preference for heterosexuality, homosexuality, bisexuality, or identification with one of these preferences. Sexual orientation may also be referred to as lifestyle.

Eight states have comprehensive nondiscrimination laws and more than 25 cities and 100 counties in the United States now have ordinances and policies banning discrimination based on sexual orientation since the widespread attention given to Anita Bryant's campaign to repeal a Dade County, Florida, gay rights ordinance in 1977. Cities and counties across the United States have either decided to include sexual orientation in their antidiscrimination statutes or have repealed such ordinances. Fully one-fifth of the American population is covered by such ordinances or policies as of mid-1994. The ordinances differ greatly from one locale to another, but they typically amend the human rights or antidiscrimination statute by adding "sexual orientation" to the list of protected categories. Most of the ordinances and policies are found in large cities with virtually none in smaller communities. Employee protections on the basis of sexual orientation or individual lifestyle are afforded only to those in communities with ordinances.

As an example of a library organization's stand on the issue, the American Library Association's (ALA) antidiscrimination policy (54.3) states, "ALA is committed to equality of opportunity for all library employees or applicants for employment, regardless of race, color, creed, sex, age, or physical or mental disability, individual life-style or national origin."[1] By advertising through ALA services, libraries and other organizations agree to comply with the policy. Direct or implied biases are edited out of ads placed in ALA publications. Controversies surrounding gays in the military and discrimination against gays in federal hiring demonstrate that the issue of discrimination based on sexual orientation remains largely to be resolved.

DISABLED WORKERS

The Vocational Rehabilitation Act of 1973 was passed by Congress to protect the employment rights of disabled workers. That act applied only to federal contractors and subcontractors. The Americans with Disabilities Act (ADA), which took effect in 1992, extends coverage to all employers of 15 or more workers. A disabled individual, for the purposes of the law, is a person who has a physical or mental impairment that limits one or more major life activities, has a record of such impairment, or is regarded by others as having such an impairment. Impairments that limit major life activities must be substantial as opposed to minor and include impairments that limit seeing, hearing, speaking, walking, breathing, performing manual tasks, learning, caring for oneself, and working. An individual with paralysis, substantial hearing or visual impairment, mental retardation, or learning disability would be covered, but an individual with a minor, nonchronic condition of short duration such as a sprain, broken bone, or infection would normally not be covered. A person with a history of cancer or of mental illness would be covered. The third part of the definition protects individuals who are regarded and treated as though they have a substantially limiting disability, for example, the law would protect an individual who is disfigured from adverse employment decisions because the employer feared negative reactions from coworkers. AIDS victims are included in the latter definition as well.

The basic provision of the ADA prohibits discrimination against qualified disabled persons by requiring that the employer make reasonable accommodation for those who can perform the job unless that accommodation would create an undue hardship for the employer. To be a qualified disabled person, the individual must have an impairment that limits one of the major life activities yet must be able to perform the essential functions of the job. The sole fact that an individual is disabled can't eliminate the individual from consideration. Reasonable accommodation requires that the employer modify the job application process so disabled persons can apply in the first place and adjust the work environment in such a way that the disabled individual can perform the job. It should be noted here that the employer may make preemployment inquiries into the ability of a job applicant to perform job-related functions However, an employer cannot ask whether the applicant is an individual with a disability.

A reasonable accommodation might include altering the structure of the work area to make it accessible, acquiring new equipment, modifying work schedules, or simply putting a desk on blocks to accommodate a wheelchair. An accommodation does not have to be made if it would create an "undue hardship." An undue hardship on an employer depends in large part on the type and cost of the accommodation needed, the size of the organization, and the size of the budget. A large organization would have to go to greater lengths than a small business to make a reasonable accommodation. An accommodation could also be considered an undue hardship if it would unduly disrupt other employees or customers, but not if the disruption is caused simply by fear or prejudice. Even in the case of undue hardship, an employer may be required to provide an alternative accommodation.

The ADA excludes from coverage applicants and employees who are currently illegally using drugs but not those individuals who have been successfully rehabilitated. ADA calls largely for common sense solutions to making accommodations for disabled workers who, with the accommodation, can perform the essential functions of the job. A larger, more difficult problem revolves around those few individuals who would take advantage of a disability to find a way to sue.

Vocational Rehabilitation Act of 1973 (Rehab Act). This legislation extended Title VII antidiscrimination protections to disabled individuals. The act prohibits discrimination in employment on the basis of a mental or physical disability. The act defines a disabled person as one who "has a physical or mental impairment which substantially limits one or more of life's major activities, has a record of such impairment, and is regarded as having such an impairment."
REFERENCE: Title 29, *U.S. Code*, Sec. 701 et seq.

Americans with Disabilities Act (ADA). Prohibits discrimination against qualified disabled workers in hiring, compensation, and other terms and conditions of employment. Requires employers to make reasonable accommodations for individuals who are otherwise qualified to perform the essential functions of the job as long as those accommodations would not be an undue hardship on the employer. Enacted in 1990.
REFERENCE: Title 42, *U.S. Code*, Sec. 12101 et seq.

AGE DISCRIMINATION

The Age Discrimination in Employment Act (ADEA) protects employees from discrimination because of age. Workers over the age of 40 are protected by the ADEA, and state laws have been passed to extend that protection in many cases. The law forbids employers from specifying any age preference in job ads except minimum age requirements, for example, for an individual who will serve alcoholic beverages. Employers can't refuse to hire, pay employees less, or discriminate in any way because of age. Courts recognize four elements necessary for a prima facie for age discrimination:

1. The individual is in the protected age group—over 40 under the ADEA or younger for some states.
2. The individual was terminated, not promoted, or was the object of an adverse employment decision.
3. The individual was qualified for the position.
4. The adverse decision was made under circumstances that give rise to an inference of age discrimination.

In 1989, the Supreme Court ruled that the ADEA did not apply to employee benefit plans; however, in 1990, Congress passed the Older Workers Benefit Protection Act, which extended age discrimination prohibitions to benefits. The Act states that if an employer has an employee benefit plan, the employer has to expend the same amount of money for the older worker's benefits as for the younger worker, even though the resulting coverage may be less; for health insurance coverage, premiums, and benefits must be equal.

Age Discrimination in Employment Act (ADEA). Enacted in 1967and amended by additional law, including the Older Workers Benefit Protection Act (OWBPA) of 1990. Prohibits discrimination against workers between the ages of 40 and 70 on the basis of age.
REFERENCE: Title 29, *U.S. Code*, Sec. 621.

NATIONAL ORIGIN DISCRIMINATION

The only question relating to citizenship an employer can ask a prospective employee related to country of origin is whether or not the applicant is authorized to work in the United States. Once hired, the individual must comply with the provisions of the Immigration Reform and Control Act (IRCA), under which the employer and employee complete applicable sections of the INS I-9 form. Under federal law, employees cannot be discriminated against because of place of origin or because employees have physical, cultural, or linguistic characteristics of a certain nationality. Simply put, employees are protected from employment discrimination because they "look foreign" or have a "foreign accent."

The prohibitions against harassment on the basis of national origin are the same as for sexual harassment. Title VII of the Civil Rights Act of 1964 protects workers against ethnic slurs or conduct that serve to create a hostile working environment.

Immigration Reform and Control Act (IRCA). 1986. Makes it illegal to recruit, hire, refer for hire any unauthorized alien; requires documentation of identity and eligibility of workers to work in the United States; and prohibits discrimination on the basis of national origin or citizenship status. Employer and employee complete applicable sections of the INS I-9 form.
REFERENCE: Title 8, *U.S. Code*, Sec. 1324.

RELIGIOUS DISCRIMINATION

Individuals are protected from discrimination based on religion by the First Amendment of the U.S. Constitution.

Amendment I (1791). "Congress shall make no law respecting an establishment of religion, or prohibiting the free exercise thereof; or abridging the freedom of speech, or of the press; or the right of the people peaceably to assemble, and to petition the government for a redress of grievances."

The overriding concern in employment is that all individuals be treated equally, whether equally good or equally bad. Inasmuch as more than 70 percent of the employees in an organization are likely to fall into one of the protected groups discussed in this chapter, the minority, in effect, are the majority. Thus, it simply makes sense to treat all employees equally.

RIGHT TO A HARASSMENT-FREE WORKPLACE

Harassment can be verbal abuse, subtle pressure for sexual activity, or physical aggressiveness. Verbal abuse may also be discrimination in the form of ethic, racial, or sex-related jokes, slurs, or name-calling. Employees have a right to expect their supervisors to put an end to this form of harassment. Victims of verbal abuse that is discriminatory may file a grievance or a complaint with the Equal Opportunity Employment Commission.

While sexual harassment most often takes place in a situation of power differential between the persons involved, sexual harassment may occur between persons of the same status: student-student, librarian-librarian, or staff-staff. It may take place between two males or two females and is not restricted to male-female or female-male incidents. While the vast majority of victims are female and the vast majority of offenders are male, the prohibition of sexual harassment applies regardless of the genders of the parties. Guidelines issued by the Equal Employment Opportunity Commission define sexual harassment as unwelcome sexual advances, requests for sexual favors, and other verbal or physical conduct of a sexual nature occurring under any of the following three conditions:

1) Submission to the conduct is an explicit or implicit condition of an individual's employment.
2) Submission to or rejection of such conduct by an individual is used as the basis for employment decisions affecting the individual.
3) Such conduct has the purpose or effect of interfering with an individual's work performance or creating an intimidating, hostile, or offensive work environment.

As a supervisor, it is extremely important that you know that the employer is liable for sexual harassment charges if the supervisor is aware of, or should have known about, such activity taking place. The supervisor must be aware of what is happening in the work area and put an immediate end to any activity that even hints at sexual harassment. It is critical that you, the supervisor, be familiar with your library/university's policy on sexual harassment.

LAST-RESORT TERMINATION RIGHTS

Student employees have certain rights relating to the termination of their employment with the library. Legally, an employee's termination may be declared invalid if any of the following conditions exist:

1) Discharged for a reason specifically prohibited by federal or state standards. Termination that is in direct violation of Title VII of the Civil Rights Act of 1964, or the Occupational Safety and Health Act, for example, is illegal.
2) Discharged for complying with a statutory duty. Termination for performing jury duty, for example, is illegal.
3) Discharged in violation of implied promises made at employment. For example, if your handbook says employees may be terminated only for unsatisfactory performance, what happens if the student employee is caught stealing the overdue fine money?
4) Discharging an employee without providing due process. The employee has the right to certain procedural steps and the right to know the reason for termination. A reason for termination may not be needed during a probationary period.
5) Discharge that is motivated by malice or retaliation may be ruled to be invalid.

Of course, there is a right way and a wrong way to terminate student employees. Your library's policies should be clear on how termination is to be handled. For additional suggestions on how to handle termination of student employees, review Chapter 14.

PRIVACY RIGHTS

Employees have the right to keep personal information from those who have no need to know. This privacy includes employment references, personnel files, and protection from unreasonable searches.

The best practice to follow when prospective employers contact you for employment references for current student employees is to provide only the most basic employment information to them. Basic information includes a confirmation of employment, dates of employment, and the specific position held. Many libraries have policies forbidding supervisors from giving employment references for their staff or student employees. One exception is that an employer is ethically bound to pass on negative information about the moral character of a former student employee, if relevant. For example, if a student employee discharged for stealing, who has applied for a position with a financial institution, the prospective employer has a right to know.

Student employees have a right to expect that the information contained in their personnel files is confidential. Employees have a right to see most of the information in their files. Management has the right to withhold some information, for example, a confidential memorandum discussing a promotion that was not given. Information that is irrelevant to the employees' jobs or performance should be purged from all personnel files. Supervisors tend to keep their own personnel files, duplicating the centralized files. If those files contain information not relevant to the student employees' jobs or performance, remove and destroy it.

Constitutional protection against unreasonable searches is provided by the Fourth Amendment of the U.S. Constitution. Although it appears that the focus is on searches by government officials and not private employers, it appears that private employers can conduct searches without fear of constitutional violation. Employers considering establishing a search policy must make sure that it provides for giving employees adequate advance notice. The best policy is to seek advance consent before any search of employees' lockers, desks, etc. The following guidelines apply:

1) The search policy should be based on legitimate employer interest. The prevention of theft, drinking, or the use or possession of drugs are legitimate employer interests.
2) The policy should include all types of searches, including searches of the person, lockers, and personal possessions.
3) The policy should advise employees that lockers are library property, and that lockers may be routinely searched.
4) The search procedure should be applicable to all employees.
5) A statement should be included that a request to undergo a search does not imply an accusation.
6) The search policy must be communicated to all employees. It should be included in handbooks, and employees should be asked to sign a consent statement at the time of employment.
7) Those responsible for conducting searches should be given explicit instructions regarding search procedure.

8) The search should be conducted in a dignified and reasonable manner. Never conduct a search of an employee's person in the presence of other employees.

Those libraries that have access to the services of a campus police department should seek their advice and assistance in all matters regarding employee searches. Remember, employees have a right to expect that unreasonable searches will not be conducted.

UNION PARTICIPATION RIGHTS

Although this does not apply to the majority of libraries, it should be noted that union and nonunion employees have the right to participate in organizing and maintaining membership in a union. This right is guaranteed by the National Labor Relations Act (Wagner Act).

THE SUPERVISOR AND UNIONS

YOU MAY tell employees about current wages and benefits and how they compare to other jobs.

YOU MAY tell employees you will use all legal means to oppose unionization.

YOU MAY tell employees the disadvantages of having a union (especially the cost of dues, assessments, and requirements of membership).

YOU MAY show employees articles about unions and negative experiences others have had elsewhere.

YOU MAY explain the unionization process to your employees accurately.

YOU MAY forbid distribution of union literature during work hours in work areas.

YOU MAY enforce disciplinary policies and rules in a fair manner.

YOU MAY NOT promise employees pay increases or promotions if they vote against the union.

YOU MAY NOT threaten employees with termination or discriminate when disciplining employees.

YOU MAY NOT spy on or have someone spy on union meetings.

YOU MAY NOT make a speech to employees or groups at work within 24 hours of the election.

YOU MAY NOT ask employees how they plan to vote or if they have signed authorization cards.

YOU MAY NOT urge employees to persuade others to vote against the union (such a vote must be initiated solely by the employee).

—Adapted from Robert L. Mathis and John H. Jackson. *Personnel*. 4th ed. St. Paul, MN: West Publishing Company, 1985, p. 576.

UNIVERSITY-GRANTED RIGHTS

In addition to those rights granted to employees by law, there are rights that are granted by the employing institutions. Rights granted by universities usually include the right to an appeal and grievance process and the right to equitable compensation. Those rights are usually described in detail in the policies of the college or university personnel handbook.

RIGHT TO AN APPEAL AND GRIEVANCE PROCESS

Universities, and in turn their libraries, grant to all employees the right to a grievance and appeal process. Some universities grant the same rights to student employees and permanent staff while other universities provide slightly different processes to the two groups. The difference is commonly in how far a grievance may be taken. Temporary employees and employees during their probationary period are often given access to only the first step of the process. Student employees may be considered as temporary employees in some libraries.

The primary purpose of an appeal and grievance procedure is to provide a means by which employees, without jeopardizing their jobs, can express complaints about their work or working conditions and obtain a fair hearing through progressively higher levels of management. Complaints charging discrimination based on race, creed, sex, age, sexual preference, national origin, or handicap may be handled by the regular grievance procedure or be dealt with by the university's affirmative action office. The appeal and grievance procedure serves to avoid the high costs of court action, both in terms of dollars and morale.

Two-Step Grievance Procedure

A two-step grievance and appeal process is common in university libraries. The time limits for the process may vary. In Step One, a grievance must be filed in writing by the employee within five working days following the act or discovery of the condition that gave rise to the grievance. Normally, the written grievance is submitted to an office in University Personnel. A personnel officer will conduct a preliminary investigation of the grievance and attempt to mediate the dispute. If the grievance is resolved to the satisfaction of both parties, the officer prepares a report of the resolution, provides copies to both sides, and the grievance is considered closed. If the grievance is not resolved through mediation, a report to that effect is prepared and provided to both parties. If student employees are given access to the second step, an appeal to Step Two of the procedure may be made.

An appeal must be filed in writing by the employee within five working days from receipt of the Step One report. Failure to file within the specified period constitutes forfeiture of the right to appeal, and the grievance will be considered closed. The appeal is heard by a Grievance Review Committee, which is composed of the director of personnel, the dean/director of the library, and one other uninvolved employee selected by the aggrieved employee. The written decision of the Review Committee, including a discussion of the case and the rationale for the decision, is provided to the employee and employer, usually within 15 working days of the hearing. There is no further right to appeal in the procedure. Any further action by the employee must be taken in civil court.

Mediation and Arbitration

In the previous two-step grievance procedure, both mediation and arbitration are utilized. Mediation is provided by the personnel office and arbitration by the review committee.

Mediation is a procedure by which an impartial third party helps the employee and the employer to reach a voluntary agreement on how to settle a grievance. The mediator often makes suggestions or recommendations and attempts to reduce the emotions and tensions that prevent resolution of the complaint. In order to be successful, the mediator must have the trust and respect of both parties. If, in Step One, the mediator is unable to get the parties to agree, the mediation effort is ended without resolution.

If an appeal is made, arbitration is required. Arbitration is a procedure in which a neutral third party, in this case, the Grievance Review Committee, studies the grievance, listens to the arguments on both sides, and makes recommendations that are binding on both.

Common Types of Grievances

The grievance is a formal charge made by a student employee that the employee has been adversely affected by a violation of university or library policy. Grievances always allege that there has been a violation. Often the situation begins as a gripe by the employee, and when it is not handled by the supervisor to the employee's satisfaction, a grievance is filed. Some of the most common types of grievances deal with the following situations:

1) Discipline or termination for absenteeism, insubordination, misconduct, or substandard work.
2) Promotion or transfer of student employees.
3) Complaints charging discrimination based on race, creed, sex, age, sexual preference, national origin, or handicap.

When a Grievance is Filed against You

It is hoped that library supervisors do not cause student employees to file grievances, yet few libraries are able to completely avoid them. That is not to say that libraries that have no grievances all have student employees who are completely pleased with their jobs and their supervisors. Of course, it is better to have the problems openly discussed than to have a staff who do not express their feelings. It is hoped that complaints and employee concerns are addressed by the supervisor and that grievances will not have to result. When there are a lot of grievances, management must look at its supervisors.

Supervisors must know how to handle a complaint before it becomes a grievance. If a grievance is filed, it is important that the supervisor not consider it an attack on supervisor authority, only that a situation has not been resolved to the employee's satisfaction. Remember that it is the employees' right to file grievances without jeopardizing their jobs.

If you can determine the nature of the grievance, you have taken the first step to successfully handling it. Determine if the stated complaint is the problem or if it is only a symptom of the real problem. Investigate the grievance objectively and thoroughly. One of the biggest mistakes supervisors make is to make light of complaints. If the employee files a grievance, it is important and the employee will not be satisfied until the grievance is resolved. The supervisor must be willing to work with the mediator in a grievance, and if you've made a mistake, admit it. When the grievance is resolved one way or the other, do not punish the grievant. The employee is exercising a right given by the university.

RIGHT TO EQUITABLE COMPENSATION

In addition to the right to an appeal and grievance process, employees have a right to fair and equitable compensation for the work they perform. Student employees should be made aware of the pay schedule for different jobs in the library and are entitled to pay equity. All student employees should be rewarded fairly in relation to what other student employees are paid for the work they perform. Pay rates for student employees are discussed in Chapter 6.

EMPLOYEE RESPONSIBILITIES

Employees must recognize that in addition to their rights, they have responsibilities as well. The legal responsibilities of employees are the responsibility to perform the work for which they were hired and the responsibility to follow the library's policies, procedures, and rules.

Employees also have a responsibility to contribute positively to the library's image. In the eyes of many people, student employees are the library. Their image of the library is often formed by their view of the student employees. Loyalty to the library is an ethical responsibility of student employees. Given the opportunity, student employees should speak positively about the library and if employees have gripes, they should be taken to their supervisors, not to persons outside.

Other specific moral and ethical actions for which student employees should be held responsible include:

1) Come to work for all scheduled hours, unless excused.
2) Comply with instructions issued by the supervisor.
3) Complete assigned work.
4) Be safety-conscious.
5) Take care of library materials and property.
6) Be honest in dealings with the public and the library.
7) Avoid abusive, threatening, coercive, indecent, and discourteous language.
8) Be sober and drug-free on library time, library property, or while conducting library business.
9) Keep accurate records and avoid any hint of intentional falsification of time reports.
10) Cooperate with coworkers.

ETHICS FOR SUPERVISORS

Student employees and the public make few distinctions between lower level and upper level management of the library. To most of the university community, supervisors are part of library management and you can be expected to be tarred with the same brush as your supervisor and the dean/director. As a result, you must be concerned with managerial ethics.

Ethics is concerned with what a person does that is right or wrong according to what the individual, friends, coworkers, and society think is right or wrong. There is a fine line between acceptable and unacceptable behavior in organizational life. The following questions present problems that have answers that society judges as ethically correct. It is a rare individual who would not bend one of these ethical standards.

Answer the following questions as truthfully as you can. Only you can judge their significance or the correct answers.

- Would you ask a maintenance person employed by the university to do a small repair job at work on your own kitchen appliance?
- If offered a chance, at no cost to you, would you go on a vacation sponsored by the company that sells supplies to the library, if your supervisor has said it is okay?
- If you had the opportunity to approve a promotion for a family member who was less qualified than other candidates, would you do it?
- Would you take home for your personal use such office supplies as pencils or scratch pads?
- If no one said you could not, would you use the library's telephone to conduct a private business of your own?
- Would you use the library's telephone to make long-distance personal calls at university expense?
- If given the opportunity, would you work on a personal, non-job-related project on library time?
- If you discovered a technicality that enabled you to dismiss a particularly troublesome employee, even though in this instance the employee was blameless, would you do it anyway?

The concern for ethics must be addressed by both the individual and the organization. Supervisors of student employees must adhere to the same ethical standards as their supervisors and the librarians in the organization. The American Library Association has had a Code of Ethics since 1939.

AMERICAN LIBRARY ASSOCIATION STATEMENT ON PROFESSIONAL ETHICS, 1981

Introduction

Since 1939, the American Library Association has recognized the importance of codifying and making known to the public and the profession the principles that guide librarians in action. This latest revision of the Code of Ethics reflects changes in the nature of the profession and its social and institutional environment. It should be revised and augmented as necessary.

Librarians significantly influence or control the selection, organization, preservation, and dissemination of information. In a political system grounded in an informed citizenry, librarians are members of a profession explicitly committed to intellectual freedom and the freedom of access to information. We have a special obligation to ensure the free flow of information and ideas to present and future generations.

Librarians are dependent upon one another for the bibliographical resources that enable us to provide information services, and have obligations for maintaining the highest level of personal integrity and competence.

CODE OF ETHICS

    I. Librarians must provide the highest level of service through appropriate and usefully organized collections, fair and equitable circulation and service policies, and skillful, accurate, unbiased, and courteous responses to all requests for assistance.

    II. Librarians must resist all efforts by groups or individuals to censor library materials.

    III. Librarians must protect each user's right to privacy with respect to information sought or received, and materials consulted, borrowed, or acquired.

    IV. Librarians must adhere to the principles of due process and equality of opportunity in peer relationships and personnel actions.

    V. Librarians must distinguish clearly in their actions and statements between their personal philosophies and attitudes and those of an institution or professional body.

    VI. Librarians must avoid situations in which personal interests might be served or financial benefits gained at the expense of library users, colleagues, or the employing institution.

—American Library Association, 1981.

INSTITUTE OF CERTIFIED PROFESSIONAL MANAGERS CODE OF ETHICS

While the American Library Association Code of Ethics should guide you, the following code of ethics relates directly to managers and supervisors:

CODE OF ETHICS FOR MEMBERS OF INSTITUTE OF CERTIFIED PROFESSIONAL MANAGERS

I will recognize that management is a call to service with responsibilities to my subordinates, associates and supervisors, employer, community, nation, and world.

I will be guided in all my activities by truth, accuracy, fair dealings, and good taste.

I will earn and carefully guard my reputation for good moral character and citizenship.

I will recognize that, as a leader, my own pattern of work and life will exert more influence on my subordinates than what I say or write.

I will give the same consideration to the rights and interests of others that I ask for myself.

I will maintain a broad and balanced outlook and will look for value in the ideas and opinions of others.

I will regard my role as a manager as an obligation to help subordinates and associates achieve personal and professional fulfillment.

I will keep informed on the latest developments in the techniques, equipment, and processes associated with the practice of management and the industry in which I am employed.

I will search for, recommend, and initiate methods to increase productivity and efficiency.

I will respect the professional competence of my colleagues in the ICPM and will work with them to support and promote the goals and programs of the institute.

I will support efforts to strengthen professional management through example, education, training, and a lifelong pursuit of excellence.

—Institute of Certified Professional Managers (ICPM) 2210 Arbor Boulevard, Dayton, Ohio 45439.

The resources mentioned in the bibliography below should be consulted for more information on employee/employer rights and responsibilities.

NOTE

1. "Career Leads: ALA Guidelines," *American Libraries* 26(8) (September 1995): 832. ALA's guidelines appear each month in the classified advertisements section of *American Libraries*.

BIBLIOGRAPHY

The Americans with Disabilities Act: Questions and Answers. Washington, DC: U.S. Equal Employment Opportunity Commission, U.S. Dept. of Justice, Civil Rights Division, 2004.

Bagenstos, Samuel. "The future of disability law." *Yale Law Journal* 114(1) (October 2004): 1–83.

Boland, Mary L. *Sexual Harassment: Your Guide to Legal Action : What You Should Know and What You Can Do*. Naperville, IL: Sphinx Pub., 2002.

Brostrand, H. L. "Tilting at Windmills: Changing Attitudes toward People with Disabilities." *Journal of Rehabilitation* 72(1) (January–March 2006): 4–9.

DelPo, Amy, Lisa Guerin, and Janet Portman. *Dealing with Problem Employees: A Legal Guide*. Berkeley, CA: Nolo, 2003.

Dobrich, Wanda, Steven Dranoff, and Gerald Maatman. *The Manager's Guide to Preventing a Hostile Work Environment: How to Avoid Legal and Financial Risks by Protecting Your Workplace from Harassment Based on Sex, Race, Disability, Religion and Age*. New York: McGraw-Hill, 2002.

Federal Laws Prohibiting Job Discrimination: Questions and Answers. Washington, DC: U.S. Equal Employment Opportunity Commission, 2003.

Foos, Donald D. and Nancy C. Pack, eds. *How Libraries Must Comply with the Americans with Disabilities Act*. Phoenix, AZ: Oryx, 1992.

Gregory, Raymond F. *Unwelcome and Unlawful : Sexual Harassment in the American Workplace*. Ithaca, NY : Cornell University Press, 2004.

———. *Women and Workplace Discrimination: Overcoming Barriers to Gender Equality*. New Brunswick, NJ: Rutgers University Press, 2003.

Guerin, Lisa, Amy DelPo, and Shannon Miehe. *Everyday Employment Law: The Basics*. Berkeley, CA: Nolo, 2002.

Gutek, Barbara. "Sexual Harassment: Rights and Responsibilities." *Employee Responsibilities and Rights Journal* 6(4) (December 1993): 325.

Hames, David S. "Disciplining Sexual Harassers: What's Fair?" *Employee Responsibilities and Rights Journal* 7(3) (September 1994): 207.

Hasty, Keith N. "Worker's Compensation: Will College and University Professors Be Compensated for Mental Injuries Caused by Work-Related Stress?" *The Journal of College and University Law* 17(4) (Spring 1991): 535.

Jasper, Margaret C. *Harassment in the Workplace*. Dobbs Ferry, NY: Oceana Publications, 2002.

———. *You've Been Fired: Your Rights and Remedies*. Dobbs Ferry, NY: Oceana Publications, 2005.

Kulik, Carol T. *Human Resources for the Non-HR Manager*. Mahwah, NJ: Lawrence Erlbaum, 2004.

Larson, Lex K. *Civil Rights Act of 1991*. New York: Matthew Bender, 1992.

Lees, Tammi J. "The Individual vs. the Employer: Who Should Be Held Liable under Employment Discrimination Law?" *Case Western Reserve Law Review* 54(3) (Spring 2004): 861–888.

Lindemann, Barbara and David D. Kadue. *Sexual Harassment in Employment Law*. Washington, DC: Bureau of National Affairs, 1992.

MacKinnon, Catharine A. and Reva B. Siegel. *Directions in Sexual Harassment Law*. New Haven, CT: Yale University Press, 2004.

Minow, Mary and Tomas Lipinski. *The Library's Legal Answer Book*. Chicago, IL: American Library Association, 2003.

Mook, Jonathan R., ed. *Americans with Disabilities Act: Employee Rights & Employer Obligations*. New York: Matthew Bender, 1992.

Muir, Dana M. *A Manager's Guide to Employment Law How to Protect Your Company and Yourself*. San Francisco, CA: Jossey-Bass, 2003.

Nager, Glen D. and Edward K.M. Bilich. "The Civil Rights Act of 1991 Going Forward." *Employee Relations Law Journal* 20(2) (Fall 1994): 237.

O'Brien, Gerald V. and Christina Ellegood. "The Americans with Disabilities Act: A Decision Tree for Social Services Administrators." *Social Work* 50(3) (July 2005): 271–279.

Parliman, Gregory C. and Rosalie J. Shoeman. "National Origin Discrimination or Employer Prerogative? An Analysis of Language Rights in the Workplace." *Employee Relations Law Journal* 19(4) (Spring 1994): 551.

Paul, Niall A. "The Civil Rights Act of 1991: What Does It Really Accomplish?" *Employee Relations Law Journal* 17(4) (Spring 1992): 567.

Repa, Barbara Kate. *Your Rights in the Workplace*. Berkeley, CA: Nolo, 2005.

Simon, Howard A. and Erin Daly. "Sexual Orientation and Workplace Rights: A Potential Land Mine for Employers?" *Employee Relations Law Journal* 18(1) (Summer 1992): 29.

Smith, James Monroe. "The Legal Rights of People with HIV/AIDS." *EAP Digest* 13(5) (July 1993): 30.

Stein, Michael Ashley. "Same Struggle, Different Difference: ADA Accommodations as Antidiscrimination." *University of Pennsylvania Law Review* 153(2) (December 2004): 579–673.

Steiner, Alison. "The Americans with Disabilities Act of 1990 and Workers' Compensation: The Employees' Perspective." *Mississippi Law Journal* 62(3) (Spring 1993): 631.

Steingold, Fred and Amy DelPo. *The Employer's Legal Handbook*. Berkeley, CA: Nolo, 2005.

Susser, Peter A. "The ADA: Dramatically Expanded Federal Rights for Disabled Americans." *Employee Relations Law Journal* 16(2) (Fall 1990): 157.

Warner, Daniel M. "'We Do Not Hire Smokers': May Employers Discriminate Against Smokers?" *Employee Responsibilities and Rights Journal* 7(2) (June 1994): 129.

Waxman, Merle. "Constructive Responses to Sexual Harassment in the Workplace." *Employee Responsibilities and Rights Journal* 7(3) (September 1994): 243.

6

Compensation for Student Employees

"Far and away the best prize that life offers is the chance to work hard at work worth doing."

—Theodore Roosevelt (1858–1919)

DIFFERENTIATED PAY

The compensation system for student employees is well established at most academic institutions. These guidelines will likely permit only so much flexibility in setting student pay rates. It is advisable, however, to examine the library's internal compensation guidelines for student workers to assure that they are fair.

A fair compensation system should be logical, consistent, equitable, and competitive. A compensation system that pays all beginning searchers in the acquisitions department the same wage is fair. A system that pays the same wage to student employees who reshelve books as those students who supervise circulation operations during late evening and weekend hours is illogical, inequitable, and inconsistent. There are good reasons to compensate different students for different work if the level of that work differs. To be fair to all student employees, it is necessary to pay at different rates for different work. The job descriptions in Chapter 3 provide for several levels of positions based on responsibility and difficulty.

The steps in this schedule can be used for longevity increases to student employees. For example, all Group II student employees would start work at $6.55 per hour and after 500 hours or two semesters' of work experience, be given an increase to $6.70 per hour. Longevity increases permit the library to reward students for staying in their positions. Of course, they could also be promoted to higher level positions if qualified. Group III positions would be used for advanced positions requiring specialized knowledge, skills, and experience.

HOURLY PAY RATE STRUCTURE FOR STUDENT EMPLOYEES

GROUP	STEP I (START RATE)	STEP II	STEP III	STEP IV
I	Base	Base + $0.15	Base + $0.30	Base + $0.45
II	Base + $0.15	Base + $0.30	Base + $0.45	Base + $0.60
III				
LEVEL 1	Base + $0.30	Base + $0.45	Base + $0.60	Base + $0.75
LEVEL 2	Base + $0.65	Base + $0.80	Base + $0.95	Base + $1.10
LEVEL 3	Base + $0.90	Base + $1.20	Base + $1.35	Base + $1.50

Example: Where the Base is a minimum wage of $6.55 (effective July 24, 2007), the following schedule would apply:

GROUP	STEP I (START RATE)	STEP II	STEP III	STEP IV
I	$6.55	$6.70	$6.85	$7.00
II	$6.70	$6.85	$7.00	$7.15
III				
LEVEL 1	$6.85	$7.00	$7.15	$7.30
LEVEL 2	$7.20	$7.35	$7.50	$7.65
LEVEL 3	$7.45	$7.75	$7.90	$8.05

Use this table after July 23, 2008:

GROUP	STEP I (START RATE)	STEP II	STEP III	STEP IV
I	$7.25	$7.40	$7.55	$7.70
II	$7.70	$7.55	$7.70	$7.85
III				
LEVEL 1	$7.55	$7.70	$7.85	$8.00
LEVEL 2	$7.90	$8.05	$8.20	$8.35
LEVEL 3	$8.15	$8.45	$8.80	$8.75

STUDENT EMPLOYEE ALLOTMENTS

The allocation of student work-study funds differs widely among academic libraries. The two primary means of setting allocations are to have those allocations of hours or dollars established by the student employment office for libraries or for the libraries to establish their own budgets for students that are then coordinated with student work-study awards.

The student with a work-study award typically receives notification of the amount of the award and the period during which that amount can be earned, i.e., academic year, summer session, etc. The number of hours that a work-study student can work depends on the pay rate for the position. It is important for the student employee supervisor to know the total number of hours that a student may work, based on the award and pay rate. If there are twenty pay periods (biweekly payroll) in the Fall and Spring semesters, does the work-study student you are hiring have an award large enough to get through the entire academic year before exhausting the award amount? Will you be faced with having the student terminated because the award has run out, leaving desks unattended and hours not covered in your department's schedule? Constructing a table like the following is useful in determining how many hours per pay period may be worked in order for a work-study student to be able to work all year and earn the entire award amount.

NUMBER OF HOURS PER PAY PERIOD THAT CAN BE WORKED IN TWENTY PAY PERIODS BASED ON AWARD AMOUNT (DIVIDE HOURS BY TWO TO DETERMINE HOURS PER WEEK)

EFFECTIVE JULY 24, 2007 THROUGH JULY 23, 2009				HOURLY PAY RATE						
AWARD	$6.55	$6.70	$6.85	$7.00	$7.15	$7.30	$7.45	$7.60	$7.75	$7.90	$8.05
$1,000	7.6	7.5	7.3	7.1	7.0	6.8	6.7	6.6	6.5	6.3	6.2
$1,200	9.2	9.0	8.8	8.6	8.4	8.2	8.1	7.9	7.7	7.6	7.5
$1,400	10.7	10.4	10.2	10.0	9.8	9.6	9.4	9.2	9.0	8.9	8.7
$1,600	12.2	11.9	11.7	11.4	11.2	11.0	10.7	10.5	10.3	10.1	9.9
$1,800	13.7	13.4	13.1	12.9	12.6	12.3	12.1	11.8	11.6	11.4	11.2
$2,000	15.3	14.9	14.6	14.3	14.0	13.7	13.4	13.2	12.9	12.7	12.4
$2,200	16.8	16.4	16.1	15.7	15.4	15.1	14.8	14.5	14.2	13.9	13.7
$2,400	18.3	17.9	17.5	17.1	16.8	16.4	16.1	15.8	15.5	15.2	14.9
$2,600	19.8	19.4	19.0	18.6	18.2	17.8	17.4	17.1	16.8	16.5	16.1
$2,800	21.4	20.9	20.4	20.0	19.6	19.2	18.8	18.4	18.1	17.7	17.4
$3,000	22.9	22.4	21.9	21.4	21.0	20.5	20.1	19.7	19.4	19.0	18.6
$3,200	24.4	23.9	23.4	22.9	22.4	21.9	21.5	21.1	20.6	20.3	19.9
$3,400	26.0	25.4	24.8	24.3	23.8	23.3	22.8	22.4	21.9	21.5	21.1
$3,600	27.5	26.9	26.3	25.7	25.2	24.7	24.2	23.7	23.2	22.8	22.4
$3,800	29.0	28.4	27.7	27.1	26.6	26.0	25.5	25.0	24.5	24.1	23.6
$4,000	30.5	29.9	29.2	28.6	28.0	27.4	26.8	26.3	25.8	25.3	24.8
$4,200	32.1	31.3	30.7	30.0	29.4	28.8	28.2	27.6	27.1	26.6	26.1
$4,400	33.6	32.8	32.1	31.4	30.8	30.1	29.5	28.9	28.4	27.8	27.3
$4,600	35.1	34.3	33.6	32.9	32.2	31.5	30.9	30.3	29.7	29.1	28.6
$4,800	36.6	35.8	35.0	34.3	33.6	32.9	32.2	31.6	31.0	30.4	29.8
$5,000	38.2	37.3	36.5	35.7	35.0	34.2	33.6	32.9	32.3	31.6	31.1
$5,200	39.7	38.8	38.0	37.1	36.4	35.6	34.9	34.2	33.5	32.9	32.3
$5,400	41.2	40.3	39.4	38.6	37.8	37.0	36.2	35.5	34.8	34.2	33.5
$5,600	42.7	41.8	40.9	40.0	39.2	38.4	37.6	36.8	36.1	35.4	34.8
$5,800	44.3	43.3	42.3	41.4	40.6	39.7	38.9	38.2	37.4	36.7	36.0
$6,000	45.8	44.8	43.8	42.9	42.0	41.1	40.3	39.5	38.7	38.0	37.3

EFFECTIVE JULY 24, 2009				HOURLY PAY RATE						
AWARD	$7.25	$7.40	$7.55	$7.70	$7.85	$8.00	$8.15	$8.30	$8.45	$8.60	$8.75
$1,000	6.9	6.8	6.6	6.5	6.4	6.3	6.1	6.0	5.9	5.8	5.7
$1,200	8.3	8.1	7.9	7.8	7.6	7.5	7.4	7.2	7.1	7.0	6.9
$1,400	9.7	9.5	9.3	9.1	8.9	8.8	8.6	8.4	8.3	8.1	8.0
$1,600	11.0	10.8	10.6	10.4	10.2	10.0	9.8	9.6	9.5	9.3	9.1
$1,800	12.4	12.2	11.9	11.7	11.5	11.3	11.0	10.8	10.7	10.5	10.3
$2,000	13.8	13.5	13.2	13.0	12.7	12.5	12.3	12.0	11.8	11.6	11.4
$2,200	15.2	14.9	14.6	14.3	14.0	13.8	13.5	13.3	13.0	12.8	12.6
$2,400	16.6	16.2	15.9	15.6	15.3	15.0	14.7	14.5	14.2	14.0	13.7
$2,600	17.9	17.6	17.2	16.9	16.6	16.3	16.0	15.7	15.4	15.1	14.9
$2,800	19.3	18.9	18.5	18.2	17.8	17.5	17.2	16.9	16.6	16.3	16.0
$3,000	20.7	20.3	19.9	19.5	19.1	18.8	18.4	18.1	17.8	17.4	17.1
$3,200	22.1	21.6	21.2	20.8	20.4	20.0	19.6	19.3	18.9	18.6	18.3
$3,400	23.4	23.0	22.5	22.1	21.7	21.3	20.9	20.5	20.1	19.8	19.4

$3,600	24.8	24.3	23.8	23.4	22.9	22.5	22.1	21.7	21.3	20.9	20.6
$3,800	26.2	25.7	25.2	24.7	24.2	23.8	23.3	22.9	22.5	22.1	21.7
$4,000	27.6	27.0	26.5	26.0	25.5	25.0	24.5	24.1	23.7	23.3	22.9
$4,200	29.0	28.4	27.8	27.3	26.8	26.3	25.8	25.3	24.9	24.4	24.0
$4,400	30.3	29.7	29.1	28.6	28.0	27.5	27.0	26.5	26.0	25.6	25.1
$4,600	31.7	31.1	30.5	29.9	29.3	28.8	28.2	27.7	27.2	26.7	26.3
$4,800	33.1	32.4	31.8	31.2	30.6	30.0	29.4	28.9	28.4	27.9	27.4
$5,000	34.5	33.8	33.1	32.5	31.8	31.3	30.7	30.1	29.6	29.1	28.6
$5,200	35.9	35.1	34.4	33.8	33.1	32.5	31.9	31.3	30.8	30.2	29.7
$5,400	37.2	36.5	35.8	35.1	34.4	33.8	33.1	32.5	32.0	31.4	30.9
$5,600	38.6	37.8	37.1	36.4	35.7	35.0	34.4	33.7	33.1	32.6	32.0
$5,800	40.0	39.2	38.4	37.7	36.9	36.3	35.6	34.9	34.3	33.7	33.1
$6,000	41.4	40.5	39.7	39.0	38.2	37.5	36.8	36.1	35.5	34.9	34.3

HISTORY OF COMPENSATION LAWS

It is easy to forget that that before government regulations, there were times when a laborer needed to collect his pay at the end of each day because there were no real guarantees that the employee would be paid at all. During the Depression era, the federal government stepped in to establish when employees were to be paid, where employees had to be paid, how much extra employees had to be paid for working especially long hours, how long employees could be made to work, and under what circumstances children could be employed. For example, in 1914, a majority of the workers in cotton mills were under the age of 16, with some of them aged 6 or 7. They worked 12 hours a day at a daily wage of 22 cents while women were earning 39 cents and men were earning 57 cents.[1] When the Fair Labor Standards Act was first enacted in 1938, the minimum wage was 25 cents per hour. The Fair Labor Standards Act of 1938, which has been amended numerous times, controls minimum wages, overtime, equal pay, and the employment of minors.

CHILD LABOR LAWS

When the Fair Labor Standards Act (FLSA) was passed into law in 1938, child labor was a serious social problem in the United States. Today, child labor is less of a problem but children are protected nonetheless. Under federal law, minors under 18 may not work in any job that is considered hazardous by the secretary of labor. Included in those jobs specifically designated are coal mining, logging, slaughtering and meat packing, wrecking and demolition, and roofing and excavation. Also included are working in explosives plants and any job involving radioactive substances.

Minors under 16 may not work in mining, manufacturing and processing, the operation of motor vehicles, or in public messenger service or hazardous occupations. Exceptions include delivering newspapers, agricultural jobs, and minors under 16 may be employed as actor or performers. Minors under twelve cannot be employed except on a family farm. Federal law does not restrict the number of hours that children between 16 and 18 may work, but it does state that minors between the ages of 14 and 16 may not work during school hours. They may not work more than 8 hours a day or 40 hours a week when school is not in session, nor more than 3 hours a day and

18 hours a week when school is in session. Children between the ages of 14 and 16 may not work anytime between the hours of 7 P.M. and 7 A.M., except from June 1 through Labor Day, when evening hours are extended to 9 P.M. Different rules apply in agricultural employment. Minimum wage laws regulate the wage that children must be paid.

Fines of up to $10,000 per violation may be assessed against employers who violate the child labor provisions of the law. This law prohibits discriminating against or discharging workers who file a complaint or participate in any proceedings under the Act.

WAGES AND SALARIES

Wages and salaries are simply the payment received for performing work and are probably the single most important incentive and motivation for coming to work. Although individual library employees differ on how much importance they place on pay, it is critical. Library managers need to understand how wages and salaries are determined and managed.

Although wages and salaries are often used as synonyms, they are slightly different in meaning. Wages, or hourly pay, refers to an hourly rate of pay and is the basis for pay used most often for production and maintenance employees or blue collar workers. Salary refers to a weekly, monthly, or yearly rate of pay. Professional and management employees as well as faculty are usually salaried, or earn a set salary for the week, month, or year.

Hourly, or wage earning, employees normally get paid only for the hours they work whereas salaried employees earn a set salary even though the number of hours they work may vary to pay period to pay period. Salaried employees are normally classed as exempt employees—exempt from the provisions of the Fair Labor Standards Act (FLSA).

FAIR LABOR STANDARDS ACT (FLSA)

The FLSA was enacted in 1938 and has had numerous amendments through the years revising and updating the law. Before describing the provisions of the law, let's examine who the employees are who are exempt from its provisions. Exempt workers may include executive, administrative, and professional employees, as well as outside salespeople, and computer professionals. There are two tests of whether you can be considered an executive, administrative, or professional employee and thus be exempt from the minimum wage and overtime laws. There are both long and short tests used to determine if employees qualify for exempt status. The long form is used primarily to determine whether or not lower paid (between $155 and $250 per week) employees qualify while the short test is useful for higher paid (at least $250 per week) employees qualify.

The long test:

You are an executive if you:

- Spend at least 80 percent of your time managing a department or subdivision and/or directing the work of two or more subordinates;

- Have the authority to hire and fire or to give recommendations; regarding hiring, firing, and promotion of employees;
- Routinely rely on your own discretion; and
- Are paid at least $155 a week.

You are an administrative employee if you:

- Spend at least 80 percent of your time doing office work; or
- Are on the administration of an educational institution; or
- Perform tasks requiring special training or experience with only general supervision or exercise general supervision over others; or
- Regularly help your employer or an executive or another administrative employee;
- Routinely rely on your own discretion; and
- Are paid at least $155 a week.

You are a professional employee if you:

- Spend at least 80 percent of your time doing work that requires an advanced degree or recognized artistic talent; or
- Are a certified teacher in an educational institution; or
- Do work that is primarily intellectual;
- Routinely rely on your own discretion; and
- Are paid at least $170 a week.

The short test:

Executive, administrative, and professional employees are considered highly paid employees and are highly paid if you:

- Are paid at least $250 a week;
- Spend at least 50 percent of your time performing the duties of an executive, administrative, and professional employee described in the long test above.

Computer professionals: To qualify as a computer professional who is exempt, you must be paid at least six and a half time the current minimum wage and your primary duty has to be one or more of the following:

- Applying systems analysis techniques and procedures, including consulting with users, to determine hardware and software functional specifications;
- Designing computer systems based on and related to user specifications;
- Creating or modifying computer programs based on and related to system design specifications; or
- Creating or modifying computer programs related to machine operating systems.

One other major group of individuals who are exempt are independent contractors. Many universities utilize independent contractors for specialized work. The independent contractor is sufficiently free from the employer and normally is in a trade, business, or profession independent from that of the person employing him or her. The independent contractor is essentially a nonemployee who is paid for completing a specific task and is not paid any of the employee benefits.

EXEMPT VERSUS NONEXEMPT

Having examined how an exempt employee is defined for the purposes of classification under the FLSA, it is instructive to see how the exempt and nonexempt differ from one another.

- Nonexempt employees earn an hourly wage.
- Exempt employees earn a salary.
- Nonexempt employee hours are tracked by time clock or recorded on time sheets. Employees report hours worked and hours taken as sick or annual leave on the time sheet.
- Exempt employees do not use time clocks or time sheets. Normally, exempt employees report the hours not worked, to be deducted from hours earned for sick days, annual leave, etc.
- Nonexempt employees are paid only for the hours reported as worked.
- Exempt employees are paid a salary for the month.
- Nonexempt employees are eligible for daily overtime, call-in pay, and guaranteed overtime.
- Exempt employees are not eligible.
- Nonexempt employees have a set maximum number of paid sick days, sometimes cumbersome work rules, and a formal discipline program for lateness and absences.
- Exempt employees, except in government, do not have a limit on paid sick days, they have few work rules, and no formal discipline program.

Generally, exempt employees have certain benefits or privileges that nonexempt employees do not, such as fewer work rules but exempt employees are not eligible for overtime.

VIOLATIONS OF WAGE AND HOUR LAWS

On occasion, employees file charges with the United States department of labor or a state department of labor to assist them in recovering unpaid overtime, final wages, or pay for accrued but unused vacation. During the course of investigating an employee's claim, investigators often find violations of wage-hour laws that even savvy employers did not know existed. Some of these violations can have substantial ramifications for employers, including requiring employers to pay substantial monies to employees other than the one who filed the charge.

Just because an employee is salaried does not mean the employee is exempt from the overtime provisions of the FLSA. One common misconception employers have is that all employees who are paid on a salary basis are exempt from the overtime provisions of the FLSA. However, only employees who are paid on a salary basis and who meet certain FLSA requirements for exempt status such as executives, administrators, professionals (including certain high-level computer systems analysts), and outside salespersons are exempt and need not be paid for overtime. See C29CFR Part 541 for general regulations and interpretations in order to determine whether your employees are exempt or not.

Private employers should not use comp time in lieu of paying nonexempt employees for overtime. Federal wage and hour law allows only public-sector employers to substitute comp time in lieu of overtime for nonexempt employees. This means that private-sector employers must pay all hourly and salaried nonexempt employees 1 1/2 times their regular rate of pay for all hours worked in excess of 40 hours a week. (Employers are not allowed to substitute comp time even when they correctly allow 1 1/2 hours of comp time for every hour of overtime.) However, there is no prohibition against an employer adjusting hours worked on a weekly basis to control overtime, i.e., an employee who works 12 hours on Monday, 8 hours on Tuesday, 8 hours on Wednesday, and 8 hours on Thursday can be scheduled to work only 4 hours on Friday. Adjusting hours over a two-week period also is not allowed.

Docking exempt employees for partial day absences may result in loss of the exemption. As you know, employers are not required to pay overtime to exempt employees. The department of labor takes the position that employers may deduct pay from exempt employees' salaries for full-day absences (or as discipline for major safety violations) without losing exempt status for such employees but may not dock exempt employees' salaries for partial day absences or for tardiness. A finding by the department of labor that an employer improperly docked even one exempt employee may result in loss of exempt status for all employees who are subject to the employer's docking rules. This, in turn, can result in substantial overtime payments, plus interest and penalties, to all formerly exempt employees who were not paid overtime. Another problem is that employers generally do not keep time records for exempt employees; therefore, the employees' "time records" or guesstimates may be accepted as true in the face of no employer records.

All employers should review their written pay policies and guidelines and communicate with and educate their human resources/personnel departments and payroll staff about proper pay practices. Slip-ups may be costly. If any of the foregoing situations apply to your library, you may need to immediately consult an attorney to work out a plan for correcting the problems without drawing employees' attention to them.

MINIMUM WAGE

The Federal Minimum Wage is established by legislation enacted by the United States Congress. It was last raised to $6.55 per hour effective July 24, 2007. Some states have set minimum wages higher than the federal rate. Employers must pay the higher of the two rates to its minimum wage employees. Any future increase in the minimum wage requires enactment of new legislation passed by the Congress. This wage is important to libraries because student employees are directly affected by changes in the minimum wage.

The department of labor may recover back wages, either administratively or through court action, for the employees that have been underpaid in violation of the law. Violations may result in civil or criminal action. Fines of up to $1,000 per violation against employers who willfully or repeatedly violate the minimum wage or overtime pay provisions. This law prohibits discriminating against or discharging workers who file a complaint or participate in any proceedings under the Act.

OVERTIME

The FLSA requires employers to pay time and a half (one and one half times the regular rate of pay) for every hour employees work over 40 in one week or in some states, for more than 8 hours worked in a day. All exempt employees are exempt from the overtime pay requirement. In addition, other groups such as agricultural workers, car salespeople, taxi drivers, people who work on a commission basis, merchant mariners, drivers who work for employers who are subject to the authority of the Interstate Commerce Commission, anyone whose employer is subject to the Railway Labor Act, and radio and television personnel are specifically exempted from the overtime pay requirement of FLSA. Hospitals and other health care providers are allowed to use a fourteen day work period to figure overtime, paying overtime for hours in excess of eighty. Fire fighters and police can be put on a "tour of duty," which means that they don't receive overtime pay until they work more than 212 hours.

State and local government agencies may be allowed to give compensatory time off instead of paying overtime. Unless the nonexempt employee is a public employee, he or she can not agree to waive payment of overtime, accepting compensatory time instead of overtime. FLSA requires that employers pay nonexempt employees overtime.

REQUIREMENTS FOR EXEMPT POSITIONS

Because of the exemption of groups of employees from certain requirements of the FLSA, it is necessary to review the requirements detailed by the Wage and Hour Division of the U.S. Department of Labor as to what is meant by bona fide executive, administrative, professional, and sales personnel. Staffing in libraries can be divided first by exempt and nonexempt, with the nonexempt employees being those individuals meeting production standards—student employees, clerical staff, and individual staff members performing the basic functions—lowest level cataloging, acquisitions, information services, stacks maintenance, and circulation, for example. This group is sometimes referred to as operative employees and often comprises up to 80 percent of all staff. Librarians are always exempt employees.

Increasingly in libraries, there is a need for more higher level staff to perform what at one time were duties and responsibilities assigned to librarians. The exempt group includes two levels of management, senior and operating, and professional, technical, and paraprofessional employees.

LIBRARY MANAGERS

Managers in the library are the director or dean, the associate and assistant directors, and division, department, and branch library heads. In addition, there are usually staff members who head units and are often given manager titles. The Wage and Hour Division of the U.S. Department of Labor defines senior management as being responsible for establishing organization-wide policy, laying groundwork for the strategic operations that enable the organization to meet its objectives, relate organizational activities to external organizations, and serve as the ultimate authority group. Senior management in libraries usually includes the dean/director, and associate and assistant deans/directors. Operating managers are those persons at the scene of the action and are responsible for daily operations. They are responsible for implementing operating decisions that enforce established policy. They interpret organizational objectives and relate them to their departmental activities to meet organizational goals. They filter organizational problems, passing on those that need review to the senior management. They are responsible for work schedules and for maintaining the quality and quantity standards of their workgroups.

LIBRARY ADMINISTRATORS

Administrators, as defined by the Wage and Hour Division of the U.S. Department of Labor, are involved in office or nonmanual work directly related to the management policies or general business operations of the employer or perform work that is directly related to academic instruction or training carried on in the administration of a school system or educational establishment. Administrators normally function in such areas as personnel, accounting, finance, law, medicine, research and development, and planning. Administrators in libraries are often librarians in charge of personnel or budget working with staff specialists who perform the daily personnel or accounting work. Librarians are, by definition, exempt professionals. Typically in libraries, senior management and administrators are considered as one group.

PROFESSIONALS IN LIBRARIES

The Wage and Hour Division of the U.S. Department of Labor defines professionals as those employees who work requires advanced knowledge in a field of science or learning. Although there may not be specific academic degree requirements, professionals normally have advanced degrees. There are fairly specific standards for professionals and normally they must have some form of license or certification. The master's degree in library science is the accepted requirement for librarians. In addition, most libraries require that the degree be from an American Library Association (ALA) approved university. The faculty status of many librarians also establishes their professional status and usually requires that a faculty contract be signed. In libraries, there are many instances of staff members being assigned the highest levels of duties also being performed by librarians. Staff in these positions are required to possess either the ALA accredited MLS or another advanced degree related to their assigned duties. In accordance with the FLSA, these staff members are given exempt status based on their professional responsibilities and their advanced degrees, sometimes changing the library from 80/20 nonexempt/exempt staff to a 20/80 nonexempt/exempt organization. Library managers are faced with a serious dichotomy. There are librarians and staff performing the same work while the salary disparity between the groups in quite wide, leading to one of the library's most important compensation problems.

TECHNICIANS IN LIBRARIES

Libraries are hiring more and more technicians to perform support activities including work with integrated automation systems, networks, staff computers, and computers in public areas. The Wage and Hour Division of the U.S. Department of Labor defines technicians as those employees who provide semiprofessional technical support in their specialized areas. Their activities may involve planning and conducting a complete project or a portion of a larger project in accordance with the objectives, requirements, and methods as outlined by a supervisor. There are limited licensing and academic requirements for technicians and knowledge acquired on the job or in community college technical courses are often sufficient for entry-level technical jobs. There is an overlap between advanced technicians and paraprofessionals and professionals.

PARAPROFESSIONALS IN LIBRARIES

This is the most recent and probably the most dynamic grouping of talent in many organizations. This group is wedged between the technicians and the professionals and is often absent in libraries. There may be a division of professionals and paraprofessionals in a library that divides the librarians from the staff. There may be a third group of professionals who perform some of the librarian's duties and some of the paraprofessional's duties. By definition, the paraprofessionals are not required to have the broad, extensive educational background of the professionals, but they are assuming more of the responsibilities of the professionals in many libraries.

WHAT DO WE CALL THEM?

It doesn't take long for a newcomer to figure out that there are different groups in the library. There is obviously senior management and librarians who have a varying degree of administrative or managerial responsibilities. There is also clearly a group of staff who are professionals performing duties that appear to overlap with what the nonmanager librarians do. There are paraprofessionals and technicians whose work appears to overlap with some of the professionals' work and there are student employees who do all the rest. How do you refer to the staffing in a library? Are they librarians and staff? Yes. Are they professional, technical, and clerical staff? Yes. Are they professional and nonprofessional staff? I think you will always have problems referring to staff as non-anything or even para-anything. Even if the organization has the group name of paraprofessionals, I don't think they should be referred to as such. If you want staff to act professionally, they should be called professionals or just plain staff members.

PAYMENT OF WAGES

It is not illegal to pay employees less than they feel they are worth. It is illegal to underpay employees in violation of the FLSA or state wage and hour laws. For example, it is illegal to pay an employee for 30 hours of work when the individual has worked 40 hours. One potential area of abuse is in the misclassification of hourly employees as exempt so as to avoid paying overtime. On the positive side, classifying employees as exempt sometimes gives them additional benefits, such as more annual leave.

PREVAILING WAGE ACT

A government defined prevailing wage is the minimum wage that must be paid for work done on covered government projects. In practice, these wages are the union rates paid in various geographical areas. The original purpose of prevailing wage was to prevent the government from undercutting local workers. If the government were to pay a wage lower than local rates, it would serve to drive down the pay for other jobs in the area. The main prevailing wage laws are the Davis-Bacon Act (1931), the Walsh-Healey Public Contracts Act (1936), Service Contract Act (1965), and the National Foundation Arts and Humanities Act (1965). All of these acts were aimed at providing coverage to groups of workers either working on public projects or providing services or supplies for government projects. These acts were all passed to address social issues in their time. In the 1960s, the equal rights movement pushed different social issues to the front and there was new legislation passed to protect groups of workers. These included the Equal Pay Act, the Vocational Rehabilitation Act of 1973, the Age Discrimination in Employment Act of 1967, and the Pregnancy Discrimination Act.

EQUAL PAY ACT

An important federal law that specifically addresses equality of the sexes in the workplace is the Equal Pay Act of 1963, which mandates equal pay for equal work. Equal work is that work that requires essentially the same skill, effort, and responsibility, done under similar circumstances. Fringe benefits are also considered as pay under the act, and therefore equal benefits must be provided to both men and women even if the cost of providing those benefits to both is not the same. Employers cannot lower the pay of one sex in order to remedy an unequal situation. The pay of the lower group must be raised. The Equal Pay Act does not require the employer to equalize pay in cases where different wages are paid according to a merit or seniority system, a system based on quality or quantity of production, or any other system not based on sex.

"Comparable worth" is a concept related to the Equal Pay Act. The act requires that people performing essentially the same job receive the same pay regardless of sex, while comparable worth states that people performing different jobs having essentially the same value to the employer should be paid the same regardless of sex. The justification is that historically female-dominated job classifications with lower wages should be compared with jobs characterized by the same levels of responsibility or requiring the same skill level or effort under similar working conditions.

DISABLED WORKERS

The Vocational Rehabilitation Act of 1973 was passed by Congress to protect the employment rights of disabled workers. That act applied only to federal contractors and subcontractors. The Americans with Disabilities Act (ADA), which took effect in 1992, extends coverage to all employers of 15 or more workers. A disabled individual, for the purposes of the law, is a person who has a physical or mental impairment that limits one or more major life activities, has a record of such impairment, or is regarded by others as having such an impairment. Impairments that limit major life activities must be substantial as opposed to minor and include impairments that limit seeing, hearing, speaking, walking, breathing, performing manual tasks, learning, caring for oneself, and working. An individual with paralysis, substantial hearing or visual impairment, mental retardation, or learning disability would be covered, but an individual with a minor, nonchronic condition of short duration such as a sprain, broken bone, or infection would normally not be covered. A person with a history of cancer or of mental illness would be covered. The third part of the definition protects individuals who are regarded and treated as though they have a substantially limiting disability, for example, the law would protect an individual who is disfigured from adverse employment decisions because the employer feared negative reactions from coworkers. AIDS victims are included in the latter definition as well.

The basic provision of the ADA prohibits discrimination against qualified disabled persons by requiring that the employer make reasonable accommodation for those who can perform the job unless that accommodation would create an undue hardship for the employer. To be a qualified disabled person, the individual must have an impairment that limits one of the major life activities yet must be able to perform the essential functions of the job. The sole fact that an individual is disabled can't eliminate the individual from consideration. Reasonable accommodation requires that the employer modify the job application process so disabled persons can apply in the first place and adjust the work environment in such a way that the disabled individual can perform the job. It should be noted here that the employer may make preemployment inquiries into the ability of a job applicant to perform job-related functions. However, an employer cannot ask whether the applicant is an individual with a disability.

A reasonable accommodation might include altering the structure of the work area to make it accessible, acquiring new equipment, modifying work schedules, or simply putting a desk on blocks to accommodate a wheelchair. An accommodation does not have to be made if it would create an "undue hardship." An undue hardship on an employer depends in large part on the type and cost of the accommodation needed, the size of the organization, and the size of the budget. A large organization would have to go to greater lengths than a small business to make a reasonable accommodation. An accommodation could also be considered an undue hardship if it would unduly disrupt other employees or customers, but not if the disruption is caused simply by fear or prejudice. Even in the case of undue hardship, an employer may be required to provide an alternative accommodation.

The ADA excludes from coverage applicants and employees who are currently illegally using drugs but not those individuals who have been successfully rehabilitated. ADA calls largely for common sense solutions to making accommodations for disabled workers who, with the accommodation, can perform the essential functions of the job. A larger, more difficult problem revolves around those few individuals who would take advantage of a disability to find a way to sue.

AGE DISCRIMINATION

The Age Discrimination in Employment Act (ADEA) protects employees from discrimination because of age. Workers over the age of 40 are protected by the ADEA, and state laws have been passed to extend that protection in many cases. The law forbids employers from specifying any age preference in job ads except minimum age requirements, for example, for an individual who will serve alcoholic beverages. Employers can't refuse to hire, pay employees less, or discriminate in any way because of age. Courts recognize four elements necessary for a prima facie for age discrimination:

- The individual is in the protected age group—over 40 under the ADEA or younger for some states.
- The individual was terminated, not promoted, or was the object of an adverse employment decision.
- The individual was qualified for the position.
- The adverse decision was made under circumstances that give rise to an inference of age discrimination.

In 1989, the Supreme Court ruled that the ADEA did not apply to employee benefit plans; however, in 1990, Congress passed the Older Workers Benefit Protection Act, which extended age discrimination prohibitions to benefits. The Act states that if an employer has an employee benefit plan, the employer has to expend the same amount of money for the older worker's benefits as for the younger worker, even though the resulting coverage may be less; for health insurance coverage, premiums and benefits must be equal.

It is also important that managers not assume that performance will decline with age. There are variations in performance at all ages. A pay system designed to pay for performance must insure that performance appraisal systems are not biased by age.

NATIONAL ORIGIN DISCRIMINATION

The only question relating to citizenship an employer can ask a prospective employee related to country of origin is whether or not the applicant is authorized to work in the United States. Once hired, the individual must comply with the provisions of the Immigration Reform and Control Act (IRCA), under which the employer and employee complete applicable sections of the INS I-9 form. Under federal law, employees cannot be discriminated against because of place of origin or because employees have physical, cultural, or linguistic characteristics of a certain nationality. Simply put, employees are protected from employment discrimination because they "look foreign" or have a "foreign accent."

The prohibitions against harassment on the basis of national origin are the same as for sexual harassment. Title VII of the Civil Rights Act of 1964 protects workers against ethnic slurs or conduct that serves to create a hostile working environment.

RELIGIOUS DISCRIMINATION

Individuals are protected from discrimination based on religion by the First Amendment of the U.S. Constitution.

AMENDMENT I (1791)

Congress shall make no law respecting an establishment of religion, or prohibiting the free exercise thereof; or abridging the freedom of speech, or of the press; or the right of the people peaceably to assemble, and to petition the government for a redress of grievances.

The overriding concern in employment is that all individuals be treated equally, whether equally good or equally bad. Inasmuch as more than 70 percent of the employees in an organization are likely to fall into one of the protected groups discussed in this chapter, the minority, in effect, are the majority. Thus, it simply makes sense to treat all employees equally.

JURY DUTY, WITNESS DUTY, AND VOTING TIME

Under the federal Jury System Improvement Act of 1978, the employer cannot discharge an employee for serving on a federal jury. State laws also prohibit employers from disciplining an employee in any way for responding to a summons to serve on a jury in state court. Normally, state employees have the option of either taking their regular pay or the pay offered to jurors, but not both. Federal law prohibits employers from making any deductions from an exempt employee's salary for being absent for less than a week, which would include time spent on a jury. The same rule of thumb applies when an employee is summoned as a witness for a trial. There is no federal law requiring the employer to give employees time off to vote but some states do make employers give time off if there is not enough time outside of regular working hours to get to the polls.

SENARIO ONE: PERFORMANCE APPRAISALS: PROBLEM RESOLUTION AND PREVENTION

Everything appeared to Patricia to be going smoothly enough. The circulation department was setting new highs each month for checkouts and for reserve materials use. The staff and student workers were working well together and there was virtually no turnover. But everything was about to change. Patricia carefully read the memorandum from the dean's office saying that performance appraisals were due in ten days. She reviewed her handwritten schedule. She had asked each staff member to complete a self-appraisal for her. Then she had written a draft appraisal that was discussed in a meeting with each employee set up especially to discuss the draft. Together, employee and supervisor had finalized and signed the appraisals. She was pleased with herself that she had been able to turn them into the office well in advance of the deadline. The appraisal process was usually more of a nuisance than a useful process for Patricia, except for this year. She had been planning for weeks to talk to Anthony about his work and the appraisal process provided a good opportunity to tell him that he needed to do a better job. He seemed to agree with her assessment. Now Patricia was looking at the stack of papers. The claim of racial discrimination from Anthony Chavez was on her desk. Included in the packet were copies of the previous five appraisals, all giving Anthony "superior" ratings for his work and the last one with two "needs improvement" ratings. Patricia resolved then and there never to give anyone less than a "good" rating.

Patricia scheduled a meeting with the director of library human resources to make certain she understood all of the steps of the performance appraisal system and to review all of the steps she had taken with Anthony. Patricia, the director of library personnel, and the dean would probably receive a series of questions or be interviewed by someone in the Equal Opportunity Programs Offices regarding the complaint. More than likely they would want to see what was done in other similar situations, i.e., did other employees who were not Hispanic receive similar performance reviews? What documentation was there that showed that the comments on the performance appraisal were justified? What evidence was there that Anthony was being treated consistently with other employees? All Patricia could do is wait for some response from the Equal Opportunity Programs Offices regarding the complaint. She would also have to be sure that she didn't take any action against Anthony that could be construed as retaliation. She was also concerned about their friendship.

Prevention

- Document, document, document. At every step of a progressive disciplinary action, each action must be documented and copies must be provided to the employee.

- The performance appraisal system has to be clearly understood by all and consistently applied.
- Do not wait for the performance appraisal to take action relating to performance problems. Act when those problems are first evident.
- Maintain good communication with employees on a daily basis.
- No surprises.

SENARIO TWO: MERIT DECISIONS: PROBLEM RESOLUTION AND PREVENTION

The library had done well in its campaign to raise acquisitions funds from private sources but the legislature has just adjourned and librarians and staff have learned that it would be another year of almost no increases in salary. Along with the approval of raise monies was the directive to award all of the salary increase monies based on merit. After all, there were many in state employment who didn't deserve any raises, legislators reasoned, but who in truth, should be fired. The library was required to determine who would get awards of $795, $545, or $0 increases for the coming year. Dean Rivera wanted to just distribute what little money was available in across the board increases. He knew that when there was not enough money for cost of living increases, puny merit increases destroyed morale. The dean would await instructions from the provost, but he already knew that salary determinations would be difficult. Dean Rivera reviewed in his head the process for merit determination. Performance appraisals were completed and attached to each was a merit point recommendation made by the supervisor and department head. Based on those recommendations, the library's department heads would have to get together to agree on how to match those recommendations to the university provost's directions on the awarding of merit. The dean would only need to make some decisions on awarding merit to administrative staff as soon as the guidelines were agreed upon.

On the fourth day of August, Dean Rivera received official notification that he, the head of reference, and the desk supervisor in reference were named in an equal pay suit by three women in the reference department. When analyzed, it was determined that the males in the library had received an average increase of $691 and the females had received an average increase of $548.

Dean Rivera should first meet with the individuals who have filed the complaint for the purpose of sharing relevant information with them. While the statistical information may indeed point to a gender discrimination problem, it is presumed that the merit increases were arrived at in a fair, consistent manner across the library. It is important that the individuals know how the salaries were arrived at and by whom. If the individuals wish to continue their suit, all that the dean can do is make certain that he is confident in the decisions that were made, make adjustments if there were mistakes made, and/or wait for the next step. This action will involve the university attorney's office so it would be a good idea to schedule a preliminary meeting to discuss the issues.

Prevention

- The library must have developed agreed-upon merit criteria for both faculty and staff. Long before merit points are assigned, employees need to know the ground rules. For example, if a merit system is based on five points, everyone needs to understand what it will take to earn five points, four points, etc. What constitutes "Exceeds Standards," "Meets Standards," or "Unsatisfactory"?

- The best merit systems are integrated with the performance appraisal system that requires that appraisals be completed before merit points are assigned. Ideally, employees would know at the beginning of the year what is expected of them, what it will take to earn highest merit, and the schedule for completion of appraisals and merit assignment.
- If merit is assigned based on performance, there should be few disagreements and if there appears to be inequity based on gender, it can be explained.

SUMMARY

There are ongoing debates about the role of government in compensation. Its role in resolving some of this country's early employment and social problems is well established. The government influences compensation practices and wages through laws that set minimum wages and those that prohibit discrimination. The government also influences labor supply and demand, which impacts wages. There is probably a need for balance between government intervention and the lack of regulations regarding compensation.

Laws prohibiting discrimination require the attention of library managers for several reasons. All employment discrimination law relates to pay in one form or another. These laws regulate the design and administration of pay systems. The definition of pay discrimination and the approaches used by employees to sue under these laws and the employers' defense of pay practices is continually evolving. Many of the provisions of these laws simply require that managers practice sound pay practices. Decisions on pay should be work related, related to the mission of the organization, and provide for a well-communicated appeals process. Knowledge of these laws is essential and assuring compliance is the responsibility of all managers working with a pay system that is properly designed and managed.

NOTE

1. Edwin Markham, Benjamin B. Lindsey, and George Creel, *Children in Bondage* (New York: Hearst's International Library Company, 1914), p. 25.

BIBLIOGRAPHY

Baldwin, David A. *The Library Compensation Handbook: A Guide for Administrators, Librarians, and Staff.* Westport, CT: Libraries Unlimited, 2003.

Berman, Karen. *Financial Intelligence: A Manager's Guide to Knowing What the Numbers Really Mean.* Boston, MA: Harvard Business School Press, 2006.

Brill, Allison. *Improving Compensation for Library Workers: Strategies.* Chicago, IL: American Library Association Office for Library Personnel Resources and Committee on Pay Equity, 1995.

Employment Discrimination: An Employer's Guide. Chicago, IL: American Chamber Of Commerce Publishers, 2001.

Kenady, Carolyn. *Pay Equity: An Action Manual for Library Workers.* Chicago, IL: American Library Association, 1989.

Kohl, John P. and Paul S. "The Pregnancy Discrimination Act: A Twenty-Year Retrospect." *Labor Law Journal* 50(1) (March 1999): 71–77.

Sheehan, Michael F., Robert E. Lee, and Lisa Nuss. *Oregon's Prevailing Wage Law: Benefiting the Public, the Worker, and the Employer*. Portland, OR: Oregon and Southwest Washington Fair Contracting Foundation, 2000.

Simmons-Welburn, Janice and Beth McNeil. *Human Resource Management in Today's Academic Library: Meeting Challenges and Creating Opportunities*. Westport, CT: Libraries Unlimited, 2004.

Singer, Paula M. *Developing a Compensation Plan for Your Library*. Chicago, IL: American Library Association, 2002.

United States Merit Systems Protection Board. *Designing an Effective Pay for Performance Compensation System: A Report to the President and the Congress of the United States*. Washington, DC: U.S. Merit Systems Protection Board, 2006.

Unlocking the Door to Higher Compensation: Your Key to the Salary Maze. Produced by Ernst & Young for the Special Libraries Association. Washington, DC: Special Libraries Association, 1996.

Winfeld, Liz. and Susan Spielman. *Straight Talk about Gays in the Workplace*, 2nd ed. New York: Harrington Park Press, 2001.

Working @ Your Library for Love or Money? Videorecording. Chicago, IL: ALA-Allied Professional Association, 2004.

7

Hiring Student Employees—The Employment Relationship

> The best executive is the one who has sense enough to pick good men to do what he wants done, and self-restraint enough to keep from meddling with them while they do it.
>
> —Theodore Roosevelt (1858–1919)

HIRING AND FIRING

Probably the single most important part of your job as supervisor is hiring the right persons for the work. Any supervisor who has fired student employees realizes how important it is to hire the right people and train them well in order to reduce the possibility that they will have to be discharged. In this chapter, we will discuss how to effectively recruit, screen, and interview student employees. Suggestions on handling corrective discipline and termination are offered in Chapter 14.

REFERRAL OF STUDENT WORKERS

The referral of student workers to the library has been improved in recent years. Thankfully, gone are the days when this exchange was common in university financial aid offices:

Student Employment Counselor: "Do you have any preference as to where you'd like to work?"
Student: "No."
Counselor: "Do you have any special skills?"

Student: "No, but I am carrying 17 hours."

Counselor: "Oh, OK, Go to the library. They don't need special skills and they let you study."

Student: "Where's the library?"

Today, in the Student Financial Aid Office, you are more likely to hear a conversation like this:

Student Employment Counselor: "Do you have any preference as to where you'd like to work?"

Student: "Not really."

Counselor: "Do you know any languages?"

Student: "Besides English?"

Counselor: "Spanish, German, French?"

Student: "Yes, I am fluent in German and can read Spanish."

Counselor: "How about computer keyboard skills?"

Student: "Yes, I'm pretty good at that."

Counselor: "Good, I have a request from the Acquisitions Department in the library for someone who can read German and can learn their automated system. It pays $6.25 to start. Interested?"

Student: "Yes, where's the library?"

A slight improvement in the college-wide orientation program is still needed; the student can now be interviewed by a hiring supervisor in the library.

RECRUITING STUDENT WORKERS

The recruitment and screening of student employees for library employment varies greatly from one university to another. Recruitment depends on the available pool of student workers, their funding sources, and on how prospective employees find their way to the library's hiring supervisors for interviews. On some campuses, the library has a part-time budget that does not depend on work-study students and may not require that part-time employees be current students. Most campuses rely very heavily on work-study funding or have a combination of work-study and other part-time employee budgets.

One aspect of recruitment for the library involves keeping the student employment office up to date on the skills needed by prospective student employees. Work in the library can be made quite attractive to students looking for employment. Night and weekend hours are a selling point as are the opportunities for students to set their own schedules in some jobs. Some students are attracted by the prospect of learning more about the library, which they hope will help them in their coursework. Capitalize on that interest if you can.

Recruitment for library work can be quite extensive. Some libraries take part in job fairs on campus, advertise in the student newspaper, post job openings around campus, post "help wanted" signs on bulletin boards, or ask present student employees to recruit their friends. The hope is that libraries are such attractive places to work, that you will have many more applications for jobs than you have openings.

SCREENING STUDENT EMPLOYEES

The initial screening process begins when a student completes an application. In some universities, the student employment office screens students for jobs throughout campus. Depending on the system, students who seem to have no usable skills may all be ticketed for the library, making the library's hiring process more difficult. At other universities, the student employment office carefully reviews the library's needs and refers highly skilled students to the library. Many libraries also have their own personnel offices which screen student employee applicants for departments of the library.

In order to effectively screen applicants it is essential that the hiring supervisors provide those who screen applications with job descriptions that not only describe the work but also the skills required to do that work. The screening process is nothing more than a comparison of applications to the skills required for the jobs available. Effective screening will greatly improve the hiring supervisor's ability to hire qualified people.

PREPARING FOR THE INTERVIEW

It is desirable for students who have gone through the screening process and met the qualifications for the job to be asked to report to a central location in the library to meet the hiring supervisor. The best place for students to meet the interviewer is in the dean/director's office area, branch library office, or the personnel office. The supervisor as well as the applicant must prepare for the interview. The following are suggestions for preparing for the interview:

1) One of the best ways for the supervisor to prepare is to review the job description for the position as well as the job application.
2) Set the stage for the interview by planning to conduct the interview in a comfortable private office or conference room. Keep in mind that the interview is a two-way street. You want to give the interviewee a good first impression of the library just as much as the interviewee wants to make a good impression on you.
3) Be sure to set aside enough time for the interview and make certain that there will be no interruptions.
4) Review the application. Is it filled out completely, with no blanks? Is it legible? Does it present a sequential outline of the applicant's work history and education? Does it tell why the applicant left each job?
5) When preparing questions for the interview, don't include questions that are answered on the application.
6) Do prepare most of the questions that will be asked in the interview. The questions asked in the interview should focus on the applicant's employment history, education, schedule, outside activities and interests, and strengths and weaknesses. A list of possible questions as well as questions that are inappropriate in the interview are presented later in this chapter.
7) Make certain you are prepared to answer any questions the interviewee has about the job, the department, and the library. Know ahead of time how soon you will make a decision about hiring for the position.

INTERVIEWING TECHNIQUES

There are three different techniques used in employment interviewing. Those techniques are: the directed interview, the nondirected interview, and the stress interview.

- The directed interview usually involves use of a predetermined set of questions that are asked of the interviewee. The primary advantage is that of thoroughness and consistency. All interviewees are asked the same questions, usually in the same order. The disadvantages of directed interviews are that interviewers sometimes get caught up in asking questions without listening to the answers, and structured interviews tend to cause anxiety in applicants.
- The nondirected interview is usually unstructured. The purpose is to allow the interviewees to talk about what is on their minds. The interviewer knows what information needs to be obtained and does so by skilled questioning. The use of the nondirected approach by skilled interviewers can be very effective but much less so by unskilled interviewers.
- The stress interview technique is seldom used. It relies on a series of tough, unexpected, anxiety-producing questions designed to place the interviewee in an uncomfortable situation and forces instinctive reactions. Its purpose is to determine how an individual reacts under pressure. It is a technique sometimes used to screen people for higher level management positions.

Probably the best approach is a combination of the directed and nondirected interview techniques. Using this approach, the interviewer uses a broad list of prepared questions, asking them in no particular sequence. The interviewee is given latitude in responding to questions, some of which are not scripted. The interviewee feels more at ease and yet it provides the interviewer with some structure. It is still necessary to ask essentially the same questions for all applicants for a position.

CONDUCTING THE INTERVIEW

The purposes of the interview should always be kept in mind. They are: to gain information that supplements the application; to find a fit between the supervisor, employee, and the job; to begin building external motivators by communicating the importance of the job and your expectations. The following are suggestions on how to conduct the interview meeting:

1) Begin the interview by putting the student at ease. Spend a few moments in small talk but be careful to avoid asking questions that might be considered discriminatory.
2) Let the applicant know the purpose of the interview is to try to determine if there if a fit between the applicant and the position opening in the department.
3) Keep in mind that the interview should provide you with information about the applicant that may not be completely covered in the application and the interview meeting should provide the applicant with more complete information about the job.
4) Listen to the student's answers. One of the most common mistakes made by interviewers is to concentrate so much on the questions they ask, that they forget to listen to the answers.
5) You should maintain control of the interview by establishing the direction of the questions and not allow the interviewee to wander off in other directions.
6) Never help the interviewee by suggesting the answer to a question but don't use Gestapo interrogation techniques either.

7) Keep the interview friendly and comfortable.

8) Take notes during the interview to refresh your memory when making a decision. Another school of thought claims that taking notes disrupts the interview and that the interviewer should develop the ability to remember responses and take a few minutes after the interview to make notes.

9) The interview is completed when you are sure that you have gotten the information you need to make a decision and when the student's questions have been answered.

10) Close the interview by thanking the interviewee and providing information regarding when a decision will be made. If you are able to hire on the spot, discuss schedules, pay rates, starting date, etc.

11) Check references. This step is sometimes left out when hiring student employees but it is good practice nonetheless.

SAMPLE QUESTIONS WHICH MAY BE ASKED

The following are suggested questions that may be asked in the interview. Job-specific questions should be prepared for specific positions in the library.

Work Experience

- Describe your work experience at your last job.
- What was the most fulfilling aspect of the job?
- What was the least fulfilling?
- Why did you leave?
- What skills did you develop in your previous job?

Education

- What is your major? This will probably be on the application.
- Why did you select that major?
- What is your minor?
- What courses do you prefer? Why?
- What courses do you dislike? Why?
- What courses do you find most and least valuable? Why?
- What extracurricular activities are you involved in?
- What are your short-term goals?
- What are your long-term goals?

Leadership/Initiative/Persistence

- How do you feel about making decisions? Why?
- How do you feel about supervising others? Why?
- What is your idea of challenging work?
- How do you feel about working in an unstructured environment?
- How do you feel about increasing your job responsibilities?
- How do you feel about working in a high-pressure area?
- How would you react if given an unpleasant task?

Library Job-Specific

- Tell me about experience you have had with computers.
- Tell me about experience you have had in working with customers or patrons.
- Describe your experience in using libraries.
- What times during the day and week are you available to work?

TYPES OF QUESTIONS TO BE AVOIDED

In order to gain the type of information you need in an interview, it is advisable to avoid the following types of questions:

1) Questions that can be answered with a "Yes" or" No." These should be changed to open-ended questions that allow the interviewer to see and hear the interviewee use communication skills.
2) Leading questions. Questions that telegraph the expected answers are of little use. For example, "Would you say that you have good interpersonal skills?" definitely calls for a positive response.
3) Obvious questions. "So you graduated from Midvale High School?" is a question that is answered on the application and a waste of time. Ask questions for which the application does not supply the answers.
4) Questions that are not related to the job. "Do you think the Chicago Cubs will ever win the pennant?" has nothing to do with the job, even if you are a Cubs fan.
5) Questions that may be considered discriminatory. It is not only advisable but mandatory that you avoid these types of questions. Examples are given later on in this chapter.

LEGAL IMPLICATIONS OF EMPLOYMENT DECISIONS

All employment decisions, including hiring, promotion, transfer, and termination, must be made on the qualifications of the individual, not on race, creed, sex, age, sexual preference, national origin, or handicap. In order to avoid charges of discrimination in employment, supervisors must be aware of laws that protect certain groups from discriminatory practices. At the federal level, there are laws governing equal employment opportunity and protection of employees:

1) Title VII of the 1964 Civil Rights Act, as amended, protects against discrimination in employment decisions based on race, color, religion, sex, and national origin.
2) The Equal Pay Act of 1963 makes it unlawful to pay females less than males who do similar work.
3) The Age Discrimination in Employment Act of 1967, as amended, protects against discrimination on the basis of age. It protects all persons over the age of 40.
4) The Vocational Rehabilitation Act of 1973 prohibits discrimination in employment on the basis of a mental or physical handicap.
5) The Americans with Disabilities Act (ADA), which took effect in 1992, prohibits discrimination against qualified disabled persons by requiring that the employer make reasonable accommodation for those who can perform the job unless that accommodation would create an undue hardship for the employer. Reasonable accommodation requires that the

employer modify the job application process so disabled persons can apply in the first place and adjust the work environment in such a way that the disabled individual can perform the job.

6) The Vietnam Era Veterans' Readjustment Assistance Act of 1974 requires federal contractors and subcontractors to take affirmative action to employ, and advance in employment, qualified disabled veterans and veterans of the Vietnam era.

7) The Pregnancy Discrimination Act of 1978 protects against discrimination in employment because of pregnancy. Pregnancy should be treated as any other temporary disability and an employer may not refuse to hire a qualified female because she is pregnant.

8) The Immigration Reform and Control Act of 1986 (IRCA) makes it illegal to recruit, hire, refer for hire any unauthorized alien; requires documentation of identity and eligibility of worker to work in the United States; and prohibits discrimination on the basis of national origin or citizenship status.

9) The Employee Polygraph Protection Act of 1988 protects employees from wrongfully being subjected to polygraphs in prehiring or employment.

THE SUPERVISOR'S RESPONSIBILITY

As a supervisor, it is your responsibility to assure that discrimination does not occur in hiring or employment. It is also your responsibility to report any instances of discrimination to the appropriate person. Even the perception of discrimination based on race, creed, sex, age, sexual preference, national origin, or handicap in the library must be avoided at all costs. Although it is not expected that supervisors will become experts in employment law, it is the responsibility of supervisors to be familiar with the applicable laws.

Student employees who believe that they are victims of employment discrimination have the right to avail themselves of the library's grievance process. The student may also file a complaint with the local or regional office of the Equal Employment Opportunity Commission. If you are named in a discrimination grievance, be prepared to present documentary evidence that will clearly show nondiscriminatory intent or action. The grievance procedure is described in Chapter 5.

NONDISCRIMINATORY INTERVIEWING

Nondiscriminatory interviewing simply means asking questions that are job-related. In order to avoid charges of discrimination in hiring, supervisors must be aware of the types of questions that can not be asked in the interview. The following are some guidelines:

1) Do not discuss age.
2) Do not ask female applicants about child care arrangements.
3) Do not discuss religious preferences.
4) Do not ask about the employment of a spouse.
5) Do not discuss matters relating to the applicants race, ancestry, or national origin.
6) Do not attempt jokes related to race, national origin, religion, or sex.
7) Do not ask about military discharge or rank at time of discharge.
8) Do not ask a handicapped applicant about the severity of the handicap.
9) Do not ask questions about civil rights litigation with former employers.

10) Do not ask questions about arrests because a person is not judged guilty by an arrest.
11) Do not discuss political affiliation or membership.

REFERENCE CHECKS

You have a right to collect information about prospective student employees regarding past employment, including duration, absences, punctuality, skills, and reasons for leaving previous positions. In most instances, the references provided by the employee will confirm your impressions of the applicant. However, there are times when contacting those references will help you make a final decision between two applicants or even avoid a hiring mistake. When you contact references supplied by the applicants, you must ask the same questions about all applicants for a particular position and you must have a good business reason for seeking the information. The following are suggested areas for reference check questions:

1) Relationship to the applicant
2) Length of time the reference has known the applicant
3) Length of time the reference has supervised the applicant
4) Applicant's employment dates
5) First and last position held
6) Starting and leaving salary
7) Duties and responsibilities
8) Quality of work
9) Quantity of work
10) Attendance and punctuality
11) Cooperation with other employees and supervisors
12) General work habits
13) Amount of time required to learn new jobs
14) Willingness to accept responsibility
15) Reason for leaving position
16) Eligibility for rehire

COMMUNICATING THE HIRING DECISION

The final step in hiring is the offer. Communicating your decision to applicants is important and should not be unnecessarily delayed. Your choice for the position may well find another job if you do not act within a reasonable time period and it is unfair to all applicants to be kept waiting. Care should be exercised in communicating either acceptance or rejection. It is always easier to give someone good news than bad news. Whether you communicate the bad news in person, by phone, or in writing, you may consider beginning with, "we have a very strong pool of applicants for this position," and mention the strengths of this individual's application. It is possible to reject people in a kind way, without adding to the disappointment unsuccessful applicants already feel. Too often, hiring supervisors forget to consider the feelings of the persons being rejected. Consider how you would like to be informed that you were not the successful applicant.

INTERVIEW SITUATIONS

The hiring interview is only one of the many face-to-face situations a supervisor experiences. Interviewing isn't just talking with someone. The process has a purpose and structure. Interviews are also used in performance appraisal, termination, and some problem-solving situations. Interviewing, if done well, is a very important skill to possess. The resources provided in the bibliography will help you develop hiring skills.

BIBLIOGRAPHY

Adler, Lou. *Hire with Your Head: A Rational Way to Make a Gut Decision.* New York: Wiley, 1998.

Fox, Jeffrey J. *How to Become a Great Boss: The Rules for Getting and Keeping the Best Employees.* New York: Hyperion, 2002.

Gresko, Amy Beth. Recruitment to the profession: student workers in academic libraries as potential future librarians. Thesis (MSLS), University of North Carolina at Chapel Hill, 2003.

Kennedy, R. Bryan and Nicole K. Harris. "Employing Persons with Severe Disabilities: Much Work Remains to Be Done." *Journal of Employment Counseling* 42(3) (September 2005): 133.

Kenney, Donald J. and Frances O. Painter. "Recruiting, Hiring, and Assessing Student Workers in Academic Libraries." *Journal of Library Administration* 21(3–4) (1995): 29–45.

Rosen, C. Martin. "Student Employees and the Academic Library's Multicultural Mission." *Reference Librarian* (45–46) (1994): 45–55.

Wu Qi. "Win-win Strategy for the Employment of Reference Graduate Assistants in Academic Libraries." *Reference Services Review* 31(2) (2003): 141–153.

8

Orienting and Training
Student Employees

Creative minds have always been known to survive any kind of bad training.
— Anna Freud (1895–1982)

TRAINING IS EVERYTHING

Why is good training necessary? Won't employees learn without being trained? Yes, they will but that's the danger. Whether you train them or not, employees will learn, but not the right way. Some people cringe at the word "training." "Training is what you do to monkeys; development is what you do to people." In fact, training is a very specialized and practical form of education that prepares employees to do their jobs and to do their jobs well. In academic libraries, supervisors must train student employees to do their jobs but they also have an obligation to develop student workers. A development program is needed that provides them with a broadening experience designed to build on their strengths and give them positive work experiences. In this chapter we will discuss the first step in training, orientation, as well as training and development programs.

WHY PROVIDE ORIENTATION?

Providing an orientation to the library, the "big picture," sets the tone for the student's employment experience. A positive beginning provides the student employee with a positive attitude toward the job, coworkers, supervisors, and the library. The major reason for providing an orientation for new student employees is that oriented workers do a better job and stay with the library longer than those who are not given an orientation. Orientation serves to reduce the anxiety associated with a new job and saves time for supervisors and coworkers. The better the orientation, the less time the new employee will take from other employees to answer questions. An effective orientation helps the new employee develop a positive attitude toward the library and the job. The result is higher job satisfaction and better performance.

Some libraries have continuous hiring processes while others tend to hire most of the student employees in the fall. Smaller libraries will often include all new student employees in their orientation while large libraries orientation may be done only at the departmental level. Orientations are sometimes provided to individual hires throughout the year.

FIRST IMPRESSIONS

Orientation training, or induction training in industry, actually begins the minute an applicant comes to the library to fill out an application or appears for an interview. First impressions will determine the student's initial feelings about the library. As discussed earlier, it is important to establish a central point for student employee applicants to report. The best place for employee applicants to report is the office of the dean/director, branch library office, or the library's personnel office. The hiring supervisors should be summoned to meet the students and escort them to the department office or work area. If handled properly, new employees will have more positive attitudes toward the library as well as toward their jobs.

THE NEW STUDENT EMPLOYEE

It is essential that you recognize how the student feels when reporting for work on the first day. Think about your first day on a new job. Did you feel anxious, out of place, concerned about how others would accept you, confused, and worried about how you would perform? Almost everyone has those feelings. Your new student employees will undoubtedly feel that way too. It is important that an employee orientation system is followed that will ease the new student employees' anxiety and that makes them feel welcome.

Effective orientation of new student employees paves the way for good relations between the employees and the library in the future. The time and personal attention given by the supervisor during the first few days on the job go a long way toward making the student employees feel wanted and important. Your personal attention to orientation gives new employees a sense of security and demonstrates that the library is interested in the employees as individuals.

Orientation begins with introductions to key staff and other students. Explain what other employees do and how they work together in the department or unit. It is worthwhile to brainstorm with your fellow supervisors and the department head about what to include in your general orientation. The supervisor should give the new employee a tour of the department—don't ask someone else to do it. You should explain how the job will be learned and who will provide the training. Orienting new employees includes discussing library rules, procedures, and policies, usually included in a student handbook. It is not advisable to simply hand the book to new employees and tell them to read it—you should sit down with new student employees and review it with them.

A student employee handbook should include the following information:

1) Eligibility for student employment. Included are definitions of the number of credit hours required in order to qualify for employment. Students must be made aware that if the

number of credit hours falls below the required number, they will be terminated. Different libraries have different policies.

2) Hours of work allowed. Many libraries limit the number of hours a student may work each week, normally 20 hours.

3) Timesheets/timeclock. Describe how time worked is to be reported.

4) Pay periods. Describe how, when, and where student employees receive their paychecks. Provide a schedule of paydays.

5) Absences. Describe the library's policy on reporting absences and what to do when they will be or are late.

6) Transfer policy. Some libraries require that students work a certain number of months before they may request a transfer to another department or campus job.

7) Personnel records. Inform student employees about employment records that are maintained and clarify how they are used.

8) Telephones. Describe the library's policy on personal use of telephones.

9) Socializing and studying. Describe the library's policy on socializing and studying on the job or in the work area.

10) Library equipment. Describe the library's policy on the use of university equipment for personal use.

11) Security/emergencies. Describe the library's policies on reporting emergencies.

12) Termination. Describe what length of notice is required or desired when terminating employment. Describe the process used for termination for disciplinary reasons.

13) Grievance procedures. Describe the library/university grievance procedures and employee rights.

14) Training. Note that the student's supervisor will provide further orientation and training.

If your library does not presently have a handbook for student employees, you should consider developing one. A handbook guarantees that all employees are given the same information, regardless of how thorough the supervisors are in providing new employee orientation. Of course, there is no guarantee that the handbook will be read, but if you review the handbook with them, later claims of ignorance about these policies and procedures will be without foundation.

ORIENTATION CHECKLIST

Does your new student orientation provide answers to the following questions?

- What does the organization do?
- How does the student's work group or job fit into the overall library organization?
- How important is the work to the library?
- What do the other departments do?
- What do the other libraries on campus do?
- What is the chain of command?
- What exactly will the student do?
- What equipment will the student employee be using?
- What other employees will the student be working with daily?
- What are the work hours?
- Are there scheduled breaks?
- How long is the employee's probationary period?

- When and how will the student employee be evaluated?
- How and how much will the student be paid?
- When is payday?
- Will the employee be paid after the first pay period or is there a delay of one pay period?
- What will be deducted from paychecks?
- How will time worked be reported?
- If a timeclock is used, where is it and how do you use it?
- If timesheets are used, how are they filled out, and when?
- How are pay increases determined?
- When the student employee has questions, who should the student ask?

If the new student employees have the answers to these questions, whether provided by a library-wide orientation program or by you, your employees will be ready for job training.

TRAINING AND DEVELOPMENT ARE NOT THE SAME

We have all heard the terms "training" and "development" used interchangeably. The two words do not mean the same thing and it is important to know the difference. Training for the job emphasizes the skills and knowledge necessary to achieve and maintain an acceptable level of performance. Development goes beyond training. It focuses on the growth and improvement of employees as members of the organization and as human beings. The payoffs for training tend to be for the short run, while the benefits of development programs are felt over the long run.

ROLE OF THE STUDENT EMPLOYEE SUPERVISOR IN TRAINING

Your job description may simply say, "supervises student employees," or "hires, trains, supervises, and evaluates student workers." Training is in fact a very important part of your supervisory role. The role of the supervisor in training varies with different organizations. In industry, the personnel department is often charged with the responsibility for training new employees or there may be a separate training division. In libraries, the student employee supervisor is usually directly responsible for teaching new employees all of the skills and information necessary to become full contributing members of the department. Typically, the supervisor is given latitude in developing a training program as long as the training has the desired results. Frequently, the student employee supervisor inherits a training program from a previous supervisor who may no longer be in the department.

Training can be accomplished by the use of handbooks, computer-assisted instruction, videos, hands-on-practice, and so forth. It can be handled by other staff or by experienced student employees but above all, the immediate supervisor must be involved in the training process. The main reasons for being involved are the following:

- The supervisor can begin to establish a good working relationship and communications with the new employee;
- The supervisor knows the job (or should) better than anyone else;
- The supervisor knows what has worked well in training other student employees;

- The supervisor can set the tone for the quality and quantity of the work expected of the new employee.

SHOULD THE SUPERVISOR DO ALL THE TRAINING?

Supervisors approach training in one of two ways. The supervisor may elect to do all the training or place the new student with an experienced employee. By doing all of the training, the supervisor can be assured all employees are trained the same way, but training is very time consuming, taking time from other responsibilities. Having another experienced employee handle the training can be effective, depending on how well the training is done. The best approach is probably a combination of the two.

TWO TYPES OF TRAINING

There are two types of training that you may use in preparing student employees for their jobs: off-the-job or vestibule training and on-the-job training.

- Vestibule training takes place away from the site where the actual work will be done. It may take place in a classroom or at a desk away from the work station. The advantage is that the new employee is given "hands-on" experience without interfering with the flow of work in the department.
- On-the-job training is conducted in the department at the actual assigned work station. Most library training is done on-the-job.

WHAT DO YOU TRAIN FOR?

It is obvious that you can not train immediately for everything there is to do on the job. The basic rule is to train for those things that are vital to the job that will protect the employee and equipment from harm. You should divide the job into "have to know now," "have to know soon," and "have to know one of these days." The "have to know now" are those things that a person has to know without which nothing can be done until they are learned. If they are not learned now, employees could damage a piece of equipment, hurt themselves, or turn away a patron with an incorrect or improper response. You can avoid some training by determining what a student employee already knows.

FOUR-STEP METHOD FOR TRAINING

For supervisors, training can be very simple or very difficult. If you can remember just four fundamental steps, you can be a good trainer. If you do not use this approach, training will always be difficult and may not be effective. The foundation of systematic, structured job training has four steps:

- Step 1. PREPARATION. Get the workers ready to learn.
- Step 2. PRESENTATION. Demonstrate how the job should be done.
- Step 3. PERFORMANCE TRYOUT. Try the workers out by letting them do the job.
- Step 4. FOLLOW-UP. Put the workers on their own gradually.

Step 1. Preparation of the Learner

Until individuals are psychologically and emotionally ready to learn, it is difficult to teach them. It is the supervisor's responsibility to help the trainee prepare for what you will teach. The following will help get the trainee ready to learn the job:

1) Put the student employee at ease—relieve the tension.
2) Explain why the trainee is being taught.
3) Create interest, encourage questions, and find out what the student employee already knows about the job.
4) Explain the why of the whole job, and relate it to some job the trainee already knows.
5) Place the student employee as close to the normal working position as possible.
6) Familiarize the trainee with the work area and equipment and materials that will be used.

Step 2. Presentation of the Operation

After preparing the student employee to learn, you are ready to begin demonstrating how the job should be done. In this step you will describe and demonstrate one step at a time; stress each key point of the job, and patiently, without giving the trainee more than can be mastered, teach the steps of the job in sequence. The following steps are followed in presentation:

1) Explain requirements for quantity and quality.
2) Go through the job at the normal work pace.
3) Go through the job at a slow pace several times, explaining each step. Between operations, explain the difficult parts, or those in which errors are likely to be made. Repeat several times.
4) Go through the job at a slow pace several times, explaining the key points.
5) Have the trainee explain the steps as you go through the job at a slow pace.
6) Have the trainee explain the key points as you go through the job at a slow pace.

Step 3. Performance Tryout

In this step of training, you will give the trainee the opportunity to actually perform the job while you observe. Performance tryout includes the following:

1) Have the student employees go through the job several times, slowly, explaining to you each step. Correct trainee mistakes, and, if necessary, do some of the complicated steps for them the first few times.
2) You, the trainer, run the job at the normal pace.
3) Have the trainees do the job, gradually building up skill and speed.
4) As soon as the trainees demonstrate proficiency, put the trainees on their own, but don't abandon them.

Step 4. Follow-Up

Sometimes, the most difficult step is the last because of the tendency to think that once the employee is trained, you're done. To guarantee long-term performance, you need to be sure the employee knows where to go for help and to check back frequently to see if all is going well. During this step, you will taper off coaching so the employees don't feel you're watching over their shoulders. Follow-up entails these activities:

1) Designate to whom the trainees should go for help or to ask questions.
2) Gradually decrease supervision, checking student employees' work occasionally against quantity and quality standards.
3) Correct faulty work patterns before they develop into habits. Demonstrate why the method taught is superior.
4) Compliment good work and provide encouragement until the trainees are able to meet quantity and quality standards.

EXTENDING THE TRAINING

Some libraries use the mentor or buddy system to extend the training of student employees after the initial training. Experienced student employees are assigned to new employees to serve as role models and as sources of help after new employees are put on their own in their jobs. If the mentor or buddy is a willing participant in the training process, the relationship can be a positive training support system. It goes without saying that care must be taken to assure that the assigned mentor or buddy will be a positive influence on the new student employee.

COMMON TRAINING ERRORS

Experience, like practice, makes us perfect only if we're doing the right thing. Many of us do things wrong day in and day out, simply because we learned incorrectly in the first place. If you follow the four-step training method but discover that your training is not effective, the cause may be one of the following common training errors:

1) Failure to devote enough time to teaching. A common error for supervisors is to let other responsibilities hurry their training. Remember that the time devoted to training new employees properly is time well spent if the workers are productive.
2) Failure to follow the system step by step. The four-step system takes time but it works if followed correctly. If you skip a step, the system will break down and you will fail. Don't cut corners.
3) Failure to show enough patience with the slow learner. Some new employees will learn more slowly than others. When you teach someone who learns more slowly, you must slow your own pace or you will surely be disappointed in the results. Cover each of the four steps, even if it takes you twice as long. Keep in mind that many slow learners make excellent workers once they master a job, so your time will not be wasted.

JOB INSTRUCTION TRAINING (JIT)

The theory and practice of management is constantly evolving and changing but one constant over many years is training. The structured four step on-the-job training method has been in use ever since it was developed during World War II to improve production. The four-step method is called Job Instruction Training (JIT). During and after World War II, special trainers first trained the supervisors in the four-step instruction method.

The process was printed on a "trainer card" for quick reference by supervisors. To demonstrate that the method has changed little in fifty years, the text of the "trainer card" is reproduced below:

JOB INSTRUCTION TRAINING (JIT)

First, here's what you must do to get ready to teach a job:

1. Decide what the learner must be taught in order to do the job efficiently, safely, economically, and intelligently.
2. Have the right tools, equipment, supplies, and material ready.
3. Have the workplace properly arranged, just as the worker will be expected to keep it.

Then, you should instruct the learner by the following four basic steps:

Step I—Preparation (of the learner)

1. Put the learner at ease.
2. Find out what he or she already knows about the job.
3. Get the learners interested in and desirous of learning the job.

Step II—Presentation (of the operations and knowledge)

1. Tell, show, illustrate, and question in order to put over the new knowledge.
2. Instruct slowly, clearly, completely, and patiently, one point at a time.
3. Check, question, and repeat.
4. Make sure the learner really knows.

Step III—Performance tryout

1. Test learner by having him or her perform the job.
2. Ask questions beginning with why, how, when, or where.
3. Observe performance, correct errors, and repeat instructions if necessary.
4. Continue until you know the learner knows.

Step IV—Follow-up

1. Put the employee "on his own."
2. Check frequently to be sure learner follows instructions.
3. Taper off extra supervision and close follow-up until person is qualified to work with normal supervision.

Remember—If the learner hasn't learned, the teacher hasn't taught.

Source: Training Within Industry Report, War Manpower Commission, Bureau of Training, 1945.

TIPS FOR IMPROVEMENT OF TRAINING

DON'T:
- Don't assume that everyone you train will learn at the same pace. We all learn at different rates. Be patient.
- Don't assume a task is easy because you found it easy. We all find different tasks easy to learn.
- Don't assume that because employees are trained, they will continue to do things the way they were taught. Skills slip, and you will have to retrain some people.

- Don't assume that because employees have experience, that they know how to perform some tasks. They may have experience performing tasks incorrectly.
- Don't forget that it takes time for good habits to develop.
- Don't act interested in your student employees' learning; be interested in their learning.
- Don't make fun of employees who make mistakes. We all learn from our mistakes.

DO:

- Do follow the four-step training method.
- Do let your student employees know that you expect them to continue doing things correctly.
- Do let them know you are always willing to help them learn.
- Do give encouragement and recognition for work done well.
- Do keep student employees informed on how well they are doing and where they need improvement.
- Do ask your student employees what you can do to help them do a better job. Ask them often.

ACTIVE VERSUS PASSIVE LEARNING

We assume our student employees are adults and need to be treated as such. In planning training programs, it is important to understand the adult learning process. Your training program is aimed at adults who learn differently from children. Children are passive learners who are taught to sit quietly, absorb what they are told, and repeat it on command. Adults, on the other hand, demand active learning that is relevant and participative.

Your student employees have learned how to learn, and are in fact engaged in learning daily as part of their undergraduate or graduate experience. Unless student employees see the relevance, your training will not accomplish much. You can establish the relevancy of training by explaining why it is given, how it will benefit them, and why it is important to the work group's productivity.

Adults learn by doing so there should be as much activity as possible throughout the learning process. Because student employees are subjected to being lectured to all day, they will respond better to doing than to hearing about doing. Student employees will absorb an enormous amount of learning by actively participating, far more than from studying manuals. Don't use the same teaching methods you use with children to teach your student employees. Remember, your student employees are adults.

IMPLEMENTING YOUR TRAINING PROGRAM

The following are suggestions on how to prepare and implement your training program:

1) Be sure that you have done your homework. Do some reading in the psychology of learning and motivation.
2) Make notes to yourself about the four step training process and resolve to follow the system.
3) Develop a plan for training and write it down.
4) A checklist of tasks to be taught and how proficiency will be measured is extremely useful.
5) When training, use your checklist to be sure everything is taught.

6) Recognize that training takes time and that retraining is an integral part of your job. At times you will feel that all you accomplish is training but remember, don't cut corners.

7) Identify experienced student employees in the department who can help you and possibly act as mentors to new student employees.

8) Discuss your training plan with your supervisor, ask for suggestions, and get support.

9) Discuss training plans with other student employee supervisors and consider using their ideas.

DEVELOPMENTAL TRAINING

A part of your training responsibility as supervisor is developmental training. Developmental training usually refers to long-term growth: training to improve performance and preparation of employees for higher level positions. In libraries, the emphasis is normally on preparing regular staff for managerial positions or for other advancement. For student employees, developmental training usually is limited to preparing them for supervisory duties within the department, night supervisor, for example, or for higher level positions in other departments of the library.

The first step is to determine what kinds of training your student employees need. Developmental training is designed primarily for experienced employees, because new employees must concentrate on learning the basics of the job. For experienced employees, training must meet one of two needs: training to improve performance on the present job and training to prepare them for higher level jobs. Both types of training are needed for all employees.

TRAINING PRESENT EMPLOYEES TO IMPROVE PERFORMANCE

Training to improve performance hinges on the difference between "can do" and "will do." If the student employee "can't do" a task, ask yourself these questions: Has this employee ever done the task correctly? Has this employee been taught to do it correctly? If offered a reward to do the task correctly, could the employee do it? If the answer to any of the questions is "no," you have a training problem—the employee "can't do" the task.

If you can answer "yes" to the previous questions, you must determine if you have a "won't do" problem on your hands. If the employee can do the task but won't do it, this becomes a management, not a training, problem. The way the employee is supervised, the way the job is organized, or the employee's attitude must be examined. No amount of training will solve the "won't do" problem.

To attack the "can't do" problem, the trainer must isolate the task that cannot be performed. Have the employee demonstrate how the employee performs the task. Physically demonstrated skills under your observation are the best way to separate the employee's abilities from inabilities. Once identified, the task that is not performed properly can be taught using the four-step training procedure described earlier.

TRAINING TO PREPARE STUDENT EMPLOYEES FOR HIGHER LEVEL WORK

Training to prepare student employees for higher level jobs depends greatly on what those jobs are. Generally speaking, providing opportunities for student employees to learn a wide range of jobs and develop skills that will help them in any future work situation would be useful. Such things as computer and keyboard skills, telephone skills, interpersonal relations skills, and the development of good work habits are all useful in future employment. This may also be an opportunity to mentor student employees who express interest in librarianship as a career.

Opportunities for student employees to take advantage of staff development programs in the library or development programs offered by the university should be investigated. Find out whether or not student employees can avail themselves of programs offered to library staff. If so, make every effort to communicate those opportunities to your student employees.

DEVELOPMENTAL TRAINING METHODS

Libraries with active staff development programs often invite student employees to participate. You, as their supervisor, should encourage participation in those programs that will provide enrichment to their jobs and help them prepare for future careers. There are at least a dozen developmental training methods used in industry and education. The most common methods used by libraries are:

1) Conference: This training normally involves verbal interaction between an instructor and participants.
2) Lecture: Presentation by a knowledgeable person given to a group of employees.
3) Programmed/computer assisted instruction: Instruction in which the learner must respond correctly to each part before proceeding.
4) Case study: This method involves the use of a written description of a situation that the trainee must read and analyze.
5) Role playing: Learners assume the role of other people and interact with other learners in acting out a situation.

Talk to your supervisor and to other student supervisors to learn how they provide developmental training for staff and student employees. Ask questions about programs offered and find out how your student employees can participate. Remember that one of your responsibilities as a supervisor of student employees is to help them grow and develop. Through counseling and coaching, you can provide the ongoing informal training intended to refine skills and give assistance for personal growth.

SUPERVISOR TRAINING CHECKLIST

If you can honestly answer "yes" to all of the following questions, you are well on your way to becoming an effective trainer of student employees:

1) Do you accept full responsibility for training your student employees?
2) Do you consider training to be a continuous, ongoing activity?
3) Do you have an orientation checklist and religiously cover each item on the list?
4) Do you have a training checklist and use it every time you train a new student employee?
5) Do you use the four step training process without skipping any steps?
6) Do you recognize that individuals learn at different rates and are you patient with those who learn slower than others?
7) Do you stay in touch with new employees to be sure they know they can ask questions?

8) Do you have a way to identify present employee performance deficiencies and can you differentiate between "can't do" and "won't do" problems?

9) Do you have a developmental training program for your student employees?

ORIENTATION, TRAINING, AND DEVELOPMENT

The supervisor's responsibility for preparing workers, training them to perform their jobs, and developing employees can not be understated. How well these are accomplished may well determine whether you succeed or fail as a supervisor.

BIBLIOGRAPHY

Albrecht, Steve. *Tough Training Topics: A Presenter's Survival Guide*. San Francisco, CA: Pfeiffer, c2006.

Allan, Barbara. *Training Skills for Library Staff*. Lanham, MD: Scarecrow Press, 2003.

Arthur, Diane. *Recruiting, Interviewing, Selecting & Orienting New Employees*. New York: American Management Association, c2006.

Avila, Antionette, Collette Ford, and Rayna Hamre. "Library Training Day: Developing an Effective Academic Library Student Training Program." *Library Mosaics* 16(1) (January/February 2005): 18–19.

Baird, Lynn N. "Student Employees in Academic Libraries: Training for Work, Educating for Life." *PNLA Quarterly* 67(2) (Winter 2003): 13, 23.

Bell, Chip R. *Managers as Mentors: Building Partnerships for Learning*. San Francisco, CA: Berrett-Koehlers, 1998.

Borin, Jacqueline. "Training, Supervising, And Evaluating Student Information Assistants." *Reference Librarian* (72) (2001): 195–206.

Christopher, Connie. *Empowering Your Library: A Guide to Improving Service, Productivity, & Participation*. Chicago, IL: American Library Association, 2003.

Creth, Sheila. *Effective On the Job Training: Developing Library Human Resources*. Chicago, IL: American Library Association, 1986.

Epstein, Carmen. "Using Blackboard for Training and Communicating with Student Employees." *College & Undergraduate Libraries* 10(1) (2003): 21–25.

Gibbs, William J., Carrie Chen, Ronan S. Bernas. "Group Instruction and Web-based Instructional Approaches for Training Student Employees." *Journal of Computing in Higher Education* 13(1) (Fall 2001): 71–90.

Guerin, Lisa and Amy DelPo. *Create Your Own Employee Handbook: A Legal and Practical Guide*. Berkeley, CA: Nolo, 2003.

Heller, Paul C. and Stuart Kohler. "Take This Book and Shelve It!" *College & Research Libraries News* (7) (July/August 1996): 425–426.

Holliday, Wendy and Cynthia Nordgren. "Extending the Reach of Librarians: Library Peer Mentor Program at Utah State University." *College & Research Libraries News* 66(4) (April 2005): 282–284.

Holtze, Terri L. and Rebecca E. Maddox. "Student Assistant Training in a Multi-library System." *Technical Services Quarterly* 19(2) (2001): 27–41.

Jones, Phillip J., Janet H. Parsch, and Vijith M. Varghese. "Graduate Assistants at the University of Arkansas Libraries: Past, Future, and Significance, Part II." *Arkansas Libraries* 62(2) (Summer 2005): 6–11.

Kathman, Jane McGurn and Michael D. Kathman. "Training Student Employees for Quality Service." *Journal of Academic Librarianship* 26(3) (May 2000): 176–182.

Lancaster, Lynne C. and David Stillman. *When Generations Collide: Who They Are, Why They Clash, How to Solve the Generational Puzzle at Work*. New York: HarperCollins, 2002.

Lucas, Robert W. *The Creative Training Idea Book: Inspired Tips and Techniques for Engaging and Effective Learning*. New York: AMACOM, American Management Association, c2003.

Manzoni, J. F. and Jean-Louis Barsoux. *The Set-Up-To-Fail Syndrome: How Good Managers Cause Great People to Fail*. Boston, MA: Harvard Business School Press, 2002.

Neuhaus, Chris. "Flexibility and Feedback: A New Approach to Ongoing Training for Reference Student Assistants." *Reference Services Review* 29(1) (2001): 53–64.

Rielly, Loretta J. and Garry A. Browning. "Point-of-use Instruction: The Evolving Role of Stacks Support Staff and Student Assistants in an Academic Library." *The Reference Librarian* (51–52) (1995): 195–208.

Riley, Cheryl A. and Barbara Wales. "Introducing the Academic Library to Student Employees: A Group Approach." *Technical Services Quarterly* 14(4) (1997): 47–59.

Wesley, Threasa L. "Beyond Job Training: An Orientation Program for Library Student Assistants." *Catholic Library World* 61(5) (March–April 1990): 215–217.

9

Teamwork and Group Dynamics

Time is a great teacher, but unfortunately it kills all its pupils.

—Hector Berlioz (1803–1869)

LOOKING AT TEAM MANAGEMENT

Teams in libraries are the "in" thing to do. As libraries face "downsizing" or "right sizing," demands for more participation by all levels of staff, and the realization that participation is desirable, administrators are looking at teams. Total Quality Management imposed from higher levels of administration utilizes quality teams and teamwork. A more horizontal organization of libraries seems an appropriate, almost inevitable outcome for many hierarchical organizations.

TEAMS IN ACADEME ARE "NOT ATTAINABLE"

In his book, *Academic Librarianship in a Transformational Age*, library consultant Allen Veaner contends that an academic community cannot be made into a team. Fundamentally, team structures spell the redistribution of power in an organization. In the strongly elitist and highly stratified microcosm of academe, however, all members of the group are not peers. It is quite impossible to give everyone an equal voice in programmatic affairs. As stated [in another chapter], an academic community cannot and should not be turned into a team; the concept implies a degree of unity and intimate cooperation that is not attainable in academe. The stratified groupings in an academic library have their own informal structures, separate agendas, group and individual goals, all of which are more in conflict than in congruence. To claim that such diversity can be welded into a team is more than wishful thinking, it is nonsense. Within this arena of conflict, management is an integrating force acting to assure the achievement of institutional mission, goals, and objectives in spite of all of these differences. Managers are expected to find or invent ways to get different groups of employees to work together as a coordinated group. Among other things, management is paid to do exactly that.[1]

Traditional middle managers typically find team structures threatening and adapt uneasily. Unions continue to view labor-management relations as basically adversarial and see team setups as a possible deterrent to unionization; thus they are slow to give up their rights. The new paradigm's highest rates of success occur in new plants or offices where semicollegial team structures can be installed without the agonies of trying to resocialize an established middle management and/or persuade unions to surrender some power.[2]

Can team management be implemented successfully in academe? If by successful, one means having a favorable outcome or having obtained something desired or intended, seeing is believing. Team management has been successfully implemented in libraries. The implementation of team management in the library has not and will not have a significant impact on the rest of the university. Its impact on academe is that the library is known as a well-managed college with high morale and a highly respected faculty and staff. It is not the library's purpose to change academe, only to be effective in its own mission.

DISADVANTAGES OF USING TEAMS

There are potential shortcomings of the team management approach. The disadvantages are as follow:

1. Teams in academe can experience burnout and become complacent, exhausting their ideas without fresh input from new members. The more cohesive a group becomes, the more likely it is that members will not censor what they say out of fear of antagonizing the leader or other members. Members also may deliberately censor themselves because of the desire to maintain group unity and to adhere to its norms.
2. When the team has a high degree of cohesiveness and esprit de corps, its members may fall victim to groupthink. The process is characterized by a marked decrease in the exchange of potentially conflicting data and an unwillingness to critically examine that data. In their desire for unanimity, team members may become insulated in their thinking, discounting negative information from outsiders, or they may reach consensus simply to please the boss. Groupthink may be diagnosed when the following symptoms are present:
   • The team has the illusion of unanimity and an emphasis on team play,
   • The team views the "opposition" as generally inept, incompetent, and incapable of countering any action by the group,
   • Group members censor themselves, overt disagreements are avoided, faulty assumptions go unchallenged, and personal doubts are suppressed in the interest of group harmony,
   • Collective rationalization is utilized when an agreed-upon decision is clearly unworkable,
   • The team has self-appointed mind guards within the group who prevent unwelcome ideas and adverse information that may threaten unanimity,
   • The team applies direct pressure on dissenting group members who threaten consensus,

- The team develops a sense of self-righteousness that leads group members to believe their actions are moral and ethical, thus allowing them to ignore ethical or moral objections to their behavior.
- The team exhibits a shared feeling of unassailability marked by a high degree of esprit de corps, implicit faith in the wisdom of the group, and optimism that leads the team to believe it can take excessive risks.

3. A team does not possess clarity unless the team leader creates it. A team has poor stability. Its economy is low; a team demands continuing attention to its management, to the relationships of people within the task force, to assigning people to their jobs, to explanation, deliberation, communication, and so on. A large part of the energy of all the members goes into keeping things running. Although everybody on the team understands the common task, team members do not always understand their own specific tasks. They may be so interested in what others are doing that they pay inadequate attention to their own assignments.[3]

4. Teams do only a little better than straight functional organizations in preparing people for higher management responsibilities or in testing their performance. A team makes neither for clear communications nor for clear decision making. The whole group must work constantly on explaining both to itself and to managers throughout the rest of the organization what it is trying to do, what it is working on, and what it has accomplished. The team must constantly make sure that the decisions that need to be made are brought into the open, when it is much easier to do the opposite. Teams fail, and the failure rate has been high, primarily because they do not impose on themselves the self-discipline and responsibility that are required as a result of the high degree of freedom team organization gives. No task force can be permissive and function. This is the reason why the same young educated people who clamor for teamwork tend so often in reality to resist it. It makes tremendous demands on self-discipline.[4]

5. The greatest limitation for the team structure is size. Teams work best when there are few members. The aboriginal hunting band had 7 to 15 members. So do the teams in team sports. Although athletic team rosters may be large, participation of more than a dozen members simultaneously is rare. If a team gets much larger than the aboriginal hunting band, it becomes unwieldy. "The team's strengths, such as flexibility and the sense of responsibility of the members, attenuate. Its limitations—lack of clarity, communication problems, overconcern with the internal mechanism and internal relationship—become crippling weaknesses."[5]

To summarize the argument against management by teamwork in libraries:

- Administrators and middle managers do not wish to share authority, do not have a unity of purpose, and will not cooperate in the elitist, stratified academic environment.
- Administrators and middle managers do not possess teamwork skills or knowledge.
- Unions dislike teams because they disrupt the adversarial relationship between labor and management.
- Teams are inefficient because they demand continuing attention to their development, operation, and maintenance. They do not on their own make for clear communication or decision making.
- Teams tend toward inaction until consensus is reached.
- Teams must continually explain themselves and may succumb to groupthink. The size of teams is a severe limitation, and all teams are prone to burnout.

- Team members may ignore their own work when paying attention to team activity. They may not have the self-discipline or skills required of teamwork.
- Empowered employees may not know their limits, and outsiders view teamwork with distrust and dismay.
- Who is in charge?

All of the above arguments against teamwork are grounded in low expectations and a low regard for the individual.

ADVANTAGES OF USING TEAMS

People have great talents that are often barely tapped by organizations. Work groups, task teams, matrix organizations, project teams, and the team management environment offer opportunities for people to accomplish more by making better use of their talents and by reducing barriers to communication and cooperation. Innovative patterns of organization call for a high degree of enlightened and supportive leadership from top management. Success is not guaranteed just because individuals are organized in teams, but there are clear advantages to individuals and the organization in the team management approach. Both scientific research and successful experience by managers indicate that individuals functioning as members of a team can perform better than those working alone.[6]

Individuals working as a team can usually pool their ideas and come up with solutions to problems more effectively than can a single person working on the same problems. Not only can a team generate better ideas, but also the chances that decisions will be successfully implemented are much improved. Teamwork recognizes that individuals assembled into teams can maximize their potential. A major advantage of teamwork is the positive feeling generated in team members. Individuals have high self-esteem in cohesive teams.

Cohesiveness in groups also increases the power of the team over the individual, which has both positive and negative aspects. Team membership has many benefits for individuals, but teams must be aware of and careful to avoid groupthink.

ADAPTABILITY OF TEAMS

The team organization has great adaptability. In a team, everybody always knows the work of the whole and holds himself responsible for it. The team is highly receptive to experimentation, new ideas, and new ways of doing things. Its size limitation determines the scope of applicability of the team principle in management. It is the best available design principle for top management work (probably the only appropriate design principle for top management work). It is the preferred design principle for innovative work. But for most operating work the team is not appropriate by itself and alone as the design principle of organization. It is a complement—though a badly needed one. It may well be that team organization will make the functional principle fully effective and enable it to do what its designers had hoped for. But the area where team design as a complement to functional organization is likely to make the greatest contribution is in knowledge work. Knowledge work by definition is specialized work. A good deal of knowledge work will undoubtedly be organized on a strictly functional basis. A good deal will also be done by individuals who, in effect, are an organizational component by themselves.[7]

Teams are the best means for overcoming functional insulation and parochialism. Any career professional should serve on a few teams during his or her working life.[8]

TEAMS EMPOWER INDIVIDUALS IN FLATTENED HIERARCHIES

Peter Block, in his book, *The Empowered Manager*, suggests radically changing the hierarchy in order to develop an entrepreneurial organization. Among the suggestions Block makes are to flatten out the organization, reverse the performance appraisal process, and introduce self-managing teams.[9]

Flattening the organization reduces the layers of staffing from top to bottom, making individuals more responsible for the success of the organization. In the team management environment, layers of administration and barriers between divisions are removed. Reversing the performance appraisal process serves to allow the supervisor and supervisees to have a common interest in each other's success. Evaluation of supervisors is an important component in the team management environment. Self-managing teams are the engines in the team management environment. Teamwork is most successful when the members are entrepreneurs who are willing to harness their abilities to the team's objectives.

THE POWER OF TEAMS

In his book *Thriving on Chaos*, Thomas Peters contends that wholesale worker involvement must become a national priority if the United States is going to maintain, let alone improve, national economic well-being.[10]

At the top of the list is the use of teams. He exhorts managers to make self-managing teams the basic organizational building block. Peters contends that "the power of teams is so great that it is often wise to violate apparent common sense and force a team structure on almost anything." He urges readers to "emphasize mainly self-sufficient units, or what I call the small-within-big principle, throughout the organization."[11]

Another of Peters' 45 prescriptions for U.S. business is to pursue "horizontal" management by bashing the bureaucracy. He suggests managing the organization horizontally, insisting that vertical obfuscating be replaced with proactive, horizontal cooperation in pursuit of fast action.[12] The team management environment actively works toward that end.

HUMANISTIC VALUES OF TEAMWORK

Douglas McGregor asserts in *The Human Side of Enterprise* that teams can be effective: The face-to-face group is as significant a unit of organization as the individual. The two are not antithetical. In a genuinely effective group the individual finds some of his deepest satisfactions. Through teamwork and group activity many of the difficult organizational problems of coordination and control can be solved. However, these values can be realized only if certain requirements are met.[13] McGregor explains how thinking must change in the team management environment:

First, we will have to abandon the idea that individual and group values are necessarily opposed, that the latter can only be realized at the expense of the former. If we would look to the family, we might recognize the possibilities inherent in the opposite point of view.

Second, we will have to give serious attention to the matter of acquiring understanding of the factors which determine the effectiveness of group action and to the acquisition of skill in utilizing their skills in group membership.

Third, we will need to distinguish between those activities which are appropriate for groups and those that are not.

Finally, we will need to distinguish between the team concept of management as a gimmick to be applied within the strategy of management by direction and control and the team concept as a natural correlate of management by integration and self-control. The one has nothing in common with the other.[14]

McGregor goes on to describe the benefits of teams:

1. Group target-setting offers advantages that cannot be achieved by individual target-setting alone. The two are supplementary, not mutually exclusive.
2. An effective managerial group provides the best possible environment for individual development. It is the natural place to broaden the manager's understanding of functions other than his own and to create a genuine appreciation for the need for collaboration. It is the best possible training ground for skill in problem solving and in social interaction.
3. Many significant objectives and measures of performance can be developed for the group that cannot be applied to the individual. The members of cohesive groups will work at least as hard to achieve group objectives as they will to achieve individual ones.
4. In an effective managerial team the aspects of "dog-eat-dog" competition, which are actually inimical to organizational accomplishment, can be minimized by the development of "unity of purpose" without reducing individual motivation.[15]

The team management environment is founded on McGregor's Theory Y, characterized as follows:[16]

1. The expenditure of physical and mental effort in work is as natural as play or rest. The average human being does not inherently dislike work. Depending upon controllable conditions, work may be a source of satisfaction (and will be performed without threat of punishment).
2. Human beings will exercise self-direction and self-control in the service of objectives to which they are committed.
3. Commitment to objectives is a function of the rewards associated with their achievement.
4. The average human being learns, under proper conditions, not only to accept but to seek responsibility.
5. The capacity to exercise a relatively high degree of imagination, ingenuity, and creativity in the solution of organizational problems is widely distributed in the population.
6. Under the conditions of modern industrial life, the intellectual potentialities of the average human being are only partially utilized.

Humanistic Management by Teamwork is founded on the principle that library employees are characterized by McGregor's Theory Y concept. Library employees can thrive in the team management environment.[17]

METHODS OF ORGANIZING

The methods of organizing in today's academic libraries are governed by the characteristics of the people, the task to be performed, and the environment. All three of these have been changing in recent years and will continue to change rapidly into the future. Much of what can be seen in today's organizations is a carryover from past models of organization. Industrial organizations, for decades, have been based on the breakdown of tasks. Large areas of responsibility were broken down into lesser responsibilities and assigned to specific jobs. These organizations were structured to perform well-defined tasks with workers having predictable qualifications. Technological considerations were more important than human considerations, and the gulf between what people were capable of doing and what they were required to do played little part in the design of the organizations. Specialization was thought to be the key to efficiency.

The breakdown of work into small segments in organizations is changing because the nature of the work is changing. Work is becoming more complex, requiring more specialists who are needed to handle a narrower scope of work in greater depth. Rapid technological changes requiring specialization and problem solving in the more complex work environment have spawned a variety of professional specialties. Common databases make it feasible to blend functions, until now quite separate, into innovative combinations. The increasing complexity of work, the need for more specialization, and automation that has reduced the need for lower skilled workers require that today's organizations examine alternatives to traditional patterns of organization. There is a need for more coordination and integration in order to improve the way groups work together. Organizations that in the past have been based on analysis are now being based, at least in part, on synthesis. Teams and work groups are being combined, often composed of members of different departments, to make a whole that is more effective than the individuals spread through several units.

EFFECTIVE GROUPS

Knowledge of group behavior can be applied to improve the functioning of teams. What distinguishes effective groups from those that are ineffective?

1. The effective group tends to be informal and relaxed. There are no obvious tensions; instead there is a comfortable atmosphere that can be observed after only a few minutes. It is a working atmosphere in which people are interested and involved and there are no signs of boredom.

2. Nearly everyone participates in the discussions. If someone strays off the subject at hand, another team member brings the discussion back on track.

3. Members of the team understand and accept the objective or task of the group. The objective has been discussed until it is formulated so that members can commit to it.

4. The members of the group listen to one another. Every idea is given a hearing, and members do not fear expressing their ideas.

5. There is disagreement. Team members are comfortable with conflict over ideas. Disagreements are not suppressed or covered up by premature group action. The group works to resolve disagreements rather than turning on the dissenter. Individuals who disagree are not attempting to dominate the group or be obstructive. Disagreements are genuine expressions

of difference of opinion, and those opinions are given a hearing. The effective group deals with ideas and opinions, not personalities.

6. The effective team may have basic disagreements that cannot be resolved. The group accepts them and may elect to defer action to allow further study, or, if action is required, it will be taken with the understanding that the action may be subject to reconsideration at a later date.

7. The team makes decisions by consensus in which everyone is in general agreement and willing to go along. There is little tendency for individuals who disagree with the decisions to keep their opposition private. Instead, those in disagreement are willing, once their positions are known, to go along. Formal voting is kept to a minimum and utilized only if consensus cannot be reached.

8. Criticism is frequent and relatively comfortable. There is little evidence of personal attack, either open or hidden. The criticism is constructive in that it is intended to remove obstacles that face the group and hinder its work.

9. Team members freely express their feelings and ideas on the problem at hand as well as on the performance of the team. There are few hidden agendas. Everyone appears to know how everyone else feels about any matter under discussion.

10. When decisions are made, it is clear who has responsibility for taking action.

11. The team leader does not dominate, nor does the team defer unduly to the leader. Leadership of the team shifts from one member to another depending on the issue being discussed. This shift takes place because individuals on the team have different kinds of knowledge or expertise, and the team relies on individuals to take leadership on certain issues.

12. There appears to be no struggle for power in the effective team. It is not important who controls but that the job gets done.

13. The team performs maintenance on itself. If the team is not functioning properly or effectively, the problem or individual behavior interfering with group effectiveness will be openly discussed and a solution found before it proceeds.

14. In order for the team to be effective, a great deal of sensitivity, understanding, skill, and trust on the part of all members of the team are required.

INEFFECTIVE GROUPS

What are the characteristics of ineffective groups?

1. The atmosphere of the group is one of indifference and boredom, manifested in people whispering to one another or carrying on side conversations. There may be obvious tensions in the form of hostility, antagonism, or undue formality. The group is clearly not challenged or interested in its task.

2. A few members of the group dominate the discussion, and little is done to keep the discussion on track.

3. From observing the group's discussion, it is difficult to determine what its objectives are. The group may have a stated objective, but the members either don't understand or don't accept the objective. It is usually evident that individuals in the group have personal objectives that are in conflict with one another and with the group objective.

4. Members of the group do not really listen to one another, and ideas are either ignored or overridden. The discussion wanders from the task at hand, and individuals appear to be making speeches intended to impress rather than to further the group objective.

5. Members of the group fail to express their feelings or ideas for fear that other members will disagree or that the group leader is evaluating their contributions. Individuals are extremely careful about what they say.

6. The group does not effectively deal with disagreements. The leader may suppress dissension. Disagreements may result in open warfare between subgroups. Votes may resolve the issues at hand, but a small majority may be satisfied at the expense of the minority.

7. An aggressive individual or faction may dominate the majority of members who wish to preserve the peace and get back to work. Less aggressive members are not heard.

8. Action is taken before sufficient discussion, Individuals who disliked the decision will complain after the meeting about not being able to voice their opinions. A simple majority vote is considered sufficient for action, and the minority remains resentful and uncommitted to the decision.

9. When decisions are made, it is unclear who will take action. Even when assignments are made, group members have doubts that action will be taken.

10. The chair is clearly the leader. Leadership does not pass to other members regardless of their abilities.

11. Criticism often appears to involve personalities rather than issues. Members are uncomfortable with the criticism of ideas, because the criticism tends to be destructive rather than constructive. When seemingly every idea gets clobbered, the ideas stop coming out in discussions.

12. The general attitude about personal feelings is that they are explosive and should not be discussed. Therefore, personal feelings are hidden.

13. The group avoids discussion of its own operation. Instead, discussions about what went wrong and why generally take place outside the meetings.

14. Members of the group have low expectations of group accomplishment, partly because so many groups are ineffective.

15. Members of the group have little knowledge about effective group functioning and are fearful of conflict in group meetings.

TEAM REQUIREMENTS

What characterizes a team is not free form or the absence of regimentation. The team must have a continuing mission and clearly defined objectives. Team design requires a continuing mission in which the specific tasks change frequently. If there is no continuing mission, there might be a need for an ad hoc temporary task force but not an organization based on the team as a permanent design. If the tasks do not change, or if their relative importance or sequence remains unchanged, there is no need for team organization and no point to it. Without clearly defined objectives, the team will drift from one activity to the next, devoting its efforts to nonproductive goals. It is the team that must help define objectives, but it is the team leader who must see that there are objectives. It is not leadership's responsibility to make the decision and give the command. It is leadership responsibility to decide who among the team members has responsibility for a particular phase or challenge. A team is therefore not democratic, if by that is meant that decisions are taken by vote. It emphasizes authority, but the authority is task-derived and task-focused. It is always the team as a whole that is responsible for the task. The individual contributes his particular skill and knowledge. But every individual is always responsible for the output and performance of the entire team rather than for his own work.

MEMBER REQUIREMENTS

People are put on teams because of their authority, knowledge, and motivation. The crucial qualifications for team membership are knowledge and authority. Members must bring their knowledge to bear on the team, and where expertise is needed, it must be available to the team. All members of a team should have or be given authority to make decisions that are consistent with other members of the team and with the team. Team members need not know each other well to perform as team. But they do need to know each other's function and potential contribution. Rapport, empathy, and interpersonal relations are not needed. Mutual understanding of each other's job and understanding of the common task are essential.

Some managers believe that all employees prefer a job that requires interaction with others and that everyone wants more autonomy. Not everyone wants to interact with a group. There are highly motivated and productive people who are ill equipped or simply not interested in functioning on teams or in a team environment. Their contributions are as individuals and those individual contributions should be recognized and valued by the organization. In order for any team to be effective, members must be motivated to work with others; they must bring their knowledge to the team; they must have the needed authority to make decisions; and the team membership must be changed as the situation or goal of the team changes. A note of caution: There is a point at which coordination can be carried too far. When people begin to feel that they are spending a disproportionate amount of their time coordinating their efforts with the work of others, you should be concerned about the design of the organization. Individuals who aspire to an organization based on teamwork would do well to assess their own abilities with regard to positive teamwork behaviors.

The following statements, answered affirmatively, indicate an aptitude for success as a team member or team leader.

> I cooperate with my colleagues.
> I collaborate, whenever possible, with people from other disciplines, departments, and work units.
> I seek input from diverse sources for problem solving and decision making.
> I recognize the interdependence of technical and service staff with others within and outside of the library.
> I can function effectively as a member of a team or task force.
> I am willing to consider issues from varied perspectives, even those that are very different from mine.
> I can tolerate ambiguity.
> I can tolerate uncertainty.
> I can tolerate a seeming lack of structure.
> I take an interest in each co-worker's achievements.
> I take an interest in the organization's achievements.
> I am able to give and receive feedback in an objective, nondefensive manner.
> I encourage an atmosphere that is informal, relaxed, comfortable, and nonjudgmental.
> I seek group participation, consensus, and shared decisions.
> I clarify roles, relationships, responsibilities, and expectations.
> I have the capacity for establishing temporary, meaningful, and intense relations.
> I can facilitate group communication on objectives, goals, and missions.

I can synthesize diverse input, information, and insights.

I encourage authentic communication, enabling employees to speak freely and express feelings.

I emphasize the constructive channeling of energy caused by disagreements and difference.

I seek group support, recognition, and encouragement for individual employees.

I attempt to draw everyone into discussions, even the silent and insecure.

I share the leadership role by fostering others to initiate, clarify, summarize, and decide.

I model ethical behavior to others.

PITFALLS IN TEAM STRUCTURES

Practicing team management is not without its pitfalls. The top management of the organization must take into consideration a number of factors and realities before deciding to implement a team-based organization.

Don't ignore the fact that attitudes may be a problem. Middle management must be as willing to change as top management, and that may take time. Unions may be reluctant to accept changes that give employees more autonomy. If employees feel that the organization is encouraging them to express their ideas, it might make them question the value of union representation. The groundwork for change to a team management environment must be laid in order to alleviate distrust of management. The solution is to make participation voluntary and to assure them that their jobs will be secure.

Don't ignore middle management. They must be prepared to change. One of the greatest pitfalls in introducing team management is that managers are hesitant to relinquish to subordinates what they believe is their decision making prerogative. They not only must share decision making with teams but also must share information with others to a greater extent than before. The established department heads may see the change as degrading to their self images. It is obvious that if the perception of managers doesn't change, infighting will result.

Don't hesitate to call in outside help. Changes in organizations will be more readily accepted if employees know that their top management is on solid ground with its plan for change. Training sessions on team building can be conducted by consultants brought in for that purpose.

Don't sacrifice a logical structure for a behavioral theory. Base your organizational design on a proven structure. The notion that individuals will achieve higher levels of satisfaction by eliminating all rules and structure is faulty thinking. Individuals and groups need some structure and guidance. Take care that you do not abandon well-defined responsibilities and channels of communication.

Don't allow teams to become independent. In order to serve the goals of the organization, groups cannot be isolated from it. Teams are part of the larger organization and must serve its goals. Communication must be maintained both horizontally between teams and vertically between teams and higher management.

Don't let the new system become rigid. Just when you think the organization is perfectly aligned, it is time to think about changes that will have to be made because the tasks and challenges to the organization are changing. Top management must also be cautioned that too many changes are disruptive and result in inefficiency. The management team has a responsibility to monitor the organization's work and its goals to assure that teams have not become rigid.

Don't assume that training is a one time thing. A training program needs to accompany changes in the organization that radically alter worker responsibilities. Training must continue in order to maintain the skills and knowledge of team members and to improve understanding of the team management environment.

Don't assume that teams don't need to be managed. The team management environment focuses work on results and it enlarges the scope of responsibility of individuals. The team organization will not, however, replace the need for performing traditional tasks. Each team must understand its goals and its decision-making processes. There must be ground rules, and the supervisor still has an extremely important role in the team management environment. Control is essential in the team management environment. An eye must be kept on the bottom line and on project timetables. The tendency to "let George do it" in the team management environment is a real danger. The team leader has a responsibility to assure that the "it's everybody's responsibility and no one's" mentality does not pervade the team management environment.

Don't underestimate people. When individuals are given a larger sense of responsibility and opportunity, they will usually rise to the occasion. If the work is important to individuals, it is hoped that their sense of dedication and responsibility will rise accordingly, manifested, for instance, in reduced absenteeism.

Don't overestimate people. Given the freedom to manage themselves to a greater degree, some individuals will take advantage of you and the system. Absenteeism may in fact increase for some employees. The team management environment encourages cross departmental teams and, as a result, multiple bosses at times. Some individuals cannot cope and become distressed over the ambiguities inherent in the team management environment. If these problems cannot be overcome, these individuals should be excluded from task groups, etc. There are some individuals who are incapable of planning their own work, who do not wish to have more autonomy or responsibility, or who do not wish to participate in team activities. There are a few individuals who would prefer to sabotage a system in which others are succeeding. None of the individuals, if proven they will not or cannot participate, should be excluded from critical team operations.

Don't believe that results will be immediate. There is often a time lag of 7 to 18 months between a change in leadership behavior and improved performance. In addition, it requires from 6 to 12 months for top management to be able to change leadership behavior down through the organization. Therefore, it can be expected that it will take more than a year for a change in the organization to be established.

Five kinds of inequalities can drive a wedge between individuals and the team.

1. The seductiveness of the hierarchy. Teams that are pulled together from different departments, with the awareness that they will be returning to them, may slip into deference patterns which give those with higher status more authority in the group. So teams may end up duplicating the organization hierarchy in miniature inside the team.
2. Participators are made, not born. It takes knowledge and information to effectively contribute to group tasks. Persons in some positions have greater access to information than other members of the team. The knowledge gap needs to be closed before team meetings in order for all to participate.
3. Differential personal resources. Members of the team have various levels of participation skills, including verbal skills. There are often coalitions within groups wherein individuals support one another. Skills including those involved in articulating opinions, developing arguments, and reaching decisions differ among members.

4. The seniority or activity gap. Newcomers or outsiders often feel uncomfortable about speaking up. The group may have developed its own language, acronyms, and understandings that are not obvious to newcomers and that may inhibit participation.

5. Internal politics. The team may also develop factions and subgroups that inhibit group progress.

NOTES

1. Katherine W. Hawkins, "Implementing Team Management in the Modern Library," *Library Administration and Management* (Winter 1989): 11–15.

2. Allen Veaner, *Academic Librarianship in a Transformational Age: Program, Politics, and Personnel* (Boston, MA: G. K. Hall, 1990), p. 447.

3. Veaner, *Academic Librarianship in a Transformational Age*, p. 460.

4. Peter Drucker, *Management: Tasks, Responsibilities, Practices* (New York: Harper & Row, 1974), pp. 567.

5. Drucker, *Management*, p. 568.

6. Drucker, *Management*, p. 568.

7. Drucker, *Management*, p. 569.

8. Drucker, *Management*, p. 578.

9. Peter Block, *The Empowered Manager: Positive Political Skills at Work* (San Francisco, CA: Jossey-Bass, 1987), pp. 68–70.

10. Thomas J. Peters, *Thriving on Chaos: Handbook for a Management Revolution* (New York: Knopf, 1987), p. 297.

11. Peters, *Thriving on Chaos*, p. 302.

12. Peters, *Thriving on Chaos*, p. 459.

13. Douglas McGregor, *The Human Side of Enterprise* (New York: McGraw-Hill, 1960), p. 240.

14. McGregor, *The Human Side of Enterprise*, pp. 240–241.

15. McGregor, *The Human Side of Enterprise*, pp. 241–242.

16. McGregor, *The Human Side of Enterprise*, pp. 247–248.

17. Robert LaLiberte Migneault, "Humanistic Management by Teamwork in Academic Libraries," *Library Administration & Management* (June 1988), 132–136.

10

Supervisory Techniques for Student Employee Supervisors

Great things are accomplished by talented people who believe they will accomplish them.

—Warren G. Bennis

MANAGING AND BEING MANAGED

Every person and every organization manages, is managed, or is affected by management. The largest of all of the groups of managers in organizations are the first-line managers, or supervisors. As the term implies, first-line managers are the first line of contact with workers. In the case of libraries, there may be two groups of first-line managers: supervisors of student employees and supervisors of permanent/regular staff. First-line managers direct those they supervise and serve as a conduit for communication with library administration. They must also work with their peers and supervisors. Normally, supervisors of student employees do not supervise other supervisors.

The organization of the academic library determines, to a large degree, how the supervisor of student employees manages and is managed.

HIERARCHICAL LIBRARY ORGANIZATION

Most academic libraries are organized in hierarchies with a dean or director, associate/assistant deans or directors for public and technical services, department heads within each division, and unit heads within departments. There are formal lines of communication and specialization of worker function within each department. Normally an administrative group led by the dean/director and that includes the assistant/associate deans/directors with selected others is the decision-making body of the organization. Department heads are consulted by the assistant/associate deans/directors and the department heads in turn consult with their staff. Control, authority, communication, and interactions between employees are vertical in the traditional hierarchic structure. Decisions are made by the administration and communicated down the hierarchy.

Some academic libraries are transforming their organizations in an attempt to more effectively address today's problems of shrinking budgets, increased materials costs, new technologies, and increased demands for services. One of the approaches being used is team management.

TEAM MANAGEMENT

While a hierarchy stresses control, team management stresses facilitation. Responsibility for the performance of work groups falls to the group in a team management situation rather than to the administration in a traditional hierarchy. Team members are involved in problem solving and do not rely solely on decisions from the administration. Another major difference is that team members must communicate with their peers within and outside the organization rather than relying on management as the sole source of information. Katherine W. Hawkins, in an article in *Library Administration & Management*,[1] describes how a library can implement a team management approach, emphasizing that commitment must exist for both workers and management in order for it to succeed.

PARTICIPATIVE MANAGEMENT

Participative management encourages participation of employees in decision making on matters relating to how the library should be operated. True participative management encourages the involvement of the employees' minds in their thinking and opinions of the work and how it should be performed. Participative management as practiced in the library:

- Gives people the right to be creative members of a cooperating group. Library faculty and staff serve together on numerous committees.
- Leads to new relationships being formed between employee and supervisor, and between an employee and other employees. Encourages horizontal communication among departments of the library.
- Can spur less skilled employees to greater effort, and it encourages them to accept responsibility. The attitude of cooperation among library employees is contagious.
- Usually results in more job satisfaction and greater output of employees. Morale in the library is higher when employees have a stake in the organization.
- Helps to improve job performance. When employees have a say in how their work should be done, they feel the need to prove that their way will enable the job to be performed more efficiently.
- Raises human dignity and interest in what other people are doing. Communication among departments is enhanced.
- Enables change to be accepted much more easily, particularly when those affected by it have participated in deciding its extent and how it should be implemented.

Whether it utilizes team management or participative management, the library that adopts this approach involves its staff in the operation of the library. Student employees working in this environment are expected to contribute not only their time and best effort on the job but will be called upon to participate fully as members of their teams. Regardless of the library's organizational structure, the supervisor performs five basic management functions.

FIVE FUNCTIONS OF MANAGEMENT

The traditional functions of management are the basis of every supervisor's job. The set of activities carried out by managers are: planning; organizing; staffing; leading and motivating; and controlling.

- The planning function includes determining the mission, goals and objectives, and direction of a unit and developing strategies for achieving them.
- Organizing involves creating a structure for accomplishing tasks, including assigning work.
- Staffing is the process of selecting, training, evaluating, disciplining, and rewarding staff.
- By creating a climate in which employees accomplish work, supervisors provide leadership and motivation for employees.
- Controlling is the process by which supervisors determine if and how well the unit is accomplishing its goals.

Seldom will you find a practicing supervisor who can actually name the five functions of management, let alone describe the activities or techniques utilized to perform each of the five functions, but good supervisors do perform those functions. In order for the supervisor of student employees to be successful, the supervisor must bear in mind that supervision is more than scheduling and assigning work to students. Supervisors perform the five functions of management, often without realizing it. A review of the principles and techniques of management will help you assess your own abilities. The following section expands on the discussion of authority in Chapter 3.

AUTHORITY

Authority is given to student employee supervisors by the library by virtue of having assigned them student employees to supervise. Authority is usually handed down to student employee supervisors from their immediate supervisors who in turn receive their authority from those above them. Authority is handed down from the top, beginning with the highest levels. Those who appoint the governing body of the institution give them authority. Authority for the operation of the institution is delegated to the university president, who delegates authority to the vice presidents, who delegate authority to the dean/director of the library and so on, to the supervisors of student employees. As authority is passed down the line to the student employee supervisor, the delegated authority becomes more specific. While the dean/director has the authority to manage the personnel budget and a large staff, as a student employee supervisor you have the authority needed to supervise a group of student employees with specific jobs and work to perform.

Authority is the power you need to carry out your responsibilities as student employee supervisor. A student employee supervisor who, in the opinion of employees, exceeds supervisory authority will find that employees will question or even resist that authority.

Student employee supervisors must remember that their authority is retained only so long as its use is approved by the organization and accepted by the majority of employees supervised.

According to Webster's New World Dictionary of the American Language, the definition of authority is:

- the power or right to give commands, enforce obedience, take action, or make final decisions; jurisdiction.
- this power as delegated to another; authorization: as, he has my authority to do it.
- power or influence resulting from knowledge, prestige, etc.

Authority is one of those things that is much misused and misunderstood in business and industry. Supervisors often fail to use their authority when it should be used. Other supervisors try to use authority when it does not belong to them, and some even use it to dominate other people. It is extremely important to understand that authority carries with it the responsibility to use it correctly. Supervisors of student employees must respect the problems and needs of their employees and the student employees must respect the authority of their supervisor.

The most common misuse of authority is by new supervisors and experienced ones who have been assigned special projects. Persons unaccustomed to directing or coordinating the efforts of others must be careful not to let the newly acquired authority affect how they treat people. Overuse of authority almost always causes employees to become less cooperative.

EXERTING AUTHORITY

Every supervisor wants to know how to exercise authority well and feel comfortable doing it. It is important to realize that it is not easy for those who are given authority for the first time but who are only used to following orders. Some advice may be in order from supervisors who have experience:

- Be certain you know what authority you have and don't have. Clarify this beforehand with your supervisor.
- Be careful that authority does not go to your head.
- Realize that good supervisors do not flaunt their positions.
- Always delegate authority to get the job done, not to show who is boss.
- When exercising authority, be considerate of others.
- When exerting authority, try to promote team spirit.
- Always use persuasion when you can instead of exerting your authority.

In addition to the authority given to you by the organization, you will find that you can be more successful and may reinforce your authority or power with one or more of the following:

- Your job knowledge (What do you know?)
- Your personal influence in the organization (Who do you know?)
- Your personal charm (Do you have it?)
- Your abilities (How good are you at your job?)

- Your ability to persuade (How well can you communicate?)
- Your physical strength (How strong are you? Usually not a factor in libraries.)

DELEGATING AUTHORITY

Generally, organizations have three classifications of authority with which supervisors can make decisions:

- Complete authority. You may take action without consulting your supervisor.
- Limited authority. You may take action but your supervisor must be informed of your actions.
- No authority. You may not take action without checking with your supervisor.

In order to accomplish your department's objectives, it will be necessary to delegate responsibility and authority to subordinates. Remember that the two go together. In delegating, you must make it clear what authority is being delegated and at what level. Of course, there are responsibilities and authorities, for example discipline, which cannot be delegated to student employees.

Authority is an essential part of a supervisor's job. Always be sure to find out what authority you have and set about exerting it wisely and carefully. Your success as a student employer supervisor may well depend on it.

The following section expands on the discussion of responsibility in Chapter 5.

RESPONSIBILITY

There is an important difference between the positions of worker and supervisor. A large part of that change is that by accepting a supervisory position, there is an agreement that you will accept the attendant responsibilities of the position.

According to *Webster's New World Dictionary of the American Language*, the definition of responsibility is:

- condition, quality, fact, or instance of being responsible; obligation;
- a thing or person for whom one is responsible.

Responsibility and authority go hand in hand but are quite different. Responsibilities are those things for which you are held accountable by your supervisor and library management. Authority is the power you need to carry out your responsibilities as student employee supervisor.

It is important for you, as a student supervisor, to determine with your supervisor what your responsibilities are. If asked, your supervisor may simply reply, "You are responsible for the students in this department." Your next question should be, "Do I also have the authority to take necessary actions without consulting you or do you want me to check with you first?" Your supervisor replies, "Just do what you think is right but keep me informed." In this brief conversation, you have determined that you are entirely responsible for planning, organizing, staffing, leading and motivating, and controlling all aspects of student employment in your department and that your supervisor has given you limited authority: you may take action but your supervisor must be informed.

In addition, there are obvious legal responsibilities that apply to supervisor and employee alike. They are:

- The responsibility to perform the work for which hired.
- The responsibility to follow organizational policies, procedures, and rules.

DECISION MAKING

Without question, being decisive is a valuable attribute for a supervisor. When making decisions, the supervisor exhibits leadership skills, while providing assurance to employees that everything is under control. The skill of making decisions under pressure must be developed in order to be effective.

In order to be decisive you must want to solve problems and have the confidence to do so. A good decision maker must know how and when to make decisions and be aware of the factors that influence decisions. Most importantly, you must have information with which to make good decisions. Successful decision makers don't make decisions without the facts. Find out what you need to know. Who is involved? What has been the past practice? By when must the decision be made?

The good supervisor is not reluctant to make decisions. You can and should learn to be decisive. The following suggestions will help you develop a pattern of decision making that works.

- Dispose of minor decisions quickly. By making these decisions promptly, you will have more time to devote to important matters.
- Be firm in making a decision. Don't leave any doubt about what you have decided.
- Don't waste time thinking about what you could have done.
- Dispel any thoughts that you might make a mistake.
- Carry out your decisions promptly.

MAKING GOOD DECISIONS

You can make good decisions if you do not act hastily, get the facts, and take time to think. It is not necessary to have experience with similar problems to make good decisions. There are four basic steps:

1. Be sure you understand the problem. If you are able to clearly state the problem, you are well on the way to resolving it. Writing it down often helps you define it.
2. Get information. Look for alternative answers.
3. Examine the good and bad points of each alternative. Will each alternative actually solve the problem? What are the risks of each? What is wrong with what appears to be the first choice?
4. Select the best alternative as your decision. Take action and monitor the results.

How can a supervisor determine when a decision must be made or when to leave a condition well enough alone? Even though it is your responsibility to make decisions, there are occasions when the best decision is take no action at all. Experienced supervisors have learned to distinguish real problems from conditions or situations that are merely irritating.

Supervisors are usually required to make a number of decisions each day. At times you may question whether a specific decision is really yours to make or whether it should be made at a higher level. Common sense dictates that decisions should be made at the lowest level of the organization, consistent with the functions of each supervisory position. If the problem requiring a decision fits into the normal duties and responsibilities of your position, the decision should rightly be made by you. If the decision will affect more than your unit's staff, procedures, or services, or if it is in conflict with existing policy, the decision should be made at a higher level.

There is much more to making a decision than just deciding. You have to consider the feelings of the people affected by your decision. By having others participate in the decision making, you will have much greater acceptance. Timing must be considered. Pick the time and place for announcing a decision. Be certain that you feel good about it before making an important decision.

NO ONE IS PERFECT—BAD DECISIONS

You will eventually make a bad decision. Probably more than one. The most experienced and successful supervisors make mistakes. When a bad decision is made, you must do what you can to correct it. Be sure to make the extra effort and devote the time needed to making a good decision. When considering reversing a decision, be sure to seek advice in order to avoid making another bad decision when correcting the first one.

One approach to developing decision-making skills is to examine the causes of poor decisions:

1) Insufficient or inaccurate information. Lack of information can lead to false conclusions and therefore poor decisions.
2) Insufficient time to decide. By taking the time to gather information, you increase your chance of making a good decision.
3) Fear of making a bad decision. If you lack confidence in your abilities, the quality of your decisions may be affected.
4) Overcautious. If you are overly concerned about the risks involved, you may be too cautious.
5) Not enough authority. If you have responsibility without the authority, your decisions will be unenforceable.
6) Underestimate the importance. If you misjudge the seriousness or importance of the situation, you may not give it enough attention or ignore it all together.
7) Emotion. Poor decisions result when emotion rather than reason is used in making decisions.

WHEN YOUR DECISIONS ARE CHALLENGED

Finally, not all of your decisions will be readily accepted. People have their own opinions, may think differently than you, or have more information than you have. In most cases, a decision is challenged because people do not understand it or why you made it. If you have made a good decision, you should have no trouble explaining it. Persons who have valid and logical arguments may still disagree. When questioned, calmly say that you would be glad to discuss their opinions. Listen to their points of view and if you discover that you have made a bad decision, be willing to admit it and correct it. Listening is without question, one of the most important skills in communication.

COMMUNICATION

"Communication" is defined as the process in human relations of passing information and understanding from one person to another. Communication between supervisor and employees is extremely important as are communication between supervisors and between supervisor and boss. Human communications suffer the same problems as mechanical or electronic communications: poor reception, interference, or being tuned to the wrong channel.

COMMUNICATING WITH INDIVIDUALS

For a supervisor, nothing is better than face-to-face communication with employees. A real advantage is that you can see how your words are affecting the person to whom you are talking. Your haste, tone, mood, gestures, or facial expression may affect how the individual reacts. The opportunity for two-way communication is extremely important. A disadvantage is that it takes time. At the end of the day you may feel that you have done nothing but talk.

Communication with individuals may take the form of informal talks, planned appointments, or telephone calls. Face-to-face communication should always be used when the subject is of personal importance to either person. Written communication may take the form of e-mail, letters, or reports. The advantage of written communication is that all recipients are given exactly the same information. It is needed for messages that are intended to be formal, official, or long-term. The use of e-mail should not be overdone. They should be used as seldom as possible. Face-to-face communication is much preferred.

COMMUNICATING WITH GROUPS

Effective communication with groups requires special skills. The best way of developing group cohesiveness is the use of regular, informal staff meetings, supplemented with individual face-to-face communication. Scheduling a time when all of the student employees in your unit can meet is always a problem. It is important, however, to recognize the need to schedule such meetings if at all possible. Written communication for groups normally takes the form of bulletin board notices or a "must read" notebook. The notebook is an effective way to make certain that all written information is seen by all student employees in your unit.

ENCOURAGING EMPLOYEES TO COMMUNICATE WITH YOU

In the long run, people will not listen to you if you will not listen to them. Employees will learn to talk to you if you will demonstrate that you will listen. How can you improve your listening skills?

- Don't assume anything. Allow the employee to tell you what is wanted. Don't anticipate. If the student employee feels you already know what will be said, why bother?
- Don't interrupt. Wait for the employee to finish speaking. Don't give anyone the impression that you do not have the time to listen.

- Try to understand the need. Look for the reason the employee wants your attention. Often what the employee says is wanted is not the real thing. Student employees are typically more straightforward and able to express themselves better than many employee groups.
- Don't react too quickly. Try to understand the other person's viewpoint. Be patient and do not jump to conclusions.

COMMUNICATING WITH STUDENT EMPLOYEES

Listening cannot be overemphasized. When employees come to you with a problem and the solution is very clear, offer it. If it is possible, help student employees develop their own solutions.

What is the best form of communication? For a supervisor, nothing can beat face-to-face communication. In a participative management environment, student employees are involved in the discussions and decisions on procedure and policy. Good communication is critical to your success as a supervisor.

GROUP EFFORT

Organizations depend on the effectiveness of group effort. The success of any supervisor is dependent on how well the employees in the group perform their work. The individuals assembled to perform work comprise the work group. In the library, student employees are required to work varied schedules, often with their hours spread throughout an 80–100 hour work week. In a situation where the supervisor needs a minimum of three students workers on duty all of the hours the library is open, it is not unusual for two students in the same department never to work at the same time. Turnover in the student work force also contributes to changes in the group. At any given time the supervisor is supervising different combinations of student workers in an ever-changing work group.

What groups do best is solve problems. One important technique in getting group support for problem solving is participation. In order to get individuals to work together to attain common goals, it is necessary to get individuals in groups to work with you. By sharing knowledge and information, sharing decision making, and sharing credit with the group, you can assure that the group will work most effectively.

GIVING DIRECTION

The successful supervisor is able to be the boss without being obvious about it. It used to be assumed that all a supervisor had to do was order an employee to do something and the employee would do it. This attitude will get you nowhere. Today's employees deserve more consideration. If employees feel they are offered some say in decisions that affect them, they will work harder when they have had the opportunity to participate. Student employees do not need to be ordered. Generally speaking, a request carries the same weight as an order but it implies that the employee has some choice in the matter.

GUIDELINES FOR GIVING DIRECTIONS

1) Avoid an "I'll show you who's boss" attitude when giving direction. You should project the idea that there is a situation that requires the employee's attention, and that it is based on more than your whim.

2) Be firm when giving direction. If delivered in an offhand manner, the request may not be taken seriously.

3) Watch what you say when giving direction. Be specific so there is no misunderstanding about what you want done.

4) Don't assume the employee understands. Give the student employees a chance to ask questions or to complain about the assignment if they wish. It is better to clear up any questions or concerns right away.

5) Don't overdo it. Be selective in issuing instructions and avoid giving too many orders. Don't give complex instructions when brief ones will do. Think about what information the person you are talking to really needs.

6) Avoid conflicting instructions. Make certain that you are telling your student employees the same thing as supervisors in similar departments are telling theirs.

7) Don't overwork the cooperative employee. Some people are more cooperative than others. Be sure you do not give directions only to those you know will cooperate without complaint.

8) Distribute the unpleasant tasks fairly. Resist the temptation to punish certain employees by assigning the difficult or unpleasant jobs to them only.

9) Don't flaunt your authority. You don't have to crack the whip to gain student employees' cooperation and respect.

GETTING COOPERATION

Good supervision is the art of getting others to do what you want, when you want it, and how you want it. In order to succeed as a supervisor, you must get others to cooperate with you. You have to be able to develop good relations with those you supervise and earn their cooperation. Here are eight ways to promote cooperation:

1) Stress team effort whenever possible. Use the word "we" when talking with employees.
2) Reward people who do more than you ask of them.
3) Set realistic goals with the help of your employees.
4) Praise your employees. Never criticize an employee in front of others.
5) Supervise with persuasion, not force or pressure.
6) Help your employees when they need and request it.
7) Be honest about problems and issues with your employees.
8) Involve your employees in problem solving and decision making.

WHEN EMPLOYEES DON'T DO WHAT THEY ARE SUPPOSED TO DO

BEFORE THE WORK BEGINS	WHAT TO DO
They don't know what they're supposed to do	Let them know what to do.
They don't know how to do it.	Find out if they know how to do it.
They don't know why they should do it.	Let them know why they should do it.
They think your way will not work.	Convince them that your way will work.
They think their way is better.	If not better, explain why it is not better.
They think something else is more important.	Let them know the work priorities.
They anticipate future negative consequences.	Convince them that there are no negatives.
They have personal problems.	Work around personal problems.
They have personal limits	Verify that it is not beyond their limits.
Obstacles beyond their control.	Verify that there are not obstacles.
No one could do it.	Verify that it can be done.

AFTER THE WORK BEGINS	WHAT TO DO
They think they are doing it.	Give them feedback.
No positive consequences for doing it.	Verbally reward.
There are obstacles beyond their control.	Remove obstacles.
They think something else is more important.	Let them know the work priorities.
They are punished for doing it.	Remove negative consequences.
They are rewarded for not doing it.	Remove positive feedback for poor work.
No negative consequences for poor work.	Progressive discipline.
Personal problems	Work around personal problems.

MOTIVATION

All supervisors want motivated employees. There will always be highly motivated individuals and self-starters who wish to work in the library and some of them will work for you. However, many employees are unmotivated, resulting often in low morale, absenteeism, and high turnover. Employee motivation can be defined as those techniques used that influence the action of an individual to help the employee integrate personal needs and goals with those of the organization.

The individual's motivational drives and societal attitudes toward work affect employee motivation. The supervisor can inhibit or contribute to an individual's motivation but it is primarily self-directed. Employee motivation is an important aspect of any supervisor's job and one that seems quite difficult on the surface.

Job satisfaction and motivation are closely tied. To help you understand how your employees can become motivated from the job itself, think about the worst and best jobs you've ever had. When you consider the worst jobs, more than likely what will come to mind are things that made it unbearable: long hours, bad weather, dirty, boring, bad boss, and no chance for advancement. Those things that made the job bad were mainly bad environment, rather than the nature of the job itself.

When you consider the best job you've had, you may think about how hard you worked, the long hours, how you couldn't wait to get to work, and couldn't believe how fast the time went. The best job probably provided challenge, responsibility, variety, recognition, and meaning. The good job has some of the same characteristics as the bad—long hours, poor working conditions, not enough money. In addition, however, the good job carries with it responsibility, challenge, recognition, and meaning. If your student employees' jobs carry some responsibility and provide challenge, recognition, and meaning, does it not make sense that the job itself can be a motivator to employees? Examine your students' jobs and determine how you can add some of these elements. Motivation can also be accomplished through coaching.

COACHING

Coaching can be considered as continuous training. Just as an athletic coach provides the knowledge and skill training for athletic competition, the manager is charged with the responsibility of not only training but keeping up the skills and knowledge of employees required on the job.

As employees begin to slip away from the basic skills that made them productive, coaching is needed. There are many possible reasons for slippage in a person's skills.

Boredom with routine tasks causes many employees to look for shortcuts that, taken over time, diminish the employees' ability to remember exactly what the tasks were originally. The shortcuts or changes in the job are attempts to add variety to the job. This deterioration of skills is called "professional degeneration." Another reason for skills deterioration is that employees want independence and will want to try things their way. While employees often bring fresh ideas on how the job should be done, they need to be kept on the right track so the job is done correctly and accomplished efficiently. Regular coaching is one of the best ways of getting employees back on the right track.

Certain employee behaviors can be changed by holding group meetings but individual coaching is usually the most effective means of coaching. It is not uncommon for supervisors to hold group training sessions to correct the behavior of one individual. It should be remembered that individual performance causes group performance and for the group to succeed, each individual must succeed. Coaching one-on-one is the most effective means for changing individual behavior.

COACHING PROCESS

First, you must be able to identify the behavior that needs changing and know what behavior you want. How do you change it? Saying to the employee, "Look, Mary, I've shown you twice how to do that. If you don't do it right, your replacement will do it right," will be counterproductive. Coaching is teaching, not scolding. Here is a logical step-by-step process:

1) Observe the present behavior, compare it to the ideal behavior, and identify what must be changed.
2) Discuss the needed changes with the employee. Does the student employee know the present behavior is wrong? Does the employee know the correct behavior?
3) Get the employee to talk about ideas for improving the task.
4) Demonstrate the desired behavior until the employee can do it correctly and can explain the reason for doing it that way.
5) Praise the employee for correct behavior.

A good supervisor coaches student employees in much the same manner as a football coach coaches a team. Corrective measures are taken when a change is needed in an observable behavior. Coaching is an excellent way to alter behavior, making a good employee an excellent employee. It is a continual process that is an extension of training.

COUNSELING

Counseling has a more personal aspect to it than coaching. While coaching is intended to improve a person's skills, counseling is a private discussion of problems that have a bearing on job performance. When there is something that is worrying the employee, the supervisor must discover and correct it if possible.

You will encounter two types of counseling sessions: those you initiate and those initiated by the student employee. Neither is more important than the other and you must be available whether the purpose is to discuss a personal problem or to allow the employee to "blow off steam."

You may need to call a student employee in if you have heard or observed that things were not going right for the student. The employee has exhibited behavior that tells you something is wrong and you feel that a counseling session is needed.

COUNSELING SESSIONS YOU CALL

The following is a step-by-step procedure that will help you improve the counseling sessions you call:

1) Determine why the student employee is exhibiting the wrong behavior. Talking privately with other employees and observing the employee may turn up the reasons. Try to determine the cause before you talk to the affected employee.
2) Plan ahead for the counseling session. Carefully think through what you want to discuss.
3) Notify the employee that you want to meet a day or two in advance of the meeting. Never call a counseling session on the spur of the moment unless it is an emergency.
4) Meet privately. If you can't stop the phone calls and interruptions, hold the meeting away from your office.
5) Put the employee at ease. Discuss anything but the topic at hand for a few minutes. If the purpose is to discuss poor performance, first stress the positive aspects of the job.
6) Get to the point of the session. Encourage the employee to talk while you listen.
7) Help the student employee save face by letting the employee know that you or others have faced similar situations.
8) Come to an agreement about what needs to be done.
9) Offer your assistance if possible and set a time to discuss what has been done.
10) Make a written note of the discussion for the file that includes date, time, location, subject, and outcome. File the note for future reference if needed.

COUNSELING SESSIONS THE EMPLOYEE CALLS

When you call the meeting, you have the advantage of being able to plan for it. The situation is quite different when the employee asks to talk to you. It often starts with the employee appearing at your office door and saying, "Do you have a minute, Steve? I need to talk to you," or "Mary, when could I see you for thirty minutes?" A good practice is not to jump into a counseling session unless it is an emergency. If you can, ascertain what the subject of the meeting is beforehand and then set a time later in the day or the next day if possible. It is entirely possible that you will not know the subject of the meeting until it takes place. The procedure for an employee-initiated meeting is similar to the supervisor-initiated meeting with a few differences:

1) You may only be needed as a sounding board for the employee, someone to talk to about a personal problem.
2) Know your limitations. Psychologists and psychiatrists have the proper training to counsel students with emotional problems. Your advice or answers may do more to complicate the problem than solve it for the student employee.
3) Be careful to avoid becoming involved in a student's emotional problems.
4) After the student employee has vented the problem, ask the employee to offer possible solutions.

5) After possible solutions have been discussed, offer encouragement and ask if the employee would like to schedule a future meeting to discuss the situation.

6) What the two of you have discussed is confidential. Keep it that way.

You, as the supervisor of student employees, should be familiar with all of the counseling services available on campus and be prepared to describe them to your student employees. Remember that you are not alone. Seek the advice of your supervisor or fellow student employee supervisors, making sure to maintain confidentiality. Be aware that no one may have had precisely the same problem with the same circumstances.

NOT ALL COUNSELING IS NEGATIVE

It must be noted that not all counseling sessions are negative. The student employee may be interested in discussing prospects for advancement on the job or seeking your advice. A good supervisor makes it a habit to counsel employees on a regular basis. Most of us do not consider this to be counseling, but it is good practice to regularly give student employees the opportunity to discuss the job or anything they wish to talk about.

Counseling can be used to resolve employee problems or to give them opportunities to discuss anything on their minds. It lets them know you are interested in them as employees and individuals.

SUPERVISORY PRINCIPLES

The quotation from Benjamin Spock's *Baby and Child Care* is quite appropriate here: "Trust yourself. You know more than you think you do." Many of the principles that are the basis of supervision are plain old-fashioned common sense. It is important that you develop a foundation of knowledge in supervision but when in doubt, use your common sense.

COMMON SENSE MANGEMENT

At an ALA annual conference during a session entitled, "Library Management and Leadership: Theory and Practice," Dr. Camila Alire, who was dean of Library Services at the University of New Mexico, described herself as a common sense, practical manager who through experience has come up with her own set of "rules":

- Treat people the way you'd like to be treated, given the same circumstance.
- Understand that the more staff you get to participate, the more buy-in you achieve.
- Everyone has a role in making the library function.
- Encouraging people to be innovative requires accepting risk-taking.
- Effective communication within the organization is critical.
- Build relationships on trust.
- It takes teamwork to make the organization work.
- One has to earn, not demand, respect.
- Expect integrity of person and process.
- Make decisions based on facts and on what makes sense for the organization.
- People may not like you for your controversial decisions.
- The organization is not about you.

- Lead by example.
- Organizations should be dynamic. Change is not bad.
- Let intuition be one of your guides.

Dean Alire highlighted two "awakenings" in her career:

- Realizing that library management is almost all common sense;
- Adopting humanistic management by teamwork (HMBT).[2]

NOTES

1. Katherine W. Hawkins, "Implementing team management in the modern library," *Library Administration & Management* (Winter 1989):11–15.
2. Robert LaLiberte Migneault, "Humanistic management by teamwork in academic libraries," *Library Administration & Management* (June 1988):132–136.

BIBLIOGRAPHY

Baldwin, David A. and Robert L. Migneault. *Humanistic Management by Teamwork: An Organizational and Administrative Alternative for Academic Libraries.* Englewood, CO: Libraries Unlimited, 1996.

Comer, Alberta. "Searching for Solutions Supervising Student Employees." *Journal of Access Services* 1(4) (2003): 103–113.

Conlow, Rick. *Excellence in Supervision: Essential Skills for the New Supervisor.* Menlo Park, CA: Crisp Learning, 2001.

Giesecke, Joan. *Practical Help for New Supervisors,* ed. by. Library Administration and Management Association. Personnel Administration Section. Supervisory Skills Committee. 3rd ed. Chicago, IL: American Library Association, 1997.

Good, Sharon. *Managing With a Heart.* Naperville, IL: Sourcebook, 1997.

Hawley, Casey Fitts. *201 Ways to Turn Any Employee into a Star Performer.* New York: McGraw-Hill, 2004.

Henry, Jane and Milton Keynes. *Creative Management.* Thousand Oaks, CA: Sage Publications, 2001.

Kaplan, Louis. "On the Road to Participative Management: The American Academic Library, 1934–1970." *Libri* 38, no. 4 (1988): 314–320.

Kathman, Michael D. and Jane McGurn Kathman. *Managing Student Employees in College Libraries.* Chicago, IL: College Library Information Packet Committee, College Libraries Section, Association of College and Research Libraries, American Library Association, 1994.

Lee, Dalton S., et al. *Supervision for Success in Government: A Practical Guide for First Line Managers.* San Francisco, CA: Jossey-Bass, 1994.

McDonald, James J., Jr. "Be Nice, or Be Sued." *Employee Relations Law Journal;* Spring 2006 v31 i4 p73.

McDonald, James J., Jr. "I Want a Nicer Boss." *Employee Relations Law Journal;* Autumn 2005 v31 i2 p79.

Migneault, Robert LaLiberte, "Humanistic Management by Teamwork in Academic Libraries." *Library Administration & Management* (June 1988): pp. 132–136.

Rogers, Shelley L. "Out of Theory and into Practice: Supervising Library Employees." *Journal of Academic Librarianship* v19 n3 p154–57 July 1993.

Rooks, Dana C. *Motivating Today's Library Staff: a Management Guide.* Phoenix, AZ: Oryx, 1988.

Slagwell, Jeff. "Don't Tread on Me: The Art of Supervising Student Assistants." *The Serials Librarian* v. 44 no3/4 (2003): pp. 279–284.

Stone, Florence M. *The Manager's Question and Answer Book.* New York: American Management Association, 2003.

Straub, Joseph T. *The Rookie Manager [Electronic Resource]: A Guide to Surviving Your First Year in Management.* New York: AMACOM, 2000.

11

Evaluating Student Employees—A Positive Approach

The world is filled with willing people; some willing to work, the rest willing to let them.

—Robert Frost

HOW AM I DOING?

Everyone wants to know, "How am I doing?" Performance appraisals provide one opportunity to tell student employees how they are doing. It should not be the only time workers are told how they are doing, but a performance evaluation system guarantees that they are given feedback at least that one or two times each year, depending on the schedule. Appraising the performance of employees is a basic task of managers. It is impossible to make intelligent managerial decisions about employees without measuring their performance in some manner.

Formal performance appraisal is as old as the concept of management and informal appraisal is as old as human history. All employees want and deserve to know not only how they are doing, but what's being done well, how it can be done better, and how the job itself can be improved.

"PRAISES AND RAISES"

Student employees, like all employees, want "praises and raises." Performance appraisals offer the opportunity for supervisors to formally communicate and document how their employees are doing and provide the evidence for "praises" and, if applicable, "raises." Supervisors are cautioned that performance appraisals can be debilitating for student employees if done poorly. Those individuals who have received poor evaluations from supervisors, deserved or not, know that criticism is difficult to accept and that no matter how tough-skinned a person is, or thinks he/she is, the experience can be devastating. Performance appraisals do not always result in "praises or raises," but they can and should be constructive and positive experiences for you and your student employees.

JOB EVALUATION VERSUS PERFORMANCE APPRAISAL

Job evaluation is an evaluation of the duties and responsibilities of a specific job or group of jobs. Performance appraisal is a measurement of how well an employee is doing that job. Performance appraisal or performance evaluation is sometimes called a merit rating. Essentially, job evaluation is a technique for evaluating a job; the other evaluates an individual.

PURPOSES OF PERFORMANCE APPRAISAL IN INDUSTRY

Performance appraisals have two basic purposes: employee evaluation and employee development. For most companies, evaluation for administrative purposes has been the most common use of the process. Appraisals of employee performance provide the basis for administrative decisions about promotions, demotions, terminations, transfers, and rewards. The development purpose has generally been secondary. Evaluations that are intended to improve performance on the job are becoming more common in industry. The following chart shows how companies utilized performance evaluations in 1984 and indicates a shift to a more balanced approach.

PURPOSE OF APPRAISAL	PERCENTAGE OF RESPONDENTS
compensation	85.6
counseling	65.1
training and development	64.3
promotion	45.3
manpower planning	43.1
retention/discharge	30.3
validation of selection technique	17.2

Source: Evelyn Eichel and Henry E. Bender. *Performance Appraisal: A Study of Current Techniques.* New York: American Management Association, 1984, p.7.

PURPOSES OF PERFORMANCE APPRAISAL IN LIBRARIES

Academic institutions view performance appraisal from a development viewpoint. There are three basic reasons for performance appraisal for library student employees:

1) To encourage good performance and to correct or discourage substandard performance. Good performers expect a reward, even if it is only praise. Those employees who perform below standard should be made aware that continued poor performance will at the very least stand in the way of advancement. At worst, poor performance may lead to termination.

2) To satisfy the student employees' curiosity about how well they are doing. It is a fundamental drive in human nature for individuals to want to know how well they fit into the organizations

for which they work. While a student employee may dislike being judged, the need to know is very strong.

3) To provide a foundation for later judgments concerning employees: pay increases, promotions, transfers, or termination. Supervisors are to be cautioned not to stress pay raises as part of the appraisal process. It is natural for student employees whose performance is rated good to expect a pay raise to follow. If your institution or library's compensation plan doesn't work that way, don't mislead student employees by telling them that their good work will result in a promotion or pay increase. It is important to tell students just how the appraisal will be used.

HOW FORMAL SHOULD THE PERFORMANCE APPRAISAL BE?

The formality or informality of the process varies greatly. Some libraries have detailed evaluation procedures and others leave it up to the supervisors. The relative value of student employees to the library is often reflected in its student employee evaluation process. Many formal programs are dictated by the University's Student Employment Office. Others have been carefully developed by the libraries. If given the choice of evaluating or not evaluating, you should do it. If you don't presently have a formal procedure for providing performance feedback to student employees, you should propose one.

PEER EVALUATION

The evaluation of student employees is a managerial/supervisory responsibility that is not easily shared with others and should not be delegated. Peer evaluation, however, is one technique that can be used to gain input for the appraisal. Because coworkers have more continuous contact and opportunities to observe each other's performance, peer ratings can be quite valid measurements. Peers judge performance from a perspective that is different from the supervisor's, and although subject to influence by friendships, peer comments are often very perceptive.

Peer evaluation deserves consideration by student employee supervisors in organizations that have developed a climate of interpersonal trust among coworkers and have noncompetitive reward systems. Peer evaluation is an effective tool for libraries utilizing team management. Student employee supervisors are cautioned that unless peer evaluation is an established part of your library's appraisal program, it should be avoided. Improper use of peer evaluation can cause enormous problems. It is often helpful, however, to gather input from persons the employee comes in contact with and to discuss your opinions with your supervisor as you prepare student employee evaluations.

MORE THAN THE SUPERVISOR'S OPINION

A good performance appraisal includes facts as well as the supervisor's opinion. Included in the information gathered for an appraisal are facts on quantity of work, quality of work, dependability, and records of work incidents, good and bad. These facts comprise the objective factors utilized in the evaluation. Subjective factors tend to be opinions about attitude, personality, and adaptability, which may or may not be substantiated by data.

QUESTIONS TO BE ANSWERED IN AN APPRAISAL

Although the questions that are answered in student employee evaluations vary from one appraisal plan to another, there are some basics:

1) What has the individual done since the last evaluation?
2) How well has it been done?
3) How much better could it be done?
4) In what ways have strengths and weaknesses in the student employee's approach to the job affected performance?
5) Are the weaknesses ones that could be improved upon?
6) What is the student employee's potential?
7) How well could this person do if given a chance?

HOW OFTEN SHOULD STUDENT EMPLOYEE APPRAISALS BE DONE?

If student employees are evaluated too often, those evaluations are likely to be affected too much by day-to-day occurrences. If done too seldom, the supervisor is likely to forget some of the incidents that need to be included in an appraisal. If annual evaluations are required, it is a good idea to do an informal unwritten appraisal more often. Twice-a-year performance appraisals, one formal and one informal, would serve to keep the student employees informed of their performance and would not create undue hardships for supervisors.

SEQUENCE OF ACTIVITIES IN PERFORMANCE APPRAISAL

Performance appraisal follows an established sequence of activities. This sequence is (1) to set performance standards; (2) to communicate those standards; (3) to observe employees doing their work; (4) to collect data; (5) to have employees do self-appraisals; (6) to do a supervisor's appraisal; and (7) to provide feedback.

SET PERFORMANCE STANDARDS

What are the expectations for the student employees? Performance standards are those benchmarks against which the student workers' performance is measured. In some libraries, those standards are based on historical data and the same form is used for all student employees. An example of the standards (rated on a scale of "exceeds objective," "meets objective," or "does not meet objective") found on one library's student employee performance evaluations are the following:

1. QUANTITY OF WORK: (Maintains a pace adequate to accomplish all assigned tasks within work period; is able to accommodate normal work flow)
2. QUALITY OF WORK: (Performs tasks with precision and neatness; meets all responsibilities; all facets of job are executed correctly and in the appropriate sequence)
3. RELIABILITY: (Punctual; able to work without direct supervision when necessary; conduct is appropriate for work environment)

4. INITIATIVE: (Commences necessary actions without direction; exercises independent judgment in problem situations; devises and applies appropriate solutions to work-related problems)

5. STAFF RELATIONSHIPS: (Works harmoniously with staff members at all levels)

—University of Rochester River Campus Libraries. "Student Performance Evaluation." Student Assistants in ARL Libraries, SPEC Kit 91. Washington, DC: Association of Research Libraries, 1983, p.96.

COMMUNICATE STANDARDS

Student employees should know from the beginning what is expected of them and what the basis of their evaluations will be. What constitutes good, acceptable, marginal, and unacceptable performance? The evaluation form in use by the library should be shown to student employees as part of their orientation. Make sure there is no question about what will be evaluated and how it will be done.

OBSERVE EMPLOYEES PERFORMING WORK

Employees should be observed during the appraisal period as they perform their daily tasks and information regarding their performance should be noted. Do not observe them only in the last minutes or days before the evaluation.

COLLECT DATA

Data for the performance evaluation should be collected throughout the appraisal period, not just prior to the evaluation. Supervisors of student employees should record both positive and negative incidents on the job. These reports become part of the file of information referred to when evaluating performance. In addition, records of attendance, etc., should be checked. Accurate, current information is critical in making objective judgments of worker performance. Unfair, inequitable, subjective decisions are often made because of incomplete data.

HAVE EMPLOYEES COMPLETE SELF-APPRAISAL

Student employees may be asked to complete an appraisal of their own performance. The following procedure should be followed:

1) Discuss the purpose of self-appraisal with the student employee.
2) Review the format and clarify what the employee should do.
3) Provide the student employee with the form at least a week before it to be completed and returned.
4) Set a specific time for the self-appraisal to be completed.
5) Stress the importance of the self-appraisal to the total performance appraisal process.

UTILIZE THE INFORMATION GATHERED

The information gained from observation, data collection, and the self-appraisal will be useful to the supervisor in completing the student employee performance appraisal.

In preparing the performance appraisal, remember that the information may be used in five primary ways:

1) To make administrative decisions, such as promotion, suspension, demotion, transfer, or termination.
2) To make decisions on who should receive merit increases.
3) To identify training needs, such as what kind of training is needed and who can benefit from it.
4) To motivate and provide feedback by letting student employees know how they are doing, what their strengths are, and what improvements are needed.
5) To validate the selection process by comparing worker performance to desired performance. If a significant percentage of the workers are performing below expected levels, the selection criteria should be examined to determine if the requirements for the job are accurate and what qualities should be sought in students to be hired in the future.

EVALUATE THE EMPLOYEE

Plan a time when you can concentrate on writing performance evaluations when you will not be disturbed. Plan a procedure that you will follow for each student employee. Gather all of the performance data and review all of the data on each employee before writing that employee's evaluation. Write a draft copy and set it aside for at least an hour. Go back to the draft and try to read it as if someone else had written it. Rewrite the evaluation as necessary. Remember to evaluate the employee on performance, not personal traits or characteristics.

In writing the evaluation, remember that performance has at least two major elements: motivation and ability. If performance is poor, a common supervisor error is to assume that if the employee doesn't perform, it is a motivation problem. While it may be true, there are many times when the employee can't do the work because of lack of ability or lack of proper training. Corrective strategies for "won't and can't" are quite different and it is very important to recognize the difference.

PROVIDE FEEDBACK

Performance appraisal feedback should be given to student employees by providing a copy of the written appraisal and by holding a meeting to discuss the evaluation. Policies on conducting a meeting with the student employee vary. Usually an invitation is made for the employee to schedule a meeting with the supervisor to discuss the appraisal. Some institutions require a meeting.

Most supervisors do not like to conduct performance appraisal meetings. Performance appraisal meetings with employees often make supervisors nervous and uncertain. The first time you conduct a performance appraisal meeting requires that supervisors is always the most difficult but careful planning can make these meetings less stressful. The purposes of the performance appraisal meeting between the supervisor and the student employee are:

1) To be sure there are no misunderstandings about the performance appraisal ratings.
2) To allow employees to share their feelings about their performance.

3) To provide an opportunity for a straightforward and honest discussion.

4) To build a better relationship between supervisors and student employees.

PREPARING FOR AN APPRAISAL MEETING

The meeting between supervisor and student employee is an opportunity for the supervisor to inform, encourage, and give recognition to the employee. The following checklist provides guidelines for preparation by supervisors for this meeting.

1) Schedule the meeting far enough in advance.

2) Ask the employees to come prepared to appraise their own performance.

3) Make it clear that the purpose of the meeting is to discuss performance on the job.

4) Find a comfortable setting for the meeting.

5) Review the employee's job description, performance standards, and the appraisal.

6) List specific good things that you can compliment.

7) List the bad things and plan to discuss them.

8) Note what reactions you think the employee might have and plan to handle them.

9) Keep a detailed list of facts supporting your evaluation.

10) Make a list of corrective actions if needed.

11) Plan how to present and gain acceptance of corrective actions.

12) Note follow-up activities that may be needed.

CONDUCTING AN APPRAISAL MEETING

If you are well prepared for the performance appraisal meetings and are comfortable with your appraisals of the student employees, the stress of conducting such meetings will be lessened. Conducting the meetings themselves requires planning. Review what you will say to the employees, define the order in which you will discuss the evaluations, and make the performance appraisal meetings productive experiences for the employees and you. Here are suggestions on how to make each experience a positive one:

1) State the purpose and create a positive attitude. Put the employees at ease.

2) Ask how they see their job and working conditions.

3) Ask if there are problems that need discussion.

4) Give your view of their performance, avoiding comparisons to other employees.

5) Mention desirable behavior you would like to continue.

6) Capitalize on their strengths.

7) Identify opportunities for self-improvement.

8) Prepare employee improvement plans which are theirs, not yours.

9) Review future opportunities for advancement, pay increases.

10) Warn poor performers, if necessary.

11) Ask if there are questions.

12) End the meetings with constructive, encouraging comments.

DISCUSSING POOR PERFORMANCE

Many supervisors find it easy, and even enjoyable, to give employees good evaluations. Often, however, you must also be prepared to give student employees unfavorable comments on their performance when needed. The following are suggestions for handling the performance appraisal meetings with poor performers:

1) Don't be too harsh.
2) Be firm, be specific, and don't rub it in. Nothing is to be gained by being soft on student employees. If their performance has been bad, tell them that performance has been bad and be specific.
3) You can be firm and direct without being cruel. Leave the student employees with their self-respect. One useful technique is the "sandwich" technique described in the next section.
4) Summarize that you have found to be satisfactory as well as things that are unsatisfactory.
5) Always end your appraisal meetings on a positive note. End the meetings with positive, encouraging comments.

Supervisors dislike giving "bad news" almost as much as employees dislike getting it. You should remember that by giving negative feedback, you are trying to correct one or two things in an employee's behavior. Yet, when the discussion gets started, the overall objectives can get lost. When a performance discussion starts to get rough, the tendency is for the participants to begin digging out all the ammunition they have. If the employee gets defensive and brings up side issues, don't retaliate even though you may feel backed against the wall. Don't allow additional issues to dilute your original objectives. Explain that those issues will be discussed at a later meeting if desired. The best strategy is to resolve the minor issues and gripes as they arise and don't let them accumulate.

THE "SANDWICH" TECHNIQUE

A technique for discussing performance that needs improvement is the "sandwich" technique. Very simply, this is done by starting the discussion with a compliment, then discuss the performance that must be improved upon, and finish with something good about the employee's work. For example, "I'm very pleased with your handling of reserve check-outs. Your accuracy, however, must be improved. You have got to remember to follow all of the steps in order for the transaction to be properly recorded. I'm sure you will be able to do that because your other work is very good." This technique can be used throughout the appraisal meeting. No matter how bad an evaluation, you should be able to stress the good things and to make the discussion a positive one.

ALLOW THE EMPLOYEE TO SAVE FACE

When discussing poor performance with student employees, be sure to give them every opportunity to explain why performance is substandard. They will, if given the chance to explain, tell you what obstacles stand in the way of their doing well. Don't interrupt their explanations or say, "That's just an excuse." Be patient and let student employees talk. If you listen carefully, the employees will tell you the real reasons for their poor performance. Don't get into an argument and don't show your anger, even if the student employee gets angry.

HANDLING CHARGES OF FAVORITISM

Unfavorable criticism that hurts the employee so much that the person being criticized may well charge you with favoritism. Your denial will likely fall on deaf ears—instead, try to determine why the employee feels that way.

Supervisor: "Judy, why do you think I might be favoring Sheila?"

Employee: "Because you give Sheila the easy jobs all the time, and you never let me do them."

Supervisor: "That may be true. I just find it easier to ask Sheila to do things. You seem hesitant to accept additional work because you just don't act like you want to be here."

Employee: "Well, I do. I don't think I'm appreciated."

Supervisor: "If you can assure me that you are willing to take on extra tasks, I will ask you more often. If I've been favoring Sheila, I will consciously make an effort to treat you more equally."

Denial is a natural reaction to criticism, but don't let a charge of favoritism divert your attention from the original point. Make sure you cover all of the items you originally planned to discuss in the appraisal meeting.

APPRAISAL ERRORS

Some of the more common errors that must be guarded against when conducting performance appraisals of workers are:

1) Personal bias: unfairly judging members of different races, religion, sex, or national origin.
2) The halo effect: letting your appraisal of one factor affect your appraisal of all other factors.
3) Central tendency: judging most workers as average, thus making no distinction between good and poor performers.
4) Harshness: judging everyone at the low end of the scale.
5) Leniency: judging everyone at the high end of the scale.
6) Similarity: judging people who are like you higher than people who are different from you.
7) Timing of events: allowing what happened recently to affect your judgment of the person's performance over the entire evaluation period.
8) Seniority: unfairly judging workers on how long they have been on the job.
9) Acquaintanceship: letting how well you know workers affect your appraisal.

VALIDITY AND RELIABILITY

Good performance appraisals measure what they should (validity), and the outcomes are consistent (reliability). When a performance appraisal is valid, it measures the things the supervisor wants it to measure. Performance evaluations are not valid when they fail to measure performance-related behaviors or when the performance measures are inappropriate to the job. When a supervisor allows a worker's hair length, style of clothing, or political beliefs to influence an evaluation, it is invalid. These are not performance-related behaviors and have no value in a performance appraisal.

When a performance appraisal is reliable, it provides a consistent measure of work performance. Supervisors must strive for consistency in evaluating every employee on the same basis. The most common types of reliability problems in appraisal are constant errors and random errors. Constant errors occur when all evaluations are in error to the same degree and in the same direction. For example, a supervisor rates all employees one point higher than their true rating is making a constant error. Who hasn't known a supervisor who rates all of the employees in a department as "excellent" when we know they should be "good"? A random error occurs whenever a rating is unpredictably higher or lower than the individual should receive.

One way to deal with reliability errors is to have multiple observations. If one of the criteria to be evaluated is job speed, then there should be two or more questions on the rating form that relate to job speed. If the rating on one shows that the worker is very slow, then the answers to the other questions relating to speed should match. If they do not, there is an inconsistency. Multiple observations help supervisors correct erroneous evaluation responses and attain consistency.

MAKING NONDISCRIMINATORY APPRAISALS

We are living in a litigious society. More and more employers are being sued by employees and former employees, therefore, it is important to be aware of what is legal and permissible in appraising employee performance. The key to making nondiscriminatory appraisals is quite simple—evaluate all employees on the basis of job performance only, be consistent in your application, and apply criteria objectively to all employees. Evaluating employees on the basis of job performance means judging them only on the way they do their jobs without regard to their age, race, sex, religion, or national origin. It also means putting aside any personal likes or dislikes.

CONFIDENTIALITY OF APPRAISALS

The entire appraisal process should be confidential. The appraisal of one student employee should never be discussed with other student employees. You cannot control what student employees discuss with one another, but the supervisor should never be the source of information for those discussions. Avoid comparisons of student employees when conducting your appraisal meetings. Make it clear that each student knows that you treat each rating and each appraisal as confidential.

GOOD EVALUATIONS DON'T ALWAYS RESULT IN ADVANCEMENT

The student employee who consistently gets very good appraisals finds it hard to accept the fact that it is not possible to move up in a seniority-based system until the person ahead gets promoted or quits.

Employee: "Every time, you tell me I'm doing a good job but it hasn't gotten me a better job. I know John is not doing as well but he still makes more money—just because he's been here longer. All the appraisal does for me is to rub salt in the wound."

A good way to handle this complaint is to admit that the situation exists. Even though the employee's claim about a coworker may be true, don't discuss relative worth of your student employees with them. Tell the student that one of the purposes of appraisals is to provide feedback on performance and that without them, performance can slip without notice. Make certain the student understands that the seniority system applies to everyone and that the time will come when less senior student employees will probably register similar complaints when the student being evaluated becomes the most senior member.

GOOD EVALUATIONS DON'T ALWAYS RESULT IN MORE MONEY

If your compensation system is not tied directly to your appraisal system, tell your student employees. Make it clear to student employees just what the appraisal process is all about. If merit increases are possible, describe the process to your employees. If longevity is the deciding factor in raises, tell them so. Misconceptions about how the performance appraisals are used must be cleared up so everyone has a common understanding of the process.

WHAT HAPPENS TO THE APPRAISAL FORMS?

Be sure that student employees know what will happen to the appraisal forms and how they may be used. Who has access to them? A written library policy is needed. Does the library give references for former student employees and are the appraisal forms used? This too, should be covered by library policy.

FOLLOW UP THE APPRAISAL

The appraisal is done, the meeting has been held, and the forms have been filed. Is that all there is? No, appraisal is not something that is done today and forgotten tomorrow. To be of value, you should follow up the appraisal meeting by:

1) Keeping your promises. If you have agreed to do something during the appraisal meeting, do it. If, for example, you've said that you will show the employee data you've referred to in the meeting, be sure to follow through.
2) Implementing employee development plan. If you said the employee needs training in an area, make arrangements to provide that training. Locate courses, workshops, or seminars that will provide the needed training, or talk to the individual who will train the employee. Communicate those arrangements to the employee.
3) Keep in touch. Continue to show interest in the development of the student employee. Monitor the employees' performance and give credit for improvement and point out deficiencies if you're not satisfied.

APPRAISAL FORMATS

The library probably has an evaluation form developed internally or by the student employment office. The form most commonly used is what is known as an absolute format: a graphic rating scale or a narrative. In order to understand evaluation forms, it is necessary to look at a number of basic types of forms. There are three basic types of performance appraisal forms: comparative, absolute, and outcome-based.

If a comparative format is used, the supervisor evaluates employees in relation to each other. Comparative methods include ranking, paired comparisons, and forced choice. When absolute formats are used, the supervisor evaluates each employee's performance without comparing employees to each other. Absolute methods include narrative, critical incidents, graphic rating scales, weighted checklists, and behaviorally anchored rating scales (BARS). If an outcome-based format is used, supervisors evaluate employees on the basis of performance outcomes. Common forms of outcome-based formats are standards of performance and management by objectives (MBO).

If you are involved in the development of an evaluation instrument, bear in mind that the form is a device to be used by human beings. Ratings on the forms will be the result of complex human processes including interpersonal perception, memory, evaluation, and decision-making. Persons using the form will typically have many other responsibilities besides supervision. Develop a form that is usable.

COMPARATIVE APPRAISAL FORMS

Employee performances are compared to one another in comparative appraisal forms. The ranking method requires the supervisor to compare employees on an overall basis and then list employees in ascending (lowest to highest) or descending (highest to lowest) order. The ranking is usually done by identifying the best performer, the worst performer, the next best, the next worst, and so on until all employees have been listed. Ranking is the simplest way to do comparative evaluation.

Supervisors using paired comparisons must compare each employee to every other employee being appraised. Employee A is compared to Employee B and given a "1" or "2", and then compared to every other employee in the same manner. The total number of points given to each results in a numerical ranking for all employees being appraised.

Forced choice is a method that requires that a percentage of employees be forced into certain groups, for example:

Excellent	10%
Above average	20%
Satisfactory	40%
Below average	20%
Unsatisfactory	10%

Comparative formats are fairly simple to use but do not provide any measure of the differences between the rankings. An employee ranked fourth in a group of eight may be considerably better than the person ranked fifth. The employee receives a ranking that provides little information and the system provides no basis for employee development. Comparative formats are seldom used in academic settings.

ABSOLUTE APPRAISAL FORMS

Absolute appraisal forms do not require comparison to other employees. The narrative form requires the supervisor to write a description of an employee's performance. The narrative describes the worker's strengths, weaknesses, and potential. Much depends on the supervisor's writing ability. A standardized form may be used to provide some uniformity to the information to be recorded. The narrative form is more commonly used for faculty and/or staff evaluations than for student employees.

Critical incidents is an appraisal form that asks that supervisors list both the good and the bad things that employees do in performing their jobs. As with narrative forms, the critical incidents form may be dependent upon supervisor writing skills.

Graphic rating scales is the oldest absolute appraisal method and the most common type of evaluation used by libraries for student employees. The scale contains a number of items relating to job performance and the evaluator checks where the employee fits on the continuum, for example, DEPENDABILITY on a scale of 1 to 5. The graphic rating scale is criticized because DEPENDABILITY has different meanings to different evaluators. To be used effectively, graphic rating scales should also include a brief description of the behavior and a definition of what is needed to earn a "1," "2," or "5."

Weighted checklists assign a value to each of the traits or job behaviors, according to the importance of the item. For example, "quality of work" may be more important than "quantity of work" and count more (20 points) than quantity (15 points).

Behaviorally Anchored Rating Scales (BARS) concentrate on job behaviors and not personal characteristics. A committee determines the "behavioral anchors" or statements that describe behaviors that are evaluated.

OUTCOME-BASED APPRAISAL FORMS

The best known forms of outcome-based methods are standards of performance and management by objectives (MBO). Standards of performance involve comparing performance to a list of standards established through negotiation between the worker and the supervisor. The list of standards provides conditions that must be met if the job is considered to have been done well.

MBO is a method of evaluation that focuses on specific objectives or goals established by negotiation between the employee and the supervisor. The employee is judged on how well those objectives are met. Performance management provides a foundation for outcome-based appraisal and is being implemented in many organizations.

DON'T WAIT FOR THE ANNUAL REVIEW

Frequently, supervisors and student employees assume too much. Supervisors assume that student employees know exactly what is expected of them and that they know how well they are doing. Student employees assume that the work is being performed to their supervisor's satisfaction. The "no news is good news" syndrome operates in many libraries until tempers flare, feelings are hurt, and productivity declines. The annual or semiannual performance appraisals are certainly useful in alleviating the problem but performance appraisal should be an ongoing activity. There should be no surprises at appraisal time if you give your employees feedback on their performance, discuss their work, and talk regularly with your student employees. The performance appraisal itself ceases to be a confrontational or traumatic experience for you or the employees if you show your interest and concern on a regular basis.

POSITIVE APPROACH TO PERFORMANCE APPRAISAL

Supervisors usually take one of two stands on performance appraisal: They see the value in the process and turn performance appraisal into a positive tool, or they don't see the purpose and fight it all the way. Supervisors who approach appraisal in a positive manner will discover that their employees will benefit from the evaluation. Those who fight the process will find that their employees mirror their feelings. Here are suggestions on how to make it a positive experience.

1) Accept the fact of performance appraisal. Of course you should make suggestions on how it can be improved, but accept the system and make it work for you.
2) Turn the appraisal meetings into profitable counseling sessions. They may be the only regularly scheduled face-to-face meetings you have with your student employees.
3) Don't take the easy way out. Be honest in your appraisals. Remember that you are evaluating performance, not personality.
4) Discuss the evaluation with the employee—don't just deliver it.
5) Don't hurry the evaluation, either its preparation or the appraisal meeting.
6) Make the appraisal a positive tool. Remember that the appraisal is not a tool used to embarrass, intimidate, or harass the employee.
7) Be careful with promises. Don't make promises to the employees you cannot keep.
8) Follow-up. Remember that good follow-up is essential to the success of the system.

The resources provided in the following bibliography provide additional information on performance appraisal.

BIBLIOGRAPHY

Bacal, Robert. *The Complete Idiot's Guide to Dealing with Difficult Employees.* Indianapolis, IN: Alpha Books, 2000.

The Basics of Advising Employers. St. Paul, MN: Minnesota Continuing Legal Education, 2002.

Belcastro, Patricia. *Evaluating Library Staff: A Performance Appraisal System.* Chicago, IL: American Library Association, 1998.

Bruce, Anne. *Perfect phrases for documenting employee performance problems.* New York: McGraw-Hill, 2005.

Kathman, Michael D. and Jane McGurn Kathman. "Performance Measures for Student Assistants." *College and Research Libraries* 53(4) (July 1992): 299–304.

Waters, Richard Lee. "Peer Review: A Team-Building Way to Evaluate Employees." *Public Library Quarterly* 16(1) (1997): 63–67.

Williams, Richard L. *Tell Me How I'm Doing: A Fable about the Importance of Giving Feedback.* New York: AMACOM, American Management Association, 2004.

12

Dealing Effectively with Student Employment Problems

Experience enables you to recognize a mistake when you make it again.
—Franklyn P. Jones

In the day-to-day management of an academic library, supervisors encounter any number of personnel problems. These problems may be seemingly minor but they can consume inordinate amounts of time. On the other hand, problems that were once small, as Lao Tzu suggests, can become major problems that challenge even the most experienced supervisor and often involve the library's administration, and even the university's administration and legal counsel.

The problems faced by supervisors may involve librarians and staff, who work with student employees. Or they might involve students, faculty, or members of the public utilizing the library. They may involve friends, relatives, or acquaintances of the employee. They may involve violations of individual employee rights, library and/or university rules, policies, or procedures, or violations of civil or criminal laws. There appears to the harried supervisor that there is no end to the kinds of difficulties that can occur. The aspect of personnel problems addressed here cover the whole span of personnel management from the minor to the major, handled easily internally or involving university administration, campus police, and attorneys.

VIOLATIONS OF EMPLOYEE RIGHTS

Although the author is not suggesting that libraries have a serious problem, an indication of how strained the employee-employer relationship is becoming in some instances, consider the advice given by Lewin G. Joel III in the book, *Every Employee's Guide to the Law: Everything You Need to Know about Your Rights in the Workplace— And What to Do if They are Violated*. Mr. Joel suggests that individuals purchase accordion file folders before setting out to get a job. He advises that everything from the first application for a job to the employee handbook to performance evaluations and every piece of paper relating to the job be kept in the file in anticipation of filing a lawsuit against the employer. He says the employer keeps a file so it is important for the employee to keep one too.[1]

As evidenced by the previous chapters, there are a large number of employee and employer rights and legal protections. We live in a litigious society, everyone seemingly ready to sue at the drop of a hat. It is important in this environment that everyone understands the ground rules established by the law and that managers be prepared to deal effectively with personnel difficulties that arise without violating anyone's rights.

Everyone in the workplace must be careful not to violate any employee's rights. Those rights apply to you as an employee as well as to the students you supervise. They fall within the following categories:

- Rights protected by a specific state or federal law;
- Civil rights laws that prohibit discrimination;
- Rights protected by the First Amendment to the U.S. Constitution;
- Employees' rights to union activity;
- Rights protected by wage and hour laws;
- Rights protected by safety and health laws;
- Rights protected by equal pay laws;
- Rights protected by laws that prohibit discipline or discharge because an employee's wages have been attached;
- Rights protected by workers' compensation laws.
- Rights protected by public policy;
- Rights protected by whistleblower laws; or,
- Rights covered by an implied contract.

MINE FIELDS

Library supervisors, managers, and administrators must be cognizant of the areas in which many personnel difficulties occur. The situations lend themselves to potential problems because either they involve legally protected rights or they involve the employer's taking action against an employee and the employee seeking to find a way out of difficulty.

Whether the situation involves a personnel action or illegal activity, library supervisors are faced with a mine field of potential difficulty. The following scenarios are presented with the purpose of providing managers with suggested solutions. The situations, circumstances, and the people involved differ from one problem to another. The supervisor will have to evaluate each problem individually and decide what course of action would be the most appropriate for the employee and the library. This determination will often involve other individuals, most notably the library's administrators and personnel specialists and often, the university's administration, law enforcement, and the legal office on campus.

Many problems can be resolved by talking to or counseling employees. Care must be taken not to cross the line into an area that must be reserved for professional psychologists and psychiatrists who have the proper training to counsel persons with emotional problems. Inappropriate advice may do more to complicate the problem than solve it for the employee.

Before labeling an employee a problem, consider the possibility that the cause may be poor management. Research studies have found that about half of the employees labeled problems by supervisors were victims of poor supervision. These employees had not been adequately trained, had not been given counseling when needed, or had not received written warnings when required. Supervisors who do not have the patience or the ability to help employees or change their behavior should resolve to improve or seriously consider getting out of supervision.

STUDENT EMPLOYEE PROBLEMS

Some of the problems most common to the supervision of student employees in academic libraries are included in this chapter. The solutions to these problems are certainly not the absolute answers. The situations, circumstances, and the people involved differ from one problem to another. You, the supervisor, will have to evaluate each problem you face individually and decide what course of action would be the most appropriate for the student employee and the library.

Remember that you are not alone. Seek the advice of your own supervisor or fellow student employee supervisors. Be aware that no one may have had precisely the same problem with the same circumstances. There are also numerous books on supervision that can be consulted. Mix all you learn from colleagues and books together with a large dose of common sense and humaneness and you will do fine in resolving student employment problems.

THE STUDENT EMPLOYEE WHO COMPLAINS

Student employees who complain are a constant source of frustration to supervisors. Student employees who are chronic complainers often do a poor job or avoid work. A poor attitude exhibited by complaining manifests itself in poor work performance and unhappiness. Supervisors need to take action when complaining affects the amount of work being accomplished or is unsettling to others in the department.

For the student employee who complains to one and all about seemingly everything, the first step is to talk privately to the student. Remember that a complaint is always justified from the point of view of the complainer and the complaint (or complainer) must be dealt with promptly. Explain that you understand that the employee is unhappy with the work and has complaints about the library. Investigate the nature of the complaint with questions. Ask, "What's wrong?" or "What happened?" Get the facts by listening carefully. Empathize with the complainer and show your concern.

Poor communications are behind many complaints. Providing a clear explanation may resolve the complaint. Some complaints are the transfer of anger type. Something may have happened to put the employee in a poor frame of mind. A few questions about how things are going in general may reveal the situation. Handling a complaint or complainer is one of the most difficult parts of a supervisor's job. You have to put yourself in the complainer's position and try to understand how the complainer feels.

THE STUDENT EMPLOYEE WHO PROCRASTINATES

People procrastinate most often when faced with unpleasant or difficult jobs to do. It is one of the biggest barriers to getting work done. Student employees are as susceptible as any other employee. Since everyone procrastinates to one degree or another, it is important to be able to overcome it in yourself and others.

You will not procrastinate nearly as often if you develop a positive attitude about work. Nothing is as difficult as it seems. Once you have completed a job you have dreaded doing, the satisfaction derived is that much greater.

Student employees who procrastinate need to learn to overcome it. If you want to help someone who is procrastinating, you must learn why the person is putting off doing something that should be done. If the tasks students avoid are either difficult or boring, sharing the load among several student workers will lessen the tendency to procrastinate.

If your boss is procrastinating on something important to you or your staff, you may be able to help. By subtly applying pressure, by persuasion, and by offering to assist with the job, you may provide the incentive that is needed. Of course, you must be very diplomatic in what you say or do. You do not want to be judgmental or seen as a nag. If the boss offers an excuse for not doing something, drop it. Your help is not wanted.

THE STUDENT WORKER WHO RESISTS CHANGE

In academic libraries today, there are changes in procedures, policies, staffing, and job duties at a greater rate than ever before. Major changes brought about in libraries have been made and continue to be made by the automation of technical and public services functions. Changes that affect the duties of student workers will sometimes require that their jobs be reclassified. Most student employees like change and accept it graciously. They are probably the most adaptable of all library staff. While change is inevitable on the job, some people do resist it. Supervisors must do all they can to help employees expect, understand, and accept change. If you do this, resistance will be greatly reduced.

One of the most effective ways to overcome resistance is to involve student workers in changes before they are made. Change is more acceptable if it is kept simple and done without a lot of fanfare. You need to give people time to adjust to change and you must recognize that some resistance may never be completely overcome.

THE STUDENT WHO IS DISHONEST

A problem that occurs rarely but is nonetheless a concern is cheating on timesheets. It is the supervisor's responsibility to review and verify reports of time worked for the purpose of determining wages. By signing a timesheet, the supervisor verifies that the student worker is entitled to be paid at a predetermined rate for the hours reported as worked. The student who arrives late, leaves early, or does not work scheduled hours and signs a timesheet that certifies that all of the scheduled hours have been worked will have cheated on the timesheet.

Falsifying a timesheet is a serious offense. The supervisor who knows that hours are incorrectly reported (and it is your responsibility to know) should first talk with the student. Point out the errors on the timesheet and allow the employee to correct them. Make certain the employee understands the importance of correctly reporting time worked and the consequences of falsifying time reports. The student employee who purposely falsifies a timesheet should be warned if there is any doubt, and terminated if it can be proven. Timesheets should never be completed by student employees in advance of time worked unless directed by their supervisors to do so.

Procedures should be established which call for auditing cash receipts and balancing the cash box or register on a regular basis. Wherever possible, establish procedures which protect student workers who work with cash from suspicion if shortages occur. The procedure should require that someone other than the persons taking in or passing out cash perform the count and do the balancing. The location of Lost and Found can also be a problem. If items are turned in at Circulation, they should be claimed in the Library Office in order that the circulation staff not be placed in the position of being accused of stealing those items.

The student employee suspected of theft (cash, personal items, library materials/supplies) should be warned if there is any doubt, and terminated if it can be proven. Involvement of campus or local police is a local issue that should be addressed by university policy.

THE STUDENT EMPLOYEE WHO VIOLATES LIBRARY RULES

Violation of company rules has always plagued business and industry. In order to deal with it, companies provide employees with handbooks with regulations and procedures. A handbook is a poor substitute for personal training because the handbooks are seldom read or understood. Supervisors should inform new student employees about library rules and regulations as soon as possible after they are hired.

When a rule is broken, the supervisor must first determine whether or not the student worker was aware of the rule and understood the reason for it. You the supervisor are responsible for disciplining chronic rule breakers because by overlooking a violation and saying nothing, you are condoning the action, making that particular rule completely unenforceable. Supervisors must speak and act with authority. Appearing unsure only causes anxiety and worry.

It is important to remember that the purpose of discipline is corrective, not punitive. Avoid using sarcasm or threats and never penalize anyone without an explanation. Spend time discussing the rule and describe what you expect of the employee in the future.

The library's policies should clearly spell out personnel rules and regulations and must be communicated to student workers. A student handbook, although not guaranteed to be read and understood, is needed. Part of the orientation of new employees is stressing the importance of reading the handbook and accepting responsibility for abiding by the policies therein.

THE STUDENT EMPLOYEE WHO VIOLATES UNIVERSITY RULES

Normally, the student government association governs the behavior of students. University rules relating to academic honesty and classroom behavior are enforced by the student government, the faculty, and the university administration. It is the duty of library employee supervisors to cooperate with those bodies. A student who is expelled for whatever reason is normally ineligible for employment by the library, especially those students who receive college work study or other university financial awards.

THE UNMOTIVATED STUDENT EMPLOYEE

The unmotivated student employee is a constant concern to supervisors. Whether the person does not like the work, appears to be lazy, dawdles on the job, is bored, or feels unappreciated, the result is usually that the employee is dissatisfied with the job. Motivation can be a severe problem for many student employees. Their primary focus is on their education. Most work in the library because they need the money. They are not interested in working in the library for a longer period of time than is necessary.

The unmotivated employee can be a poor influence on fellow workers and the problem must be addressed. The first step is to talk with the employee. Determine the cause. If the student does not like the work, there may be something else in the department or the library more suited to the employee's interests and abilities. If not, the student employee should be referred to Student Employment for reassignment.

If the student appears to be lazy or dawdles on the job, calling the student employee's attention to it may help the individual make adjustments, if only temporarily. If the student employee continues to exhibit the same behavior, make it clear in a private conversation that unless there is a change in behavior, the employee and the department would be better off if the student worked somewhere else.

If the student employee is bored, an effort should be made to see if the job can be enriched with other duties. Calling attention to the obvious boredom may help the employee make adjustments. If the student employee continues to exhibit the same behavior, inform the employee that termination may result and that the employee might be more suited to other work.

If the student feels unappreciated, the supervisor must take steps to address the problem. Inform the employee that you and the library depend on the student employee's contribution. Give your full attention and show interest when the employee communicates with you. Compliment the employee in the presence of others. It is important that you impart to the student employee that you are interested.

In dealing with the unmotivated employee, supervisors must be alert to the need to make all employees feel a part of the department's team. It is important to remember that being a member of a group is important for job satisfaction and good productivity and that good compatibility among workers promotes good performance.

Consult Chapter 10 for more suggestions on motivating employees.

THE STUDENT EMPLOYEE WITH LOW MORALE

Closely related to motivation problems with employees, low morale can disrupt the workplace. Low morale can be caused by a number of things including low pay, schedules, lack of advancement, and working conditions. Low morale is exhibited most often by student employee complaints about wages and working conditions.

To understand the causes of low morale, supervisors must know that all humans share five basic needs. These needs, which cause behavior, vary in intensity for different people and must be satisfied in order from outer needs to inner needs. These five basic needs are: physical needs; security needs; need to belong; ego needs; and achievement needs.

Physical needs are the basic animal needs for food and shelter. Until these needs are satisfied, the others are unimportant. Once satisfied, other needs emerge. The need to be protected from bodily harm, need for job and financial security are security needs. Once an individual feels secure, the need to belong must be satisfied. This is the human herd instinct: to be accepted by others, to have friends, and to identify with others. After the need to belong is satisfied, ego needs become important. Ego needs include the need to be recognized and well thought of, to be independent and avoid embarrassment, to have a good self-image, and to be in control of situations. Once ego needs have been essentially met, the last set of needs becomes important: achievement needs. Achievement or self-fulfillment needs result in the drive to be the best and to advance on the job.

The physical and security needs and the need to belong are for the most part satisfied in most student employees as are the ego and achievement needs. Those student employees with low morale most often complain about wages (security need) and lack of advancement (achievement need).

Efforts must be made to be certain that student employees are paid for work performed. First, find out whether the student is being paid fairly in relation to other student employees performing duties at the same level. If you find that the student is paid fairly, explain explicitly how wages are determined. If the student is in a position of needing more pay to meet financial obligations, refer the employee to the employment office to see if placement in another position in the library or on campus is possible. If there are other duties resulting in a higher wage that can be assigned and if it is within the supervisor's authority to do so, the student's security and achievement needs may be satisfied and the problem of low morale resolved. It is also very important that the student be made to feel that the student and his or her work is essential to the successful operation of the department.

THE DISLOYAL STUDENT EMPLOYEE

Unfortunately, not all employees are loyal to the organization they work for. So, there are student employees who are disloyal to the library. So what? The student employees are paid to work, nothing else. Of what possible harm could there be in having student employees who are not loyal? They show their disloyalty to the library in one or more ways, both on and off the job. Their actions or inactions hurt the library and themselves. Disloyalty is shown by employees who speak badly of the library, fail to keep promises, take advantage of the library in work procedures, or threaten to leave. Loyal student employees, on the other hand, are concerned about the library, its success, and its future, while disloyal student employees seem determined to oppose those things. Supervisors of must be alert to signs of disloyalty among student employees and act when they see or hear indications of it.

Employees often withhold loyalty until the supervisor and the library have earned it. As a supervisor, you must know that loyalty cannot be bought or won with favors. It must be built by making employees feel that they belong and are part of the library. Student employees must be made to feel that the success of the library depends on each of them doing their share and cooperating with coworkers and supervisors.

Student employees' value to the library depends not only on their talents and abilities but also on a willingness to use those abilities and talents to help the library. By not using those talents and abilities for the good of the library, employees are hurting themselves as well as their employer and coworkers.

Supervisors may need to examine how much their student employees are involved in planning for the department. When employees are involved in planning, they feel a commitment to helping carry out the plans they helped formulate. The student employee who is involved in planning and an important member of the team may fail to keep up the student employee's end of the bargain by not performing as expected or by being absent too often. It is important to talk to the student, making sure the importance of everyone's contribution to the accomplishment of departmental objectives is understood.

If the student fails again, inform the employee of the consequences of this action and follow through with disciplinary action at the next offense.

The student employee who criticizes the library can have a negative effect on other employees. Student workers who have contact with library users can seriously harm the library's programs. If you were to ask the student employee how loyal the student was to the library, your sanity might be questioned. Most employees tend to think about the library's loyalty to their employees rather than employees' loyalty to the library. They think of the benefits extended by the library, such as job security, etc., which help employees meet personal needs but often are taken for granted.

The supervisor must determine the cause of the criticism. Has the library in some way mistreated the student? Can the student employee give you examples of how the library has treated the student or other employees unfairly? When you learn the reasons for this attitude you can go about either proving to the student employee that it is the wrong attitude or correcting a problem if one exists.

THE STUDENT WORKER WITH ABSENTEEISM PROBLEMS

Probably the most frequent problem with student employees is their inability to work all of the hours scheduled. Student workers, whether they are scheduled to work at the circulation desk or to search new book orders are relied upon to perform those duties on a scheduled basis. The library must maintain a certain level of staffing, especially for night and weekend service hours. Students are required to meet specific requirements for courses, for example, fieldtrips, special lectures or performances. Students are not immune to illnesses or family crises that require their absence from work. The obvious solution is for the library to maintain sufficient permanent staffing so as not to rely on student workers. In the real world of academic libraries funds are not available to hire all of the new staff members needed so student employees are and will continue to be critical to the daily operation of libraries. Student employee absences must be accepted and approved policies must exist to regularize the library's response to absences.

Rules about attendance are critical to the operation of the library. Student employees are expected to establish to a schedule for work and stick to it. Because of the commitments students have for their coursework and other activities, schedule changes can be expected. Rules must be in effect relating to how much notice of schedule changes must be given, how the work or hours will be covered, and whether or not the hours missed can be made up in advance of or after the absence. Once established, these policies must be communicated to student workers and adhered to by all supervisors.

Questions that should be answered by an absence policy include the following:

1) What constitutes an unexcused absence?
2) How many unexcused absences are allowed before disciplinary action is required?
3) What disciplinary action is to be taken?
4) What constitutes an excused absence?
5) How is an anticipated absence to be reported?
6) What notice is required?
7) Will someone have to take the absent student's place during the hours missed?
8) Whose responsibility is it to find a replacement?
9) Can students switch hours with one another?
10) How is a switch to be communicated to supervisors?

11) Is there a limit to the number of excused absences allowed?
- An *unexcused* absence is normally an instance where the employee does not come to work for the scheduled hours and fails to notify the supervisor. Many libraries require that after one unexcused absence, the student employee be given a warning in writing that a second unexcused absence will result in termination.
- An *excused* absence is normally an instance where the employee makes prior arrangements to be absent during specified scheduled hours or calls in prior to the scheduled hours to report the inability to come to work. Where replacements must be found, the amount of advance notice is critical.

You will have to make a judgment as to whether these absences interfere with the department's ability to meet its objectives. Is the morale of the department affected by this employee's absences? Are you being fair in your treatment of all employees? When talking with a student worker about excessive absences, make it clear that presence on the job is important and that absences affect the department. If the student employee cannot assure you that the number absences will be reduced, you should consider reassigning the student to other duties or asking that the employee be reassigned to another department or on-campus job.

Counseling will probably help those student employees whose pressures off the job affect their commitment to work; those for whom work appears dissatisfying; those student employees who have unpleasant relationships with coworkers; those for whom a straightforward word to the wise would help. Counseling would probably not be successful for those student employees for whom the pay and the job have no attraction; those for whom off the job activities have much greater appeal than the job; and those for whom the sole purpose of their being absent is to inconvenience, punish, or disrupt the department. For this latter group, termination may be the only recourse.

THE STUDENT EMPLOYEE WITH PERSONAL PROBLEMS

All of us have personal problems of one type or another: family, financial, relationship, etc. In addition, student employees may have academic problems that most of us don't have. To a point, you can help some student employees by communicating with them, understanding them, and treating them the same way you treat all student employees.

Family problems may require that the student be absent for a period of time. The student employee is usually concerned about having a job upon return. Arrangements can usually be made to hold the position for the employee. How do you deal with financial and relationship problems? The inclination is to give students advice you would give your children. Whether or not you give advice depends on your confidence in counseling young people. It is often advisable to not get involved. Academic problems may require that the student reduce the number of hours worked. Whether this can be permitted depends entirely on your staffing situation. Tutoring help for students is available on most campuses.

If a student employee voluntarily brings a problem to you, you can be most helpful by listening without interruptions, advice, prescriptions, solutions, pontifications, or preaching. Then, recognize your own limits in dealing with situations like this.

THE STUDENT EMPLOYEE WITH PERSONALITY PROBLEMS

First, you cannot label just anyone as having personality problems. Secondly, you cannot solve real personality problems, nor does anyone expect you to solve those problems. Thirdly, extreme cases must be left to psychiatrists and psychologists. Lastly, student services on university campuses are available to students and you should know about those services and how to refer students to those services.

The definition of personality problems, for the purposes of this discussion, are those persons whose work habits, attitudes, and outlook on life are difficult to understand, and persons prone to public displays of emotion who tend to affect the morale and productivity of their coworkers. You are probably not a trained psychologist or psychiatrist but you may help some student employees by communicating with them, understanding them, and treating them the same way you treat all student employees. This common sense advice is applicable to all workers.

Types of personality problems include persons who are frequently angry, easily hurt, eccentric and unpredictable, negative and pessimistic, or who are excessive talkers.

Persons who frequently "fly off the handle" or lose their tempers are difficult to work with, and are not to be tolerated. Talking constructively to an angry person is difficult so avoid talking to anyone who is angry. Set up another time to talk and if the student becomes angry, you must listen, not talk. When you are able to talk to the individual, inform the individual that the behavior is unacceptable and that it interferes with the employee's work and the work of others. Disciplinary action may not change these individuals but will let them know that the library will not tolerate the behavior. Give a warning that if the problem is not corrected on the job, the employee will be terminated. If you are going to give a warning, be sure you are prepared to follow through.

Persons who are very sensitive to criticism and are easily hurt can be a problem. When a student employee who needs constructive criticism reacts by bursting into tears, the first inclination is to never criticize. When criticism must be given, it should be offered with kid gloves. If possible, use the words, "we" and "our" when referring to the work and how it is to be done. Avoid anything that will undermine this person's self-confidence. Praise for work well done and expressing appreciation to these persons will help them gain confidence and improve their ability to accept direction.

The eccentric or unpredictable student employee is not uncommon in university libraries because what is a university if not a place for young people to test their ideas and investigate alternative lifestyles? It is not unusual for a student to change during the college years and during employment in the library. Should you accept this behavior or try to change the person? It is unlikely that you or anybody else can change this individual or the way the job is handled. You can, however, expect the eccentric student employee to perform the assigned duties in the same manner as other student employees. This employee is to be held to the same level of accountability as other students. If the creative approach to the job does not result in acceptable performance or interferes with the work of others, this behavior needs to be addressed privately.

The negative or pessimistic student employee can be a disruption in a work group. The common sense advice for dealing with this student is to accentuate the positive. Be sure you are always positive when talking with the employee. Assign tasks at which you know the employee can excel. The secret of getting people to think positively is to convince them that positive thinking is good for them. When the supervisor conveys a positive attitude to workers, they feel better and want to do a good job.

The employee who talks excessively is usually not productive and wastes the time of others. Excessive talking on the telephone should be addressed by pointing out the library's policy on telephone use. If the employee persists in wasting time and the time of others the employee must be talked to privately. Inform the employee that the issue is time not personality. Point out that excessive talking wastes time and interferes with the work to be done. Tell the employee that you have to guard against talking too much yourself and that many people have the same problem on the job. If the problem persists, inform the employee that if the problem is not corrected, you will need to take disciplinary action.

Remember that you cannot and should not attempt to solve severe personality problems. You should be aware of student services offices on campus that are set up to assist students. If the student comes to you for help, do not hesitate to suggest an appropriate office. You can help some student employees by communicating with them, understanding them, and treating them the same way you treat all student employees.

DEALING WITH STRESS

Stress can develop on any job and in any employee. It is true however, that stress usually does not occur in employees who adjust easily to change or to persons in good mental and physical condition and who have a positive attitude. All stress is not bad. Stress that causes fear, anger, or frustration can be harmful. Employees who fear making mistakes or losing their jobs waste energy in combating those fears. Stress that challenges, encourages initiative, and raises competitive feelings can be positive.

In many cases, a heavy workload is the cause of stress. Reducing that workload may not reduce the level of stress because an individual's personality often determines the amount of stress the employee perceives. Student employees are likely to be under greater stress during mid-term or final examinations than at other times of the year. Probably as much or more than other groups of employees, student workers are likely to bring stress to the job because of their coursework.

For the student worker who is affected by stress from academics, there is not a lot that can be done. You may receive requests for time off that can be granted. Some libraries do permit students to study at work for limited periods of time during final examinations.

DEALING WITH INSUBORDINATION

Insubordination can take one of two forms: (1) An employee may willfully refuse or refrain from carrying out a direct order or (2) an employee may direct threats, abusive language, or physical violence at a supervisor.

If a worker refuses to carry out a direct order, the supervisor must first mentally reconstruct the conversation to be certain an order was given. Once certain, the supervisor should try to determine the reason for refusal. Was the employee unable to do what was requested? Did the employee feel that the order was irrational? Talk with the employee and ask for an explanation. Explain the consequences of insubordination in the library. Normally, insubordination is grounds for immediate termination. If it is determined by the supervisor that the order given was reasonable and within the capabilities of the student employee, the supervisor can warn or terminate the employee.

Insubordination that takes the form of physical violence toward the supervisor is not so easily handled. The policy in most libraries is that physical violence or the threat of physical violence in the presence of others is grounds for immediate termination. No counseling or conversation is required or expected when the supervisor's personal safety or that of other workers is threatened.

DEALING WITH RUMORS IN THE WORKPLACE

Few organizations can claim that their people don't start or spread rumors. Because one of the primary responsibilities of supervisors is to keep staff informed, rumors must not be ignored. The most effective way to dispel them is to determine whether there is any truth to the rumor and to inform your staff about what you learn. If there is no truth to a rumor, tell your staff. If you have no information, tell them that. The best way to dispel rumors is to give your staff the facts. If the supervisor keeps staff informed, there will be no need for rumors.

It is important to let your staff know that they can come to you to check out rumors and they should be encouraged not to repeat them. It is even more important to keep student workers informed because they work different schedules. A library newsletter distributed to all staff and routed to student workers is a good way to keep students informed of library activities.

DEALING WITH THE OLDER STUDENT EMPLOYEE

The average age of students enrolled in colleges and universities is becoming steadily higher. Returning students, or nontraditional students, are becoming more and more common on today's campuses. Nontraditional students can be real assets to the library. Supervisors must be careful to treat the older student in the same way as all other students.

TIME, TELEPHONE, AND DRESS POLICIES

Rules regarding arriving and leaving on time should be included in the student employee's handbook. The supervisor must speak to the student to ascertain the reasons for arriving late or leaving early. It is possible that the schedule can be adjusted to allow for a student to arrive early and leave early or arrive late and leave late, as long as the student is present during the number of hours to be worked. Disciplinary actions should include warnings and termination of habitual rule breakers.

Another common library rule relates to the use of telephones for personal calls. Common business practice is to permit employee use of the telephone as long as it is not abused and does not interfere with the work. As to what constitutes abuse, the individual supervisor will have to determine and consistently enforce.

Library rules regarding dress in public universities have become passé. A good rule of thumb can be found at the entrances to many places of business: NO SHIRT, NO SHOES, NO SERVICE. Supervisors are within their rights to require shirt, shoes, and decency but should go no farther. Some private institutions have enforceable dress codes. In matters of personal hygiene, the supervisor may privately suggest to a student that cleanliness is a concern.

MORE MINE FIELDS

In addition to those problems above, even more difficult situations potentially involve employee/employer rights and include the following: the job interview; the hiring process; performance evaluations; promotions; salary and merit determinations; dealing with poor performance; reassignment; discipline; demotion; suspension; termination;

personal problems; and the exit interview. There are also situations in which the employee is the victim or the perpetrator of an activity that is just cause for termination and/or is illegal. Occasionally, employees are the victims of stalking, obscene phone calls, harassment, theft, drug/alcohol abuse in the family, domestic violence, or personal financial problems. In instances involving these and other problem areas, be certain to talk with your supervisor in order to prevent these from becoming major problems.

PROBLEM RESOLUTION

Please remember that the suggestions offered in this book are not absolute answers. The situations, circumstances, and the people involved differ greatly from one problem to another. You will have to evaluate each instance individually and decide what course of action would be the most appropriate.

Know your limitations. Your advice or answers may do more to complicate the problem than solve it for the student employee. Remember that you are not alone. Seek the advice of your supervisor or fellow student employee supervisors. Be aware that no one may have had precisely the same problem with the same circumstances. Mix in all you learn with a large dose of common sense.

NOTE

1. Lewin G. Joel III, *Every Employee's Guide to the Law: Everything You Need to Know about Your Rights in the Workplace—And What to Do if They are Violated* (New York: Pantheon, 1993), p. 6.

BIBLIOGRAPHY

Alexander, Mark. *Employee Performance and Discipline Problems: A New Approach.* Kingston, Ontario: IRC Press, 2000.

Axelrod, Alan and James Holtje. *201 Ways to Deal with Difficult People: A Quick-Tip Survival Guide.* New York: MJF Books, 2001.

Bacal, Robert. *Managers Guide to Performance Reviews.* New York: McGraw-Hill, 2004.

Baldwin, David A., Frances C. Wilkinson, and Daniel C. Barkley. *Effective Management of Student Employment: Organizing for Student Employment in Academic Libraries.* Englewood, CO: Libraries Unlimited, 2000.

Brown, Nina W. *Working with the Self-Absorbed: How to Handle Narcissistic Personalities on the Job.* Oakland, CA: New Harbinger, 2002.

Bunzey, Marceline. *From Complaining Carl to Negative Nelli: Managing Prickly Personalities.* Palm Beach Gardens, FL: Dartnell, 2001.

Cavaiola, Alan A. and Neil J. Lavender. *Toxic Coworkers: How to Deal with Dysfunctional People on the Job.* Oakland, CA: New Harbinger Publications, 2000.

Crowley, Katherine and Kathi Elster. *Working with You Is Killing Me: Freeing Yourself from Emotional Traps at Work.* New York: Warner Business Books, 2006.

Dealing with Difficult People. Boston, MA: Harvard Business School Press, 2005.

Eitington, Julius E. *The Winning Trainer: Winning Ways to Involve People in Learning.* Boston, MA: Butterworth-Heinemann, 2002.

Fritz, Janie M. Harden and Becky Lynn Omdahl. *Problematic Relationships in the Workplace.* New York: Peter Lang, 2006.

Furnham, Adrian and John Taylor. *The Dark Side of behaviour at Work: Understanding and Avoiding Employees Leaving, Thieving, and Deceiving.* New York: Palgrave Macmillan, 2004.

Graham Leviss, Katherine. *High-maintenance Employees: Why Your Best People Will Also Be Your Most Difficult—and What You Can Do about It.* Naperville, IL: Sourcebooks, 2005.

Grote, Richard C. *Discipline without Punishment: The Proven Strategy that Turns Problem Employees into Superior Performers.* New York: Amacom-American Management Association, 2006.

Hancock, Peter A. and Paula A. Desmond. *Stress, Workload, and Fatigue.* Mahwah, NJ: Lawrence Erlbaum Associates, 2001.

Johnson, Jeffrey R. *Discipline, Documentation & Discharge of Problem Employees.* Cary, NC: North Carolina Bar Association Foundation, 2004.

Lloyd, Kenneth L. *Jerks at Work: How to Deal with People Problems and Problem People.* Franklin Lakes, NJ: Career Press, 2006.

Pincus, Marilyn. *Managing Difficult People: A Survival Guide for Handling Any Employee.* Avon, MA: Adams Media, 2005.

Schinkel, Greg and Irwin Schinkel. *Employees Not Doing What You Expect: Find Out Why, Fix It, Prevent It in Future, Turn Negative Situations into Positive Relationships.* London, Ontario: Unique Development Corp., 2004.

Shepard, Glenn. *How to Manage Problem Employees: A Step-By-Step Guide for Turning Difficult Employees into High Performers.* Hoboken, NJ: John Wiley, 2005.

Taylor, John and Adrian Furnham. *Dishonesty at Work: Myths and Uncomfortable Truths.* London: Social Affairs Unit, 2005.

Ward, Gregg. *Bad Behavior, People Problems, and Sticky Situations: A Toolbook for Managers and Team Leaders.* San Diego, CA: Winding Creek Press, 2002.

When Good People Behave Badly. Boston, MA: Harvard Business School Press, 2004.

When People Are the Problem, What Will You Do? Boston, MA: Harvard Business School, 2005.

13

Staff Development for Student Employee Supervisors

I am always ready to learn although I do not always like to be taught.
—Winston Churchill

WHY STAFF DEVELOPMENT?

Chapter 8 provides information on orienting and training student employees to perform their work. How do the student employee supervisors receive the training to perform those important responsibilities? How can the library provide that training? Why should library administrators care about and invest in building effective staff development within their organizations or the library profession?

It goes without saying that the challenges that libraries face increase by the day. Simply put, those challenges cannot be met without increasing the knowledge and skill levels of the librarians and staff in the library and within librarianship. Library patron demands, together with the complexity and rapid changes in the information world create an unprecedented need for both individual and library effectiveness that requires higher levels of sophistication in technical skills as well as increased levels of subject knowledge. In addition, individuals must be able to demonstrate creativity, flexibility, and leadership at all levels of the organization. At one time, a librarian could reach mastery in certain areas and, with relatively minor effort, maintain currency in their field. In these challenging times, we can no longer arrive at a final mastery of a body of knowledge or skill that lasts. Even as one attains mastery, there are changes that require individuals and organizations to be engaged in continuous learning. The changing environment demands that we learn how to learn and that we learn things we never dreamed we would have to know to do our work.

BASIC SKILLS DESIRABLE IN BOTH ENTRY LEVEL AND EXPERIENCED EMPLOYEES

In *Workplace Basics: The Skills Employers Want* by Carnevale, Gainer, and Melter published in 1989 by the American Society for Training & Development, the following are the basic skills considered desirable for both entry level and seasoned employees:

- Knowing how to learn
- Reading
- Writing
- Computation
- Listening
- Oral communication
- Creative thinking
- Problem solving
- Self-esteem
- Goal setting/motivation
- Leadership
- Organizational effectiveness
- Teamwork
- Interpersonal communication
- Negotiation
- Personal and career development

If these basic skills do not exist or do exist at a minimal level, there is nothing to build on. Staff development involves enhancing or building on these basic skills to allow an employee to improve and to become a more valuable contributor in the library. Student employee supervisors must possess these skills and commit to improving on them. Because of the challenges we face in the information age, library staff must also add other more sophisticated skills and knowledge to their skill/knowledge base. Statistical analysis, demonstration of creativity and initiative, shared leadership, strategic thinking, teaching, and ever-changing technology skills and knowledge are also required for many positions.

THE CONNECTIVE ERA

In *The Connective Edge: Leading in an Interdependent World*, author Jean Lipman-Blumen describes the shifts in leadership over time. In the *physical era,* the challenges posed by the environment and the elements had to be overcome beginning in prehistoric times. In the *geopolitical era,* boundaries and societal segmentation was important. Leadership and power positions were held by a very few and strategic alliances against enemies was important. This era lasted up until only recently. Lipman-Blumen proposes that we are now experiencing a shift to the *connective era.* Former boundaries are dissolving (the Internet) and connections between people, societies, and environments are becoming stronger. The connective era is the networked era of which libraries are such a critical part.

Interdependence in the connective era requires whole new skills and attitudes about the information world and, as libraries and knowledge workers, we have a unique and important role. In the new era, it is important for libraries to consider carefully their role and place. Libraries must invest in continuous learning. We must learn from the past as well as think futuristically. Libraries must form new alliances and partnerships with like-minded people, groups, and organizations in the knowledge world. While the basic skills considered desirable for both entry level and seasoned employees are important, libraries have to do more than maintain the status quo in order to provide the leadership needed in the information age and in the connective era. Staff development is critical to that effort.

WHY DON'T EMPLOYEES APPRECIATE STAFF DEVELOPMENT?

People for whom staff development is intended often do not appreciate what is being done on their behalf. Some of the possible reasons include:

- They have not been actively involved in the planning
- They have little interest in the topic
- They believe that new approaches come and go—they're just fads
- They have had previous experiences that didn't turn out well
- The motivating speaker got people excited but there was no follow-up
- They don't believe that anybody cares if there is follow-up
- Some individuals want more follow-up/individual attention than others
- They didn't get help in implementing ideas from staff development sessions
- They are asked to try several new approaches simultaneously
- Some will applaud and others will resist or complain

It is important to be aware of the differences among how individuals view staff development and to find ways to make staff development interesting to and effective with many different staff.

TEACHING ADULTS THROUGH THEIR LEARNING STYLE STRENGTHS

The following are strategies for teaching adults. We can reasonably expect that student employees, even though they may be 18-year-old college freshmen, should be treated as adults.

- Tolerate questions. Cultivate the art of asking helpful questions. It's often the quality of questions rather than answers that leads to deeper understanding.
- Think of knowledge as strategy. Work hard to experiment with ideas and make discoveries, share what you know, hang around, and observe high performers. Try for more and better ideas; keep a journal of them and reread it in a disciplined way.
- Learn to deal or negotiate with ideas: make it a point daily to play with ideas. Prioritize, categorize, correlate, recognize bias, separate fact from fiction, defend an opinion, add to, delete from, compare, and contrast.
- Enjoy surprises. It's okay to make a mistake as long as you learn something from it.
- Redefine your work as a resource for learning. Inherent in every task, job, and work process is the kernel of insight. Learn to look at your work as something to learn from; approach

your work as if you were learning to do it for the first time. Pay attention to what's great about it and to what can be improved.

- Think in terms of learning before doing your work, while doing your work, and after doing your work. Practice action and reflection.
- Be responsible. Your work is your work, not your "library's" work. Be responsible for making it the best you can make it. If changes are needed to increase the value of your work, make the changes. The value of your work as intellectual capital is your responsibility.
- Teach someone else; ask someone else to teach you.

LEARNING ORGANIZATIONS

It is past time that libraries, if they are not already, become learning organizations. Academic libraries, without question, are engaged daily in all forms of learning activities. The following are actions that you and your library can take that will enhance your library as a learning organization.

- Take time to do things. Talk with and listen to colleagues. Ask for help. The Lone Ranger died a long time ago.
- Tell people more than they need to know. Communicate widely and openly about the direction the library is going in, the values espoused by the dean and associate deans, successes and the failures.
- Involve everyone in information about the library.
- Trust people to take what information they need and to perhaps find something exciting in information for which they don't immediately see a need.
- Encourage individuals to state a personal vision for their work.
- Encourage individuals to develop a learning plan, with topics or skills they'd like to learn and when and where they could learn them. Review these regularly and assist individuals in learning what they have identified as their learning challenges.
- Promote, reward, and recognize excellence in learning. Look for all kinds of learning, not just that which happens in classrooms.
- Enlist team leaders, supervisors, shift leaders, and others to help you identify excellence in learning.
- Set up forums for ideas. Quantity of ideas leads to quality of ideas. Do this on a regular basis; record the sessions either on paper or on tape.
- Allow people the time to learn on the job from each other. Encourage teaching, coaching, and mentoring.

EVIDENCE OF A LEARNING ORGANIZATION IN PROGRESS

Use this checklist as a guideline for your leading "by walking around." As you talk with people and observe them at their jobs, see if you can find these telling signs that learning can be happening.

- The library subsidizes subscriptions to learning and training journals and pays for national conference attendance.
- The library provides easy access to databases and the Internet for all employees.
- Best practices are rewarded.
- Nobody shoots messengers.

- On-the-job training, coaching, and mentoring happen at all levels.
- Cross-training and cross-functional teamwork are apparent.
- Ideas are welcomed, not censored or ignored.
- Employees can be seen in "communities of practice" solving problems.
- "Bag More Than a Lunch" programs are available for continuous learning.
- E-learning opportunities motivate self-directed learners on the job and on library time.

MAKING STAFF DEVELOPMENT MORE VISIBLE IN THE ORGANIZATION

Staff development has functioned in libraries as a support service for far too long. It's been easy to simply provide training to people who say they want it, only loosely connected to the "real" functions of the library. It has also been easy to ignore the internal communications aspect of training, because training has seldom had to promote itself in its traditional support role. But the staff development program is enhanced when it is clearly related to business purposes. What better way to promote staff development than to establish training's visibility through the business planning process? The persons responsible for staff development should act more like the initiators of action. Here's how:

- Involve your manager peers throughout the library in staff development mission and goal statements, incorporating their input in those statements if possible.
- Communicate the training business planning documents to your supervisors in the library, so that higher management knows that training means business.
- Dovetail your goals and plans with larger library goals or plans.
- Disseminate information about staff development opportunities to all employees.
- Promote training at all levels in the library through a variety of media, including electronic bulletin boards, electronic mail, flyers, memos, and newsletters.
- Refine your formats for promoting training by seeking design ideas from graphics specialists, technical writers, and marketing specialists, and seek and incorporate feedback on your marketing efforts from users of your training services.
- Think organizationally, that is, you promote training solutions to identified problems of entire organizations, not just of individual persons.
- Promote training as a system, requiring commitment of resources at the input side and at the output side.
- Promote the idea that analysis, evaluation, and feedback are critical parts of the training system.
- Offer a variety of training seminars, on-the-job training, classroom courses, computer-based training, off-site courses, and videodisc opportunities in order to spark the imagination of all kinds of employees.
- Entice employees at all levels by the interesting and relevant training that you have in store for them.
- Don't be afraid to be a little bit of a salesman and have fun.

TRAINING MEMBERS OF A TEAM

Supervisors usually get involved early in team formation, often in designing and delivering training to the new team members in how to manage change. This kind of training often is group training, and often its immediate purpose is to help employees adopt a point of view that is "how to do more with less." Supervisors obviously need to give a lot of thought to this, because often there are natural resentments among the current employees, as comfortable ways of doing things become challenged by the ideas and actions of a team organization. Trainers need to focus on personal skill development that facilitates team growth and its consequent better ways of working. Here are some ideas for topics to cover during this kind of training:

- Team versus individual goals. Be sure that you allow each individual on the team to verbalize his or her personal goals; get it all out on the table before you facilitate definition of team goals.
- Negotiate a win-win. During this kind of initial "change management" training, help the team set up win-win situations regarding their personal goals versus the team goals.
- People are miserable if they believe that they have to compromise too much by being on a team. Help them to get to the point where they can define the added value item(s)—that is, the truly new ways of working or delivering service—so that it doesn't seem like giving up some things as much as working together, as individuals, for that something new. Don't allow people to wallow in their fond memories of the way things were but do focus on the new, and negotiate to it from the individual's point of view.
- Do scenario-planning. In the safe environment of training, engage the team in some "what if?" scenario development. Present actual challenges facing the team and real business problems in a workshop setting where trainees can develop solutions in the form of scenario A, scenario B, scenario C, asking all the time, "What if this were the case? What if we had these resources? What if these persons interacted?" etc. Scenario planning allows many individual needs and wants to become incorporated.
- Decision making. Talk about various ways of making decisions. There are a variety of decision-making models, and employees need to know that there are many acceptable ways of making decisions. How things are decided is a critical factor in how teamwork progresses and how success is measured. Individuals need to know that it's okay to try out new ways of decision making.
  Here are some common models of decision making:
  - majority rule
  - minority report
  - consensus
  - middling (going for the middle ground, compromising)
  - do what the consultant says
  - do as I say (authoritarian rule with no discussion)

Much of teamwork operates in what management experts call "the boundaries," that is, the fringe areas where innovative thinking is critical to the team's ability to get things done. Policy and procedures manuals seldom get consulted. What's more important is encouraging individuals to experiment with different ways of making decisions and encouraging and supporting them in learning from their work.

MOTIVATIONS AND REWARDS FOR TEAM MEMBERS

This checklist will give you some ideas about the motivations and rewards that are appropriate for teams. They are aimed at individuals first, then at the team.

- Persons at work want to do a good job. Tell them when and where they do good work, not just during training. Don't wait for performance review; give applause on the spot.
- Most people like to learn. Reinforce the informal learning activities that go on all around you; encourage managers and team leaders to make time for and value one-on-one peer teaching and learning within the team. Try to get away from the mind-set that "accuses" clumps of people trying to figure out a solution as wasting time—that clump might just be on the verge of a real breakthrough and could be team learning at its best.
- Reward "out of the box" thinking. Individuals are normally risk-aversive, but working in teams often requires doing things that seem uncomfortable for certain personality types. Being personally exposed at times of risk taking for the good of the project or the team deserves recognition and reward. Make it big or make it small, but do it consistently and in a timely fashion. Make this a function of the team's "personal trainer"—get the training staff out into the team—manage training by "walking around." Make it a point to know when creative and collaborative thinking occur.
- Give a lot of thought to what kind of rewards will motivate your particular employees. Here are some possibilities for rewards:
  - *Blue ribbons*—inexpensive and enough to go around; reward "most improved team member," "best cheerleader," "best networker," "most valuable player," etc. Blue Ribbons can also be adapted to photos in a hall of fame, or features in the library newsletter.
  - *Free lunch*—including items generally thought of as "travel and entertainment"; free lunches, a dinner club membership, sports tickets, concert tickets, ski weekends, a beach house for a week. For public institutions, be sure to check the policies regarding this type of expenditure. The last thing you want is your picture on the front page associated with misuse of public funds.
  - *Toys*—grownup gadgets and hardware with a wow effect; faster computers, better fax machines, cell phones, laptop computers, etc.
  - *Privilege*—company perks generally reserved only for executives; a private parking space with a name plate, guest privileges every Wednesday in the faculty dining room, a direct phone/fax line, flextime, travel on the corporate jet.

DESIGNING TRAINING FOR ADULT LEARNERS

Refresh your memory about how student learners differ from children in school and share it with student supervisors as a refresher for them, too.

- Be sure that trainees know how their work fits into the totality of work. Be sure that instruction describes the big picture. Inspect the beginnings of your course documents to be sure that instruction is designed to enable trainees to see their work in relationship to all work of the library.
- Be sure that trainees understand the requirements of the new skill, that is, give trainees a simple list of competent behaviors you expect them to exhibit after they've been through training.
- Anticipate that trainees will come to training with some gaps in prerequisite knowledge. Have reference documents, user manuals, and job aids available during training for those who might need to catch up.
- Demonstrate by your actions—the tone in which the course is written and the respect with which the instructor interacts with trainees—that the training department appreciates the past successes of trainees and will work with them to continue to build on their experiences.

- Present training as a solution to problems. Conduct training in a way that engages trainees in working out solutions. Give trainees opportunities to problem-solve individually as well as in small groups. Give them clues and ideas, but let them work through the problems.
- Provide feedback often during learning time. Adults like to know that they "got it"; if they didn't get it, they like to know what steps to take in order to do it right.
- Build in plenty of practice time, and be sure that it is "instructed" practice time, so that trainees realize their successes and failures and can learn from them in a controlled situation.
- Hand out some record or reminder of learning—a trainee manual, a course outline, a work-shop agenda, a job aid—to take back to the job. Give them a crutch to reactivate their memories after training is done.
- Give trainees a chance to evaluate their training, making suggestions for improvement.

DEALING WITH LEARNING STYLES

Personal learning style is related to an individual's values, family influences, personality, and past successes. A learner generally exhibits preference for different learning styles according to what has to be learned, often preferring to learn different things differently. The following may help you design and deliver your staff development programs to accommodate the most common learning styles:

- Present information that appeals to "left-brained" preferences, i.e., sequential, logical, organized information that requires reasoned analysis to understand.
- Present information that appeals to "right-brained" preferences, i.e., nonverbal stimuli, impulsive, simultaneous, messy information requiring intuition and synthesis to understand.
- Build in opportunities for divergent thinking, i.e., generating hypotheses, being creative, and solving problems using the concept of what might be possible.
- Build in opportunities for convergent thinking, i.e., gathering evidence, documenting, and solving problems by figuring out observable necessary components.
- Teach students to look for patterns, i.e., in verbal expression, in visual information, in situations in which touching, hearing, or smelling are important to the job.
- Teach students to understand analogies and use them to foster understanding of new concepts and skills.
- Build in opportunities for quiet individual work as well as noisy group work.
- Encourage team problem solving in small groups so that trainees can learn from each other and can develop experience working with learners of varying style preferences.
- Train your instructors to learn to listen for clues to a person's preferred style—e.g., "I see," "I believe," "I hear," "I figure," "I can prove."
- Appreciate that in the same class you'll have students on the same issue who'll always want to ask you "what" and others who will always want to ask you "why," and that both approaches are equally valid. Be sure your instructors are prepared to satisfy each kind of question—sometimes coming from the same person.
- Be sure that training is consciously designed and delivered to support both short-term and long-term memory.
  ○ short-term memory of present information delivered by current sensory inputs,
  ○ information store of past experiences in long-term memory,
  ○ and the process of associating the present and the past.
- Build in the opportunity for trainees to plan as well as to react.

CATEGORIZING TYPES OF TRANSFERABLE SKILLS

There is a need today for flexible, original, intellectually agile employees who can contribute their individual and collective expertise to the workplace. Organizationally, libraries engage in cross-training, in which workers learn new skills that can be applied to several key areas of the library. Focus on the categories of transferable skills and design learning for them:

- Think about whether you want the new skill to be transferred intact or to be a stepping stone to learning-related skills.
- Think about the work survival skills at your particular library such as following rules, using tools, dealing positively with time pressure, being a member of a team, writing reports, or analyzing spreadsheets. These are skills that the entire library values and are transferable from job to job.
- Focus on general communication skills—listening, speaking, writing.
- Focus on general mathematics skills.
- Focus on general character traits—curiosity, cooperation, initiative, persistence, competency, sharing, etc.
- Focus on reasoning skills.
- Focus on manipulative skills.
- Focus on the skills involved in learning to learn—locating information, accessing information, recognizing patterns, etc.

PROCESS WORDS FOR MANAGERS

People who study learning organizations often talk about "process"—that is, the interweaving of the way things are happening and the way people interact with each other as work progresses. One way to teach yourself to "think process" is to use the " . . . ing" form of words instead of verbs, which tend to stop the action: "planning" instead of "plan," for example. You'll be amazed at how this simple word trick can train your thinking in the direction of "process."

- *Accessing* instead of access.
- *Analyzing* instead of analyze.
- *Changing* instead of change.
- *Communicating* instead of communicate.
- *Differentiating* instead of differentiate.
- *Doing* instead of do.
- *Evaluating* instead of evaluate.
- *Finding* instead of find.
- *Interpreting* instead of interpret.
- *Leading* instead of leadership.
- *Listening* instead of listen.
- *Modifying* instead of modify.
- *Motivating* instead of motivation.
- *Revising* instead of revise.
- *Searching* instead of search.
- *Simplifying* instead of simplify.

- *Supporting* instead of support.
- *Understanding* instead of understand.
- *Verifying* instead of verify.
- *Visioning* instead of vision.

TOUGH QUESTIONS FOR LEADERS

Leadership these days is getting a lot of attention. It's clear that workers in today's flatter, less hierarchical, more empowered workplaces want and need leaders who are different mold from those of yesterday. Yesterday's leaders "looked out for number one," "walked silently and carried a big stick," or came to work to "kick butt." Leadership today, especially leadership of learning organizations, is clearly changing from authoritarian to egalitarian models. During this transition, leaders have to ask themselves some tough questions about their behaviors in their new role. These are some of them:

- How can I be comfortable facilitating team and group learning?
- What self-disciplines do I need to develop in order to be patient and truly caring about each person's growth as it impacts the growth of the team?
- How can I demonstrate my encouragement of "generative conversation" among employees?
- How can I show them that talking on the job with each other is a good thing that often leads to breakthroughs?
- How can I teach them the value of dialogue and active listening, positive evaluation, and feedback?
- How can I take steps to encourage dissent, questioning, and feedback during meetings in front of peers and supervisors?
- How can I prevent dissent from occurring behind backs and closed doors?
- What alliances within my library and organization do I need to make in order to help push the integration of learning?
- Should I have an action plan to accomplish these alliances?
- How proactive can I be?
- Where should I start?
- Have I accurately identified the stakeholders within the library and organization?
- Do I know how people learn in this library?
- Are supports in place to help them?
- What evidence is there that this library values learning?
- What can I do to help demonstrate the value of learning?
- Do employees at both ends of the longevity range get the message equally? That is, do senior employees as well as new employees know that they are expected to learn at work—from each other, by themselves, and from the work that they do?
- Do I know deep down in my heart that leadership means having followers?
- Do I conduct myself in such a way that followers happen?
- Do I earn my authority, not grab it?

LOOK AROUND

Take a look at your organization and your supervisory style. Find out if there is recognition, collaboration, listening, self-organization, and an emphasis on continuous improvement and pride in doing a job well.

- Recognition. See if recognition is lopsided in your organization and your department. Are some categories of jobs or some particular individuals always getting the lion's share of recognition? Libraries often need help in training employees to seek recognition and to give it to others who deserve it. Trusting relationships often depend on equal opportunity for recognition. All persons at all levels and in all kinds of jobs like to be recognized for what they do and for what they know.
- Collaboration. Are there rewards for seeking help, coaching, mentoring, one-to-one teaching, working in teams? If not, help to make "teamwork" more than a nice slogan and train employees in effective ways to collaborate.
- Listening. Encourage students to listen so that they hear; try to break the great American cultural habit of "speaking up" and talking fast. It's a matter of trusting the other person to be at least as wise as you are. Listening builds trust, and it is often very hard to do. Training can help.
- Self-organization. Help your coworkers and student employees to practice a "bottom-up" way of working, not a "top-down" way. People at work have very good ideas about the way in which their own jobs should be done. Get rid of rules that reinforce the top-down command and control way of organizing work. Train all employees in bottom-up approaches. Individuals on the front line with customers or at the beginning of processes need authority and support to conduct their jobs the best way they know how for the good of the library.
- Continuous improvement. Encourage everyone at all levels, in all kinds of jobs, to build quality in. Think of errors and mistakes as your friends, not as enemies. Catch the problems early, as soon as you see them. Train all employees to feel and act responsibly about feedback, in all work processes and products and at all times. Reward those who find errors the earliest; don't reward "cover your tail" behavior.
- Take pride in doing the job well. Look for individuals who are proud of what they know and how they perform their jobs. Publicize, recognize, and reward the acquisition of new skills and the development of existing skills. Make known widely the high standards by which certain jobs are done; spread the good news and make it skill-specific. Facilitate acquisition of skills at all levels through staff development.

BIBLIOGRAPHY

Allan, Barbara. *Training Skills for Library Staff*. Lanham, MD: Scarecrow Press, 2003.

Beard, Colin, John P. Wilson. *The Power of Experiential Learning: A Handbook for Trainers and Educators*. Sterling, VA: Stylus Pub., 2002.

Beck, Sara Ramser, ed. *Library Training for Staff and Customers*. New York: Haworth Information Press, 2000.

Foshay, Wellesley R., Kenneth H. Silber, and Michael B. Stelnicki. *Writing Training Materials that Work : How to Train Anyone to Do Anything: A Practical Guide for Trainers Based on Current Cognitive Psychology and ID Theory and Research*. San Francisco, CA: Jossey-Bass/Peiffer, 2003.

Marczely, Bernadette. *Personalizing Professional Growth: Staff Development that Works*. Thousand Oaks, CA: Corwin Press, 1996.

Martin, Allan and Hannelore Rader, eds. *Information and IT Literacy: Enabling Learning in the 21st Century*. London: Facet, 2003.

Massis, Bruce Eduward. *The Practical Library Trainer*. Binghamton, NY: Haworth Information Press, 2004.

Pymm, Bob and Damon D. Hickey. *Learn Library Management.* Lanham, MD: Scarecrow Press, 2003.

Trotta, Marcia. *Supervising Staff: A How-To-Do-It Manual for Librarians.* New York: Neal-Schuman, 2006.

Turner, Anne M. *It Comes with the Territory: Handling Problem Situations in Libraries.* Jefferson, NC: McFarland & Co., 2004.

14

Effective Management
of Student Employment

The difficult things of this world must once have been easy; the great things of this world must once have been small. Set about difficult things while they are still easy; do great things while they are still small.

—Lao Tzu (sixth century B.C.)

SO WHAT MAKES A GOOD SUPERVISOR?

Do you know what happens to most really good employees? They are asked to be supervisors so they can teach others how to do all the great things they do that make really good employees shine. Unfortunately, most really good employees do what they do naturally, and doing good work doesn't always translate into being a good leader, manager, or supervisor. So what makes a good supervisor? Everyone's style is different, but in my experience, a boss tells you what to do, a manager motivates you to do stuff, and a leader inspires you to be the best at what you do. A good supervisor is all three at times but most importantly, a good supervisor is a leader.

NOW FOR THE UNPLEASANT PART—DISCIPLINE AND DISCHARGE!

Two of the most unpleasant responsibilities of your job as supervisor are disciplining and terminating student employees. The most emotionally difficult task is when you have to fire an employee. Termination is very difficult for the supervisor, for the person being fired, and for the other people in the department. Any supervisor who has fired a student employee realizes the importance of hiring the right people and training them well in order to reduce the possibility that an employee will have to be involuntarily terminated.

Disciplining and discharging student employees requires that specific procedures be followed. Those procedures should be spelled out in each university's personnel/student handbooks. What follows in this chapter are suggestions on how to handle discipline and discharge but readers are cautioned to pay close attention to their library/university policies and seek the advice of their supervisors and campus legal counsel as needed.

TERMINATION OF EMPLOYMENT

As surely as student employees will be hired, they will terminate employment in the library. The very nature of student employment requires turnover in student employee positions. After all, they are students first and it is our hope and theirs that they will graduate. Termination of employment, as used here, is the process by which student employee end their employment in the library, whether voluntary (resigned) or involuntary (fired).

All terminations of employment may be categorized as one of the following:

1) Resignation. The vast majority of terminations are resignations at the employee's request (VOLUNTARY).
2) Release. Some employees are released when temporary jobs are completed (INVOLUNTARY, but usually known beforehand).
3) Relieved. Employees terminated during a probationary period are considered to have been relieved (INVOLUNTARY).
4) Layoff. In the case of a reduction in force or lack of work, employees may be laid off (INVOLUNTARY).
5) Discharge. Terminated for cause (INVOLUNTARY).

Resignation

Most student employees leave the library through resignation. While not usually specifically required, student employees are asked to give two weeks notice of resignation in order to allow supervisors to plan for replacements. In some organizations, employees are considered to have resigned if they walk off the job, fail to report to work for their scheduled hours without permission to be absent for three consecutive work days, or fail to return to work within a prescribed period of time following a leave of absence.

Release

In some libraries, all student employees are considered temporary employees. As temporary employees, they are automatically terminated at the end of each semester, academic year, or summer session and must be rehired in order to continue working during the next award period. This process allows the student employment office to clear its files for a new allocation period.

Relieved

A probationary period for all new student employees of three to six months is utilized by many libraries. The student employees are being trained and it is important for the supervisor to make an assessment of progress during this period. If a student employee appears to be ill-suited for the job, cannot perform the work, or will not work out for whatever reason, this is the time to terminate the employee. In most cases, probationary employees may be terminated any time prior to the completion of the probationary period without recourse. Employees terminated before the expiration of their probationary periods are usually not allowed to avail themselves of the grievance and appeal process.

Layoff

Student employees may be terminated because of a reduction in force due to lack of funds, lack of work, or other compelling reasons. Selection of student employees for layoff should be made on the basis of qualifications and performance but may be made on the basis of seniority if all are substantially equal.

Discharge

Sometimes referred to as "terminate," "fire," "let go," "dismiss," or even "de-recruit," this is the last resort for supervisors who have exhausted all the means available to remedy the situation. Whatever it is called, this is an unpleasant event for both parties—the supervisor and the employee. A student employee should be discharged when the seriousness of the matter is such that the student employee should not be permitted to remain on the library's payroll.

Before resorting to the termination process, the supervisor should provide the student employee with an opportunity to become aware of and correct the misconduct or substandard performance in order to restore the employee as a productive member of the work group through corrective discipline.

REASONS FOR TERMINATION

Termination, as used here, is the process by which the student employee ceases working for the library, whether it be voluntary (resigned) or involuntary (fired or discharged). The following is a list of reasons for termination:

Lack of Work
__ Reduction in force
__ Job eliminated
__ Reorganization
__ End of temporary employment
__ End of seasonal employment
__ Project completed
__ Partially unemployed reduced hours
__ Temporary

Quit
__ Reason unknown
__ Abandoned job
__ Walked off job
__ Did not return from leave
__ Did not return from layoff

__ Personal – not job related
__ Returned to school
__ Marriage
__ Relocated
__ Family obligations
__ Unable to obtain babysitter
__ Transportation
__ Accepted another job
__ Go into business
__ Illness
__ Maternity
__ Enter military
__ Dissatisfaction – work hours
__ Dissatisfaction – salary
__ Dissatisfaction – working conditions
__ Dissatisfaction – performance review
__ Dissatisfaction – supervisor
__ Dissatisfaction – policies

Discharge
__ Insubordination
__ Violation of rules or policies
__ Violation of safety rules
__ Reported under influence of alcohol
__ Reported under influence of drugs
__ Destruction of property—willful
__ Destruction of property—carelessness
__ Fighting
__ Leaving work station
__ Falsification of employment application
__ Dishonesty—falsified records
__ Dishonesty—unauthorized removal of property
__ Dishonesty—monetary theft
__ Dishonesty—other
__ Absenteeism—unreported
__ Absenteeism—excessive and/or unauthorized
__ Tardiness—frequent
__ Excessive garnishments
__ Quality of work
__ Quantity of work
__ Poor performance
__ Probationary—not qualified for job
__ Poor judgement—no misconduct
__ Lack of technical knowledge
__ Inability to work—illness

Miscellaneous
__ No information whatsoever
__ Refusal to work

___ Disciplinary suspension
___ Death

REDUCING THE NUMBER OF PROBLEM EMPLOYEES

It is not possible to entirely avoid having problem employees who must be disciplined and/or discharged but there are ways to reduce their number:

1) Don't hire persons who provide clues during the interview that there may be problems.
2) Train new employees thoroughly.
3) Make sure new employees understand organizational rules and policies and the consequences of breaking those rules or violating library or university policies.
4) Take advantage of the probationary period. Don't hesitate to let a student employee go before or at the end of a probationary period if they are not performing satisfactorily. Terminating an employee during a probationary period is much easier than doing it later.
5) Review employee performance at regular intervals and deal with problems as they occur.
6) Don't pawn off your problem employees on another student employee supervisor. Deal with your own problems.
7) Before you discharge an employee, be certain that progressive discipline is not called for instead.

For suggestions on how to deal with specific problems, consult the section, Student Employee Problem Resolution.

CORRECTIVE DISCIPLINE

Corrective discipline, also called progressive discipline, is designed to make employees aware of misconduct or poor performance and to give them an opportunity to correct their behavior or improve their performance. The first step in corrective discipline is to give the employee a verbal warning for minor infractions or to correct poor performance. A written warning addressed to the employee is used if the infraction or deficiency is of a more serious nature or if the employee does not heed the verbal warning. An employee may be suspended without pay for serious offenses or for continued poor performance or misconduct after previous attempts to bring about improvement have been unsuccessful. Termination is not necessarily a corrective discipline step but may be the result if previous steps of corrective discipline do not result in the desired behavior.

It is not essential that the steps be followed sequentially. Each situation must be judged independently and appropriate action taken. A specific situation may require, for example, a written warning or suspension as a first step or, in some instances, immediate discharge. The following are examples of when a particular step is called for:

- *Verbal warning.* Substandard work performance, unexcused absences, or tardiness.
- *Written warning.* Continued substandard work performance, unexcused absences, or tardiness.
- *Suspension.* Continuation of the above behaviors, insubordination, drinking or intoxication, gambling, fighting, or sleeping on the job.

The warnings and suspension are intended to allow an individual to correct a situation. The last step or first and only step in some situations is termination. The following are examples of when discharge is appropriate:

• *Discharge.* Applicable to all previously listed examples if continued after attempts to correct, and all of the actions listed in the earlier section on just cause for termination.

Before taking any corrective discipline steps, supervisors and managers are advised to consult with the appropriate authorities in the library and/or governing body.

PREDISCHARGE RIGHTS OF PUBLIC EMPLOYEES

One of the most important aspects of public employment is job security. Classified employees are given a "property interest" in their jobs that cannot be taken away without "due process of law" in order to put them beyond the reach of partisan political retaliation. The rights of classified employees were established by the Lloyd-LaFollette Act of 1932.[1] The act provided classified public employees the right to postdischarge appeals and established the concept of property interest for nonprobationary public employees. Under the act, the employee must receive a written copy of the charges against him or her and a reasonable period of time in which to respond in writing to the charges.

The Supreme Court ruled in the 1985 case of *Cleveland Board of Education v. Loudermill* that "the tenured public employee is entitled to oral or written notice of the charges against him, an explanation of the employer's evidence, and an opportunity to present his side of the story." It noted that "where the employer perceives a significant hazard in keeping the employee on the job, it can avoid the problem by a suspension with pay."[2] These then are the predischarge rights of public employees. When a public employee is "Loudermilled," the letter of notice has been delivered as specified in the Supreme Court ruling.

STEPS TO TAKE BEFORE TERMINATING AN EMPLOYEE

The first rule in any disciplinary situation is document, document, document. It is doubly true for situations in which the employee is to be discharged. The following steps should be followed in every situation except those instances where an employee should be immediately terminated:

1. Implement the appropriate corrective discipline steps.
2. Gather all of the facts, including any that the employee may add.
3. Determine whether there is a policy that calls for discharge in this situation and be prepared to cite it.
4. Determine whether or not the employee is or should be aware of the policy.
5. Determine whether or not, in similar situations, exceptions have been made to the policy.
6. Be absolutely certain that discrimination is not involved, especially if the individual is a member of a protected class.
7. Be absolutely certain that this action is not retaliation for an earlier, unrelated act.
8. Determine whether or not this termination will make the employee a "martyr," and if so, prepare to deal with that issue with employees who remain.
9. Make certain that the employee's file contains the proper documentation supporting the termination.

10. At the time of actual termination, arrange to have another manager present.

11. Make certain that the procedures used in this termination are the same as those used in previous terminations.

HOW TO TERMINATE AN EMPLOYEE

Before terminating an employee, make certain that the previous eleven steps have been taken. There must be written documentation defining and supporting the termination. The termination of an employee for poor performance should never come as a surprise to him or her. Through proper training, coaching, and corrective discipline steps if necessary, employees should always know where they stand. For those employees who must be terminated, however, consideration must be given to the termination interview itself and to what can and must be communicated to other employees about the termination.

Let's say that, based on all of the above-mentioned information, the decision has been made to terminate an employee. The following questions must be answered *before* calling in the employee:

1. Who should terminate the employee? The employee's supervisor must be the one who delivers the message, however, another manager should be present as a witness and for support.

2. Where should the termination meeting be held? The meeting must held in a confidential setting, ideally in an empty office or conference room. That way, when you are through with the meeting, you can leave. It is difficult to walk out of your own office, and it may be difficult to get the terminated employee to leave.

3. When should the termination meeting be held? When planning the termination meeting, review the individual's file. To lessen the impact, avoid termination on the employee's birthday or anniversary date. Consider the employee's medical and emotional state. Does the employee anticipate termination? Friday or the day before a holiday are the worst days to conduct terminations of employees. The termination meeting should be held early in the week.

4. What will the employee be told? You and the employee may want to discuss resignation instead of termination, if that is an option. If resignation is not an option, the termination message should be clear and irrevocable. Avoid debates and rehashes of the past. Do not allow the employee to trap you into "who said what" discussions. Make it clear that the decision has been made and that the decision is final. Be empathetic but uncompromising. Know ahead of time what you plan to say, and don't let the meeting become sidetracked. Make it mercifully brief.

After the termination meeting, you will also have to resolve these questions:

1. What will the individual's coworkers be told?

2. What will persons who inquire for references be told?

THE IMPACTS OF TERMINATION

Although announcement of resignations, retirements, and other voluntary terminations are often followed by departmental get-togethers, well wishes, and friendly farewells, involuntary terminations are seldom occasions for celebration. In nearly every involuntary termination, both the individuals involved and the library itself are negatively affected. The greatest impact, of course, is felt by the individual who has been discharged. Studies have shown that the level of emotional stress following termination can equal the stress of being told that one is dying of an incurable disease. The individual first suffers shock and anger, followed by the certainty that a mistake has been made. After a series of mood swings, the discharged employee may experience a period of depression. Finally, self-confidence returns. The severity of these experiences differs from individual to individual, but regardless of severity, the termination has an impact on each individual.

Coworkers may experience a mixture of shock and excitement over the news, expressing such conflicting statements as "I'm glad it didn't happen to me," "It could happen to me," "I'm sorry it happened to him," "I'm glad it finally happened to him," "I'm angry with the person who fired him," and "I wonder who's next." Employees reactions will be affected by how well the terminated employee was liked, their perceptions of the events surrounding the termination, and their opinions of the supervisor and the administration.

The supervisor of the terminated employee may experience guilt and self-pity for having to take the action, while feeling compassion for the terminated employee. Presumably the decision to discharge has been made only after the supervisor has taken every step possible to avoid the discharge. Thus, although the supervisor must be able to show compassion and empathy for the terminated employee, at the same time, he or she should feel comfortable in the correctness of the decision and the procedures taken. It is important that the terminated employee receives whatever assistance possible in finding another position if requested.

Every termination has its own circumstances and resulting impacts. The supervisor must be able to deal with his or her own emotions as the terminator, with the emotions of the individual terminated, and with the emotions of coworkers. A termination is successful when it is done objectively, humanely, and cleanly. It is a good termination when it can honestly be said that the result was best for all involved.

MISTAKES MADE IN TERMINATIONS

The following mistakes made in terminations may lead to charges of discrimination or unfair treatment by persons who are terminated.

1. Documentation was lacking.
2. Performance evaluations were poorly done or not done at all.
3. The employee was unaware of the policy or that termination could be the result of his or her actions.
4. The employee was given regular salary increases, which he or she interpreted as merit increases. In some cases, merit increases may have been given.
5. The employee was treated differently than others in similar jobs.
6. The employee had not been given sufficient help to correct substandard performance.
7. The employee had not been given a definite set of performance standards.
8. The employee was given too many "second chances."
9. The wrong person was selected to handle the termination.
10. The reasons for termination were not made clear and unequivocal.
11. Possible severe emotional reactions were not anticipated.

12. Lawsuits were not anticipated.
13. The effects on remaining employees were not anticipated.

CONSTRUCTIVE DISCHARGE

In order to make a case that he or she was wrongfully discharged, the former employee must be able to show that he or she was in fact discharged. "Terminated," "fired," "let go," "dismissed," "discharged," and "given a pink slip" all mean the same thing: You've been fired. But sometimes the sequence of events isn't quite so clear-cut. There are cases when a court will decide an employee was fired even though the individual quit because of "constructive discharge." Constructive discharge occurs when the employer does something that makes it virtually impossible for the employee to continue on the job. For example, the court may find that an employee was constructively discharged if the employer changed working conditions, which, in turn, caused the employee to quit. The change must have been recent enough to draw a cause-and-effect relationship between the change and the resignation, and the change in working conditions has to have been so demeaning or upsetting that any reasonable person in the same situation would have quit. Being able to prove that an individual was constructively discharged is important in determining whether the former employee will receive unemployment compensation.

GROSS MISCONDUCT

Gross misconduct is one of the many just causes for termination of employees. Case law has defined gross misconduct as one of the following:

- deliberate or negligent disregard of the employer's interest;
- deliberate violations of reasonable standards of conduct set by the employer;
- behavior so careless or negligent as to amount to wrongful intent.

The court, in *Paris v. Korbel & Brothers, Inc.*, noted that inefficiency, poor conduct or performance, ordinary negligence, and errors in judgment are not enough for termination on the grounds of gross misconduct.[3]

QUESTIONS ASKED BY NEW SUPERVISORS

How is this book different from all of the other employee supervision handbooks?

- This book is not designed for the first-line supervisor in a manufacturing plant, or for the meat department manager at your local supermarket. This book is written specifically for the librarian or staff member who has responsibility for the supervision of student employees by librarians with more than 20 years of experience in managing programs, staff, and student employees. It contains information basic to an understanding of supervision, student employment, and libraries and offers advice on translating management/supervision literature into usable information for library staff. If you have read sections of this book, you will have noticed that the authors have injected suggestions, opinions, and bits of advice throughout. The authors, without giving away their ages, have over 50 years of supervision experience.

Will I have to change to become a supervisor?

- Yes and no. You may have to change some of your behaviors when you become a supervisor but you will not change your basic personality. As a supervisor, you will be the same person you were before but while you should continue to be friendly, you may become less intimate with your employees. You should continue to be relaxed, but you may have to be conscious of setting a good example for your employees. You should continue to be supportive of library goals and policies, but if you have complaints or challenges to library policy, you will take them up with your colleagues or management, not with your employees. You will know when you have made the change from employee to supervisor when you start referring to library management as "we", not "they".

Why do beginning supervisors feel underpaid?

- Many new supervisors feel that their new responsibilities are so great that the difference in pay as a worker and as a supervisor is not worth it. The change in responsibilities sometimes seems overwhelming at first, but given time, the new supervisor will gain control. Secondly, it may be that the salary difference is not enough for the work involved, but it is a price one pays to reach higher levels and salaries later. The new supervisor must take the long view. This experience can help you decide whether supervision is something you wish to develop further, perhaps leading to supervision of other staff, or a unit or department leadership position.

How much can I depend on other supervisors?

- How much you can depend on other supervisors for help and advice depends on the kind of supervisors they are. In most cases, you will find that other supervisors can be of tremendous help. A good rule to follow is to seek and accept help or advice from other supervisors based on your knowledge of their skills. You are better off following your own instincts than seeking poor advice from another supervisor. Your own supervisors can be an excellent source of help but if you disagree with them, tactfully explain why. Ask the same question of several supervisors. You will soon learn whom you can go to for help.

Where else can I turn for help?

- You couldn't work in a more ideal setting when it comes to information. There are many excellent books on supervision, many of which are listed in the bibliography of this and other chapters of this handbook. Examine the supervision books and find one that best matches your supervisory style. You will also find information on supervision in the periodical literature. Four of the best periodicals containing articles for the practitioner are *Personnel*, *Personnel Journal*, *Supervision*, and *Supervisory Management*. Another excellent source may be your library's human resources person. Part of that person's role in the library is to advise managers and supervisors, especially with regard to employment practices and policies.

Is education important to advancement?

- Formal education is the best route to advancement, so take advantage of the opportunities provided by working for a university. Watch for workshops and training sessions offered through the university that will improve your skills. Experience combined with strong motivation also helps you advance. Demonstrating that you have the skills for supervision will go a long ways toward helping you succeed.

How do I cope with too much work?

- There are countless demands on your time and many of them are beyond your control. Your primary responsibility is to react calmly and keep your unit functioning while trying to squeeze in time for planning. Do your planning at home if you have to in order to get control. That planning will eventually help you to better react to all of the demands placed on you. Most supervisors of student employees also perform other job responsibilities such as cataloging, reference, selection, and instruction. Supervision may only be a portion of your job but it can consume a lot of hours. Review the section on time management in this handbook and find a way to control your time.

How can I get everything done?

- Planning is the key. Your job probably involves getting many rather routine tasks accomplished while trying to deal with all of the unplanned-for events in the workday. First, complete those routine tasks that you must perform to free yourself for more creative work and delegate, delegate, delegate. You will find it difficult at first to let go of the responsibilities you had as a worker but let them go you must. Do not allow yourself to get bogged down with routine tasks, even though they may be what you want to do. If they can be delegated, do so.

What should I do when/if I get discouraged?

- As mentioned before, supervision is not for everyone. It is a talent as well as a skill that can be developed. There are countless cases of good workers becoming promoted to supervisory positions in which they fail miserably. One piece of advice—accept a supervisory role on a conditional basis if possible with the understanding that you can return to the role you excel at. Taking on the supervision of student employees can be an excellent way to get started. While you may well have the talent for supervision, too many good workers become poor supervisors who then are either unhappy or find themselves in other jobs as good workers for someone else. So, needless to say, getting discouraged is a possibility. If you get so discouraged with your supervisory role that you feel you should resign, go to your supervisor or someone else you trust and then discuss the problem openly and honestly. It is not unusual for the new supervisor to become discouraged. It happens to nearly everyone because the adjustment is more difficult than you think. Talking things over occasionally will help you survive until you get things under control and become accustomed to the supervisory role. Resigning without talking things over with someone would be foolhardy. Remember that you are not alone. All veteran supervisors have experienced many of the same feelings you have when they were beginning to supervise.

How can I be certain that I want to be a supervisor?

- To be fair to yourself, plan to spend at least a year before making a firm commitment or requesting a change. Whether or not you should continue as a supervisor, you need to feel that you are performing close to your potential in the supervisory role and that you are able to cope with your multiple responsibilities. It may take longer than a year to know whether or not supervisory responsibilities satisfy your needs for a fulfilling, stimulating work experience. If supervision is not for you, life is far too short to spend so many hours a week doing something you don't enjoy.

Where will I be in five years?

- As soon as you have become a capable supervisor, you will be able to do some career planning. As a supervisor, you have more freedom to establish and reach career goals than if you were a worker only. Set realistic goals and don't become frustrated if you don't advance as quickly as you hoped. Much will depend on circumstances and events beyond your control but all libraries need good supervisors at all levels. Your success in the supervision of student employees will translate very well to the supervision of other staff.

How will I know when I have developed a leadership style?

- It may take a few years to develop a leadership style that works as well as you would like. You will know when you have developed a style when you feel comfortable with yourself and when those you supervise feel comfortable with you. Your department or unit will function efficiently and without turmoil. Your reputation will grow as a good supervisor but even then, don't become complacent. There will always be room for improvement.

In a few words, what is the best advice for supervisors?

- As a new supervisor of student employees, you should ask questions, seek advice, never stop learning, and the best advice, "trust yourself, you know more than you think."

NOTES

1. The processes specified in the Lloyd-LaFollette Act were incorporated into the 1978 Civil Services Reform Act.
2. *Cleveland Board of Education v. Loudermill*, 105 S. Ct. 1487 (1985), p. 1495.
3. *Paris v. Korbel & Brothers, Inc.*, U.S. District Court, Northern California, No. C-89-1278 TEH, March 14, 1990.

BIBLIOGRAPHY

Bies, Robert, Christopher Martin, and Joel Brockner. "Just Laid Off, But Still a 'Good Citizen?' Only If the Process Is Fair." *Employee Responsibilities and Rights Journal* 6(3) (September 1993): 227.

Dilts, David A., and Clarence R. Deitsch. "The Tests of Just Cause: What Price Predictability in Arbitral Decision Making." *Employee Responsibilities and Rights Journal* 5(1) (March 1992): 13.

Documenting the Hiring Process and Documenting the Termination Process. Columbus, OH: Ohio CLE Institute, 1997.

Dworkin, Terry Morehead, and Melissa S. Baucus. "Wrongful Firing in Violation of Public Policy: Who Gets Fired and Why." *Employee Responsibilities and Rights Journal* 7(3) (September 1994): 191.

Effective Interviews for Every Situation: Hiring, Performance Appraisal, Discipline, Promotion, Problem-Solving, Termination. Maywood, NJ: Alexander Hamilton Institute, 1996.

Emerging Issues in Public Sector Labor/Employment Law. Minneapolis, MN: Minnesota Institute of Legal Education, 1997.

Fox, Jeremy B., and Hugh D. Hindman. "The Model Employment Termination Act: Provisions and Discussion." *Employee Responsibilities and Rights Journal* 6(1) (March 1993): 33.

Hiring and Firing. Minneapolis, MN: Minnesota Institute of Legal Education, 1997.

How to Hire Right, Fire Right: Managing Within the Law. Pittsburgh, PA: Buchanan Ingersoll Professional Corporation, 1996.

Jacobs, Carol S. "The Use of the Exit Interview as a Personnel Tool and Its Applicability to Libraries." *Journal of Library Administration* 14(4) (1991): 69.

Joel, Lewin G. *Every Employee's Guide to the Law: Everything You Need to Know About Your Rights in the Workplace—And What to Do If They Are Violated.* New York: Pantheon Books, 1996.

Johnson, Kathryn A. "Constructive Discharge and 'Reasonable Accommodation' Under the Americans with Disabilities Act." *University of Colorado Law Review* 65(1) (1993): 175.

Kaplan, Andrew B. "How to Fire Without Fear." *The Personnel Administrator* 34(3) (September 1989): 74.

———. "How to Avoid Wrongful Discharge Lawsuits." *Journal of Accountancy* 169(5) (May 1990): 87.

Kelley, Mark W. "Constructive Discharge: A Suggested Standard for West Virginia and Other Jurisdictions." *West Virginia Law Review* 93(4) (Summer 1991): 1047.

Klaas, Brian, and Hoyt Wheeler. "Supervisors and Their Response to Poor Performance: A Study of Disciplinary Decision Making." *Employee Responsibilities and Rights Journal* 5(4) (December 1992): 339.

Kriegler, Roy. "Dismissal: Employee Rights and Procedural Fairness." *Law Institute Journal* 65(12) (December 1991): 1158.

Legal Issues in Managing Difficult Employees. Walnut Creek, CA: Council on Education in Management, 1994.

Morin, William J., and Lyle Yorks. *Dismissal: There Is No Easy Way But There Is a Better Way.* New York: Drake Beam Morin, 1990.

Petersen, Donald J. "Quits, Recision of Quits and Constructive Discharge in Arbitration." *Employee Responsibilities and Rights Journal* 3(2) (June 1990): 125.

———. "The Arbitration of Fighting Cases." *The International Journal of Conflict Management* 2(3) (July 1991): 201.

"Promoting Fairness: A Proposal for a More Reasonable Standard of Constructive Discharge in Title VII Denial of Promotion Cases." *The Fordham Urban Law Journal* 19(4) (Summer 1992): 979.

Shepard, Ira Michael. *Workplace Privacy: Employee Testing, Surveillance, Wrongful Discharge, and Other Areas of Vulnerability*, 2nd ed. Washington, D.C.: Bureau of National Affairs, 1989.

Sylvia, Ronald D. *Public Personnel Administration.* Fort Worth, TX: Harcourt Brace College Publishers, 1994.

Termination of Employment: Employer and Employee Rights. Boston, MA: Warren Gorham Lamont, 1996.

Thornton, Gene R. "Labor and Employment Review: Rights of Terminated Employees: Expanding Remedies." *Colorado Lawyer* 21(8) (August 1, 1992): 1639.

"Who Says Quitters Never Win?" *Small Business Report* 19(10) (October 1994): 45.

"Wrongful Discharge: Recovery for Emotional Distress Damages Caused by Discharge Based on Workers' Compensation Claim." *Law Reporter* 34(2) (March 1991): 74.

Wrongful Employment Termination Practice, 2nd ed. Berkeley, CA: Continuing Education of the Bar–California, 1997.

Youngblood, Stuart, Linda Trevino, and Monica Favia. "Reactions to Unjust Dismissal and Third-Party Dispute Resolution: A Justice Framework." *Employee Responsibilities and Rights Journal* 5(4) (December 1992): 283.

Glossary of Financial Aid Terms

The process of awarding student financial aid has grown more complex over the years and, as a result, has developed its own vocabulary. At times it may seem as though discussions of financial aid are conducted in a foreign language. To help reduce confusion for students, parents, and student supervisors, this section presents common-sense definitions of many of the words used by financial aid professionals.

ACRONYMS

ACT	American College Testing Program
AFDC	Aid to Families with Dependent Children
AP	Advanced Placement
BIA	Bureau of Indian Affairs
CLEP	College-Level Examination Program
COA	Cost of Attendance
CPS	Central Processing System
CSS	College Scholarship Service
CWS	College Work-Study
ED	US Department of Education
EFC	Expected Family Contribution
EFT	Electronic Transfer of Funds
ELO	Expanded Lending Option
ESAR	Electronic Student Aid Report
ETS	Educational Testing Service
FAA	Financial Aid Administrator
FAF	Financial Aid Form
FAFSA	Free Application for Federal Student Aid
FAO	Financial Aid Office
FAT	Financial Aid Transcript

FDSLP	Federal Direct Student Loan Program
FFELP	Federal Family Education Loan Program
FSEOG	Federal Supplemental Educational Opportunity Grant
FM	Federal Methodology
FWS	Federal Work-Study
GPA	Grade Point Average
GSL	Guaranteed Student Loan
HEAL	Health Education Assistance Loan
HHS	U.S. Department of Health and Human Services
HPSL	Health Profession Student Loan
IM	Institutional Methodology
IRA	Individual Retirement Account
IRS	Internal Revenue Service
ISIR	Institutional Student Information Report
MDE	Multiple Data Entry
NHSC	National health corps Scholarship
NMSQT	National Merit Scholarship Qualifying Test
NSL	Nursing Student Loan
PC	Parent Contribution
PCL	Primary Care Loan
PHEAA	Pennsylvania Higher Education Assistance Agency
PJ	Professional Judgment
PLUS	Parent Loan for Undergraduate Students
PSAT	Preliminary Scholastic Assessment Test
RA	Research Assistantship
ROTC	Reserve Officer Training Corps
SAP	Satisfactory Academic Progress
SAR	Student Aid Report
SAT	Scholastic Assessment Test
SC	Student Contribution
SEOG	Supplemental Educational Opportunity Grant
SLMA	Student Loan Marketing Association
SLS	Supplemental Loan for Students
SSIG	State Student Incentive Grants
TA	Teaching Assistantship
TOEFL	Test of English as a Foreign Language
USED	U.S. Department of Education
VA	Veterans Administration

DEFINITIONS

1040Form, 1040A Form, 1040EZ Form
The Federal Income Tax Return. Every person who has received income during the previous year must file a form 1040 with the IRS by April 15.

1090Form
IRS form 1090 is used by business to report income paid to a nonemployee. Banks use this form to report interest income.

401(k)
The 401(k) is one of several popular types of retirement funds. It is legal to borrow money from your 401(k) to help pay for your children's education.

Academic Year
The period during which school is in session, consisting of at least 30 weeks of instructional time. The school year typically runs from the beginning of September through the end of May at most colleges and universities.

Accrual Date
The accrual date is the date on which interest charges on an educational loan begin to accrue. See also Subsidized Loan.

Accrue
To accumulate.

Achievement Tests (SAT II)
The achievement tests are a collection of tests that measure the student's proficiency and accumulated knowledge of specific subject areas. Different schools require different achievement tests as part of their admissions requirements. Since March 1994, these tests are now known as the SAT II tests. See also SAT and ETS.

Adjusted Available Income
In the Federal Methodology, the remaining income after the allowances (taxes and a basic living allowance) have been subtracted.

Admit-Deny
Admit-Deny is a practice in which a school will admit marginal students, but not award them any financial aid. Very few schools use admit-deny, because studies have shown that lack of sufficient financial aid is a key factor in the performance of marginal students.

Advanced Placement Test (AP)
The Advanced Placement tests are used to earn credit for college subjects while in high school. They are offered by ETS in the spring. AP tests are scored on a scale from 1 to 5, with a 5 being the best possible score.

Alternative Loans
See Private Loans.

American College Test (ACT)
The ACT is one of the two national standardized college entrance examinations used in the United States. The other is the SAT. The ACT is widely used in the West and Midwest. Most universities require either the ACT or the SAT as part of an application for admission. See also PLAN.

Amortization
Amortization is the process of gradually repaying a loan over an extended period of time through periodic installments of principal and interest.

Appeal
An appeal is a formal request to have a financial aid administrator review your aid eligibility and possibly use Professional Judgment to adjust the figures. For example, if

you believe the financial information on your financial aid application does not reflect your family's current ability to pay (e.g., because of death of a parent, unemployment, or other unusual circumstances), you should definitely make an appeal. The financial aid administrator may require documentation of the special circumstances or of other information listed on your financial aid application.

Asset
An asset is an item of value, such as a family's home, business, and farm equity, real estate, stocks, bonds, mutual funds, cash, certificates of deposit (CDs), bank accounts, trust funds, and other property and investments.

Asset Protection Allowance
The asset protection allowance is a portion of your parents' assets that are not included in the calculation of the parent contribution, as calculated by the Federal Methodology need analysis formula. The asset protection allowance increases with the age of the parents.

Assistantship
See Graduate Assistantship.

Associate Degree
The degree granted by two-year colleges.

Award Letter
An award letter is an official document issued by the Financial Aid Office that lists all of the financial aid awarded to the student. This letter provides details on their analysis of your financial need and the breakdown of your financial aid package according to amount, source, and type of aid. The award letter will include the terms and conditions for the financial aid and information about the cost of attendance. You are required to sign a copy of the letter, indicating whether you accept or decline each source of aid, and return it to the financial aid office. Some schools call the award letter the "Financial Aid Notification (FAN)."

Award Year
The academic year for which financial aid is requested (or received).

Bachelor's Degree
The undergraduate degree granted by four-year colleges and universities.

Balloon Payment
A balloon payment is a larger than usual payment used to pay off the outstanding balance of a loan without penalty. Not all loans allow balloon payments. Simple interest loans, like many educational loans, generally do allow balloon payments.

Bankruptcy
When a person is declared bankrupt, he is found to be legally insolvent and his property is distributed among his creditors or otherwise administered to satisfy the interests of his creditors. Federal student loans, however, cannot normally be discharged through bankruptcy.

Base Year
The tax year prior to the academic year (award year) for which financial aid is requested. The base year runs from January 1 of the junior year in high school through December 31

of the senior year. Financial information from this year is used to determine eligibility for financial aid.

Borrower
The person who receives the loan.

Budget
See Cost of Attendance.

Bursar's Office
The Bursar's Office or Student Accounts Office is the university office that is responsible for the billing and collection of university charges.

Campus-based Aid
Campus-based financial aid programs are administered by the university. The federal government provides the university with a fixed annual allocation, which is awarded by the financial aid administrator to deserving students. Such programs include the Perkins Loan, Supplemental Education Opportunity Grant, and Federal Work-Study.

Note that there is no guarantee that every eligible student will receive financial aid through these programs, because the awards are made from a fixed pool of money. This is a key difference between the campus-based loan programs and the Direct Loan Program. Do not confuse the two, even though both loans are issued through the schools.

Cancellation
Some loan programs provide for cancellation of the loan under certain circumstances, such as death or permanent disability of the borrower. Some of the Federal student loan programs have additional cancellation provisions. For example, if the student becomes a teacher in certain national shortage areas, they may be eligible for cancellation of all or part of the balance of their educational loans.

Repayment assistance is available if you serve in the military. The military pays off a portion of your loans for every year of service.

Capital Gain
A capital gain is an increase in the value of an asset such as stocks, bonds, mutual funds, and real estate between the time the asset was purchased and the time the asset was sold.

Capitalization
The practice of adding unpaid interest charges to the principal balance of an educational loan, thereby increasing the size of the loan. Interest is then charged on the new balance, including both the unpaid principal and the accrued interest. Capitalizing the interest increases the monthly payment and the amount of money you will eventually have to repay. If you can afford to pay the interest as it accrues, you are better off not capitalizing it. Capitalization is sometimes called compounding. See also Unsubsidized Loans.

Collateral
Collateral is property that is used to secure a loan. If the borrower defaults on the loan, the lender can seize the collateral. For example, a mortgage is usually secured by the house purchased with the loan.

Collection Agency
A collection agency is often hired by the lender or guarantee agency to recover defaulted loans.

College Board

The College Board is a nonprofit educational association of colleges, universities, educational systems, and other educational institutions. For more information, see College Board Online (CBO).

College Work-Study (CWS)

College Work-Study is simply a part-time job. This term is sometimes erroneously used to refer to the Federal Work-Study Program.

Color of Federal Forms

The FAFSA and SAR change color each year in a four color rotation: Yellow (1995–1996), Pink (1996–1997), Green (1997–1998), and Blue (1998–1999). This will help you make sure you're filing the correct form.

Commuter Student

A student who lives at home and commutes to school every day.

Compounded Interest

Compounded interest is interest that is paid on both the principal balance of the loan and on any accrued (unpaid) interest. Capitalizing the interest on an unsubsidized Stafford loan is a form of compounding.

Consolidation Loan

A consolidation loan combines several student loans into one bigger loan from a single lender. The consolidation loan is used to pay off the balances on the other loans. Consolidation loans offer the following benefits:

- Consolidation loans often reduce the size of the monthly payment by extending the term of the loan beyond the 10-year repayment plan that is standard with FFELP loans. Depending on the loan amount, the term of the loan can be extended from 12 to 30 years. The reduced monthly payment may make the loan easier to repay for some borrowers. Of course, extending the term of a loan increases the total amount of interest paid.
- Consolidation loans also simplify the repayment process by allowing a single payment to one lender instead of several payments to different lenders.
- In certain circumstances—when one or more of the loans was being repaid in less than 10 years because of minimum payment requirements—a consolidation loan may decrease the monthly payment without extending the overall loan term beyond 10 years. In effect, the shorter term loan is being extended to 10 years. Of course, this means that the total amount of interest paid will increase. On the other hand, if you consolidate and opt to pay the same monthly payment as before, the total amount of interest paid will decrease.

Some graduate students have found it necessary to consolidate their educational loans when applying for a mortgage on a house. Consolidation loans can sometimes result in a lower interest rate, as when a consumer loan is used to pay off credit card balances. With educational loans, however, consolidation usually results in the same or higher interest rate. The interest rate on a consolidation loan is a weighted average of the interest rates on the consolidated loans, rounded up to the nearest whole percent. (The Federal Direct Consolidation Loan is a notable exception.) Consolidation can also eliminate deferment benefits, so it is unwise to consolidate while you are still in school.

Aside from the simplification of the repayment process, consolidation is usually not in the student's best interest. Instead, students who are having trouble making their payments should consider some of the alternate repayment terms provided for FFELP loans by the Higher Education Act of 1992. Income contingent payments, for example, are adjusted to compensate for a lower monthly income. Graduated repayment provides lower payments during the first two years after graduation. Extended repayment allows you to extend the term of the loan without consolidation. Although each of these options increases the total amount of interest paid, the increase is less than that caused by consolidation.

Cooperative Education
In a cooperative education program, the student spends some time engaged in employment related to their major in addition to regular classroom study.

Cosigner
A cosigner on a loan assumes responsibility for the loan if the borrower should fail to repay it.

Cost of Attendance
The cost of attendance (COA), also known as the cost of education or "budget," is the total amount it should cost the student to go to school. This amount includes tuition and fees, room and board, and allowances for books and supplies, transportation, and personal and incidental expenses. Loan fees, if applicable, may also be included in the COA. Child care and expenses for disabilities may also be included at the discretion of the financial aid administrator. Schools establish different standard budget amounts for students living on-campus and off-campus, married and unmarried students, and in-state and out-of-state students.

Credit Rating
A credit rating is an evaluation of the likelihood of a borrower to default on a loan.

Credit Bureaus and Credit Reporting Agencies provide credit information to creditors, such as banks and businesses, to help them decide whether to issue a loan or extend credit. This information may include your payment history, a list of current and past credit accounts and their balances, employment and personal information, and a history of past credit problems.

People who make all their payments on time are considered good credit risks. People who are frequently delinquent in making their payments are considered bad credit risks. Defaulting on a loan can negatively impact your credit rating.

A good credit rating is not required for most educational loans, with the exception of the PLUS Loan. However, students who have defaulted on previous educational loans may be required to agree to repay the loan and begin making payments before they can become eligible for further Federal aid.

Custodial Parent
If a student's parents are divorced or separated, the custodial parent is the one with whom the student lived the most during the past 12 months. The student's need analysis is based on financial information supplied by the custodial parent.

Default
A loan is in default when the borrower fails to pay several regular installments on time (i.e., payments overdue by 180 days) or otherwise fails to meet the terms and conditions

of the loan. If you default on a loan, the university, the holder of the loan, the state, and the federal government can take legal action to recover the money, including garnishing your wages and withholding income tax refunds. Defaulting on a government loan will make you ineligible for future federal financial aid, unless a satisfactory repayment schedule is arranged, and can affect your credit rating.

Deferment

Deferment occurs when a borrower is allowed to postpone repaying the loan. If you have a subsidized loan, the federal government pays the interest charges during the deferment period. If you have an unsubsidized loan, you are responsible for the interest that accrues during the deferment period. You can still postpone paying the interest charges by capitalizing the interest, which increases the size of the loan. Most federal loan programs allow students to defer their loans while they are in school at least half time. If you don't qualify for a deferment, you may be able to get a Forbearance. You can't get a deferment if your loan is in default.

Delinquent

If the borrower fails to make a payment on time, the borrower is considered delinquent and late fees may be charged. If the borrower misses several payments, the loan goes into default.

Dependency Status

A student's dependency status determines to what degree the student has access to parent financial resources. A parent refusing to provide support for their child's education is not sufficient for the child to be declared independent.

An independent student is one who is at least 24 years old as of January 1 (e.g., born before January 1, 1972 for academic year 1995–1996), is married, is a graduate or professional student, has a legal dependent other than a spouse, is a veteran of the U.S. Armed Forces, or is an orphan or ward of the court (or was a ward of the court until age 18). All other students are considered dependent.

If the financial aid administrator believes that you are not an independent student they can require you to provide proof of independent status to qualify, and their decision on your status is generally not subject to appeal.

For details on what constitutes a veteran, please see Veteran below.

See your financial aid administrator if you have any special circumstances. The FAA may be able to do an override of your dependency status on the FAFSA, if warranted by involuntary dissolution of the family or other very unusual situations. Special circumstances that are sometimes sufficient for an override include:

- a legal restraining order has been issued against your parents because of abusive behavior.
- both of your parents have been incarcerated.
- your parents live in another country and you have been being granted refugee status by the U.S. Immigration Service.
- your parents live in a country where they cannot easily leave or get money out.

You do not qualify for independent status just because your parents have decided to not claim you as an exemption on their tax returns or are refusing to provide support for your college education. You must provide documentation to the satisfaction of the financial aid administrator that you are truly self-supporting for them to override your dependency status. A few financial aid offices may require that you have a minimum annual income of $10,000 to establish self-sufficiency. [Several financial aid books suggest that all one needs to do for a student to become independent is for them to not be listed as a dependent on their parents' tax return for the past two years and for them to have earned at least $4,000 per year during the same period. This is the OLD definition of independence, and is no longer valid.]

Dependent

For a child or other person to be considered your dependent, they must live with you and you must provide them with more than half of their support. Spouses do not count as dependents in the Federal Methodology. You and your spouse cannot both claim the same child as a dependent.

Direct Loans

The William D. Ford Federal Direct Loan Program (aka the Direct Loan Program) is a new federal program where the school becomes the lending agency and manages the funds directly, with the federal government providing the loan funds. Not all schools currently participate in this program. Benefits of the program include a faster turnaround time and less bureaucracy than the old "bank loan" program. The terms for Direct Loans are the same as for the Stafford Loan program. For more information about Direct Loans, contact the Direct Loan Servicing Center at 1-800-848-0979.

Disbursement

Disbursement is the release of loan funds to the school for delivery to the borrower. The payment will be made copayable to the student and the school. Loan funds are first credited to the student's account for payment of tuition, fees, room and board, and other school charges. Any excess funds are then paid to the student in cash or by check. Unless the loan amount is under $500, the disbursement will be made in at least two equal installments.

Discharge

To discharge a loan is to release the borrower from his or her obligation to repay the loan. See also Cancellation.

Disclosure Statement

Lenders are required to provide the borrower with a disclosure statement before issuing a loan. The disclosure statement provides the borrower with information about the actual cost of the loan, including the interest rate, origination, insurance, and loan fees, and any other kinds of finance charges.

Doctorate

One of several degrees granted by graduate schools.

Due Diligence

If a borrower fails to make payments on their loan according to the terms of the promissory note, the federal government requires the lender, holder, or servicer of the loan to make frequent attempts to contact the borrower (via telephone and mail) to encourage him or her to repay the loan and make arrangements to resolve the delinquency.

Early Action

An early action program has earlier deadlines and earlier notification dates than the regular admissions process. Students who apply to an early action program do not commit to attending the school if admitted, unlike an early decision program. The Ivy League schools do not allow you to apply to more than one ivy early action. Do not confuse early action with early decision.

Early Admission
An early admission program allows gifted high school juniors to skip their senior year and enroll instead in college. The term "Early Admission" is sometimes used to refer collectively to Early Action and Early Decision programs.

Early Decision
An early decision program has earlier deadlines and earlier notification dates than the regular admissions process. Students who apply to an early decision program commit to attending the school if admitted. Unfortunately, this means the student has accepted the offer of admission before they find out about the financial aid package. Obviously, you can apply early decision to only one school. You should only participate in an early decision program if the school is your first choice and you won't want to consider other schools. Do not confuse early decision with early action.

EDE
EDE (Electronic Data Exchange) and EDExpress are programs used by participating schools to electronically receive SARs from the federal processor. At some schools EDE allows students to electronically file their Free Application for Federal Student Aid (FAFSA).

Educational Testing Service (ETS)
ETS is the company that produces and administers the SAT and other educational achievement tests. For more information, see their gopher.

Electronic Funds Transfer
Electronic Funds Transfer (EFT) is used by some schools and Stafford and Parent Loan lenders to wire funds for Stafford and PLUS loans directly to participating schools without requiring an intermediate check for the student to endorse. The money is transferred electronically instead of using paper, and hence is available to the student sooner. If you have a choice of funds transfer methods, use EFT.

Electronic Student Aid Report
An Electronic Student Aid Report (ESAR) is an electronic form of the Student Aid Report.

Eligible Noncitizen
Someone who is not a U.S. citizen but is nevertheless eligible for Federal student aid. Eligible noncitizens include U.S. permanent residents who are holders of valid green cards, U.S. nationals, holders of form I-94 who have been granted refugee or asylum status, and certain other noncitizens. Noncitizens who hold a student visa or an exchange visitor visa are not eligible for Federal student aid.

Emancipated
Declaring a child to be legally emancipated is not sufficient to release the parents or legal guardians from being responsible for providing for the child's education. If this were the case, then every parent would "divorce" their children before sending them to college. The criteria for a child to be found independent are much stricter. See Dependency Status for details.

Endowment

Funds owned by an institution and invested to produce income to support the operation of the institution. Many educational institutions use a portion of their endowment income for financial aid. A school with a larger ratio of endowment per student is more likely to give larger financial aid packages.

Enrollment Status

An indication of whether you are a full-time or part-time student. Generally you must be enrolled at least half time (and in some cases full time) to qualify for financial aid.

Entitlement

Entitlement programs award funds to ALL qualified applicants. The Pell Grant is an example of such a program.

Entrance Interview

See Loan Interviews.

Equity

Equity is the dollar value of your ownership in a piece of property. See, for example, Home Equity below.

Exit Interview

See Loan Interviews.

Expanded Lending Option

Under the Expanded Lending Option (ELO), some schools can offer higher annual and cumulative loan limits to students receiving the Perkins Loan. The ELO is restricted to schools with a Perkins Loan default rate of 15 percent or less.

Expected Family Contribution

The Expected Family Contribution (EFC) is the amount of money that the family is expected to be able to contribute to the student's education, as determined by the Federal Methodology need analysis formula approved by Congress. The EFC includes the parent contribution and the student contribution, and depends on the student's dependency status, family size, number of family members in school, taxable and nontaxable income, and assets. The difference between the COA and the EFC is the student's financial need, and is used in determining the student's eligibility for need-based financial aid.

If there are unusual financial circumstances, such as high medical expenses, loss of employment, or death of a parent, that may affect your ability to pay for your education, tell your financial aid administrator (FAA). He or she can adjust the COA or EFC to compensate. See Professional Judgment.

Financial Aid Form (FAF)

The Financial Aid Form (FAF) is the old name for the Financial Aid PROFILE. The Financial Aid PROFILE is a supplemental financial aid form processed by the College Scholarship Service (CSS). It is not necessary to file a Financial Aid PROFILE in order to apply for Federal student financial aid; the FAFSA is sufficient. The Financial Aid PROFILE is used by many private colleges and universities for awarding institutional funds.

Federal Direct Student Loan Program (FDSLP)

The Federal Direct Student Loan Program (FDSLP) is similar to the Federal Family Education Loan Program (FFELP). The funds for these loans are provided by the U.S. government directly to students and their parents through their schools. Benefits of the program include a faster turnaround time and less bureaucracy than the old "bank loan" program. The Federal Direct Student Loan Program (FDSLP) includes the Federal Direct Stafford Loan (Subsidized and Unsubsidized) and the Federal Direct Parent Loan for Undergraduate Students (PLUS). For more information about Direct Loans, contact the Direct Loan Servicing Center at 1-800-848-0979.

Federal Family Education Loan Program (FFELP)

The Federal Family Education Loan Program (FFELP) includes the Federal Stafford Loan (Subsidized and Unsubsidized), the Federal Perkins Loan, and the Parent Loan for Undergraduate Students (PLUS). The funds for these loans are provided by private lenders, such as banks, credit unions, and savings and loan associations. These loans are guaranteed against default by the federal government.

Federal Methodology

The Federal Methodology (FM) is the need analysis formula used to determine the EFC. The Federal Methodology takes family size, the number of family members in college, taxable and nontaxable income, and assets into account. Unlike most Institutional Methodologies, however, the Federal Methodology does not consider the net value of the family residence.

Federal Processor

The Federal Processor is the organization that processes the information submitted on the Free Application for Federal Student Aid (FAFSA) and uses it to compute eligibility for federal student aid. There are actually two different federal processors. ACT serves the east coast, Michigan, Wisconsin, Iowa, Alabama, Mississippi, and the Pacific islands. If you live in an area served by ACT, you will send in your FAFSA to the following address:

Federal Student Aid Programs
P.O. Box 4001
Mt. Vernon, IL 62864-8601

I-Net serves everyone else. If you live in an area served by I-Net, you will send in your FAFSA to the following address:

Federal Student Aid Programs
P.O. Box 60001
Cahokia, IL 62206-6001

It doesn't matter which processor an individual student uses; the only difference is in the address on the envelope that comes with the FAFSA and the address on the bottom of the last page of the form.

Federal Work-Study

The Federal Work-Study (FWS) program provides undergraduate and graduate students with part-time employment during the school year. The federal government pays a portion of the student's salary, making it cheaper for departments and businesses to hire the student. For this reason, work-study students often find it easier to get a part-time job. Eligibility for FWS is based on need. Money earned from an FWS job is not counted as income for the subsequent year's need analysis process.

Fellowship

A form of financial aid given to graduate students to help support their education. Some fellowships include a tuition waiver or a payment to the university in lieu of tuition. Most fellowships include a stipend to cover reasonable living expenses (e.g., just above the poverty line). Fellowships are a form of gift aid and do not have to be repaid.

Financial Aid

Money provided to the student and the family to help them pay for the student's education. Major forms of financial aid include gift aid (grants and scholarships) and self-help aid (loans and work).

Financial Aid Administrator

A Financial Aid Administrator (FAA) is a college or university employee who is involved in the administration of financial aid. Some schools call FAAs "Financial Aid Advisors" or "Financial Aid Counselors."

Financial Aid Notification (FAN)

See Award Letter.

Financial Aid Office

The Financial Aid Office (FAO) is the college or university office that is responsible for the determination of financial need and the awarding of financial aid.

Financial Aid Package

The financial aid package is the complete collection of grants, scholarships, loans, and work-study employment from all sources (federal, state, institutional, and private) offered to a student to enable them to attend the college or university. Note that un-subsidized Stafford loans and PLUS loans are not considered part of the financial aid package, since these financing options are available to the family to help them meet the EFC.

Financial Aid Transcript

The Financial Aid Transcript (FAT) is a record of all federal aid received by the student at each school attended. If you have previously attended an institution of higher education and are now applying for financial aid from the different university, the university will require an FAT from each of the schools previously attended, regardless of whether aid was received or not. They are required to do this by federal law. You have to submit an FAT even if you were in high school at the time. An electronic FAT process will be in place soon that will eliminate the need for the student to submit an FAT. The FAT is not the same as an academic transcript.

Financial Need

See Need.

Financial Safety School

A financial safety school is a school you are certain will admit you, and which is inexpensive enough that you can afford to attend even if you get no (or very little) financial aid.

First-Time Borrower
A first-time borrower is a first-year undergraduate student who has no unpaid loan balances outstanding on the date he or she signs a promissory note for an educational loan. First-time borrowers may be subjected to a delay in the disbursement of the loan funds. The first loan payment is disbursed 30 days after the first day of the enrollment period. If the student withdraws during the first 30 days of classes, the loan is canceled and does not need to be repaid. Borrowers with existing loan balances aren't subject to this delay.

Fixed Interest
In a fixed interest loan, the interest rate stays the same for the life of the loan.

Forbearance
During a forbearance the lender allows the borrower to temporarily postpone repaying the principal, but the interest charges continue to accrue, even on subsidized loans. The borrower must continue paying the interest charges during the forbearance period. Forbearances are granted at the lender's discretion, usually in cases of extreme financial hardship or other unusual circumstances when the borrower does not qualify for a deferment. You can't receive a forbearance if your loan is in default.

Free Application for Federal Student Aid (FAFSA)
The Free Application for Federal Student Aid (FAFSA) is used to apply for Pell Grants and all other need-based aid. An electronic version of the FAFSA called FAFSA Express will be available by disk in the 1997–1998 academic year. (Call 1-800-801-0576 for information about FAFSA Express.) As the name suggests, no fee is charged to file an FAFSA. The color of the 1997–1998 FAFSA is green.
  When filing an FAFSA, be sure to use an original form, not a photocopy. Photocopies of the form are unacceptable because photocopying alters the alignment of the forms, interfering with the imaging technology the federal processors use to process the forms.

Gapping
The practice of failing to meet a student's full demonstrated need. See also Unmet Need below.

Garnishment
Garnishment is the practice of withholding a portion of a defaulted borrower's wages to repay his or her loan, without their consent.

Gift Aid
Gift aid is financial aid, such as grants and scholarships, which does not need to be repaid.

Grace Period
The grace period is a short time period after graduation during which the borrower is not required to begin repaying his or her student loans. The grace period may also kick in if the borrower leaves school for a reason other than graduation or drops below half-time enrollment. Depending on the type of loan, you will have a grace period of six months (Stafford Loans) or nine months (Perkins Loans) before you must start making payments on your student loans. The PLUS Loans do not have a grace period.

Grade Point Average (GPA)

The GPA is an average of a student's grades, where the grades have been converted to a 4.0 scale, with 4.0 being an A, 3.0 being a B, and 2.0 being a C. Some schools use a 5.0 scale for the GPA.

Graduate Assistantship

There are two types of graduate assistantships: teaching assistantships (TA) and research assistantships (RA). TAs and RAs receive a full or partial tuition waiver and a small living stipend. TAs are required to perform teaching duties. RAs are required to perform research duties, not necessarily related to the student's thesis research.

Graduate Student

A student who is enrolled in a Masters or PhD program.

Graduated Repayment

Under a graduated repayment schedule, the monthly payments are smaller at the start of the repayment period, and gradually become larger.

Grant

A grant is a type of financial aid based on financial need that the student does not have to repay.

Gross Income

This is income before taxes, deductions, and allowances have been subtracted.

Guarantee Agency or Guarantor

Guarantee agencies are responsible for approving student loans and insuring them against default. Guarantee agencies also oversee the student loan process and enforce federal and state rules regarding student loans.

If a borrower defaults on an educational loan, the guarantee agency assumes responsibility for collecting the loan and repays the lender, usually at 98 cents on the dollar. (Legislation is pending to reduce this amount to 95 cents on the dollar.) This means that guaranteed educational loans are extremely low-risk loans for the lender, despite being unsecured.

Each state has a different guarantee agency that administers the Federal Stafford and Plus loans for students in that state. There are 41 guarantee agencies for educational loans in the United States. The state guarantee agency is the best source of information about FFELP loans in your state. Although the federal government sets the overall structure of the FFELP loan program (e.g., loan limits and interest rates), each state may set additional restrictions on the loans, within federal guidelines.

For the name, address, and telephone number of your state's guarantee agency, call the Federal Student Aid Information Center at 1-800-433-3243 (1-800-4-FED-AID). See also the State Aid and FFELP Guarantee Agencies page.

Guarantee Fee

A guarantee fee is a small percentage of the loan that is paid to the guarantee agency to insure the loan against default. The insurance fee is usually 1 percent of the loan amount (and by law cannot exceed 3 percent of the loan amount).

Guaranteed Student Loan (GSL)

The Guaranteed Student Loan (GSL) is the old name for the subsidized Stafford Loan. A guaranteed loan is a loan that is insured against default. In the case of guaranteed student loans, the Federal government agrees to repay the loans in case of default. Each loan is charged a guarantee fee to cover the costs of defaulted loans.

Half-Time
Most financial aid programs require that the student be enrolled at least half time to be eligible for aid. Some programs require the student to be enrolled full time.

Health Education Assistance Loan
The Health Education Assistance Loan (HEAL) is a low interest loan administered by the U.S. Department of Health and Human Services (HHS). It is available to medical school students pursuing medicine, osteopathy, dentistry, veterinary medicine, optometry, podiatry, clinical psychology, health administration, and public health. Undergraduate pharmacology students are also eligible.

Health Professions Student Loan
The Health Professions Student Loan (HPSL) is a low interest loan administered by the U.S. Department of Health and Human Services (HHS). It is now known as the Primary Care Loan (PCL).

Holder
The holder is the lender, institution, or agency that holds legal title to a loan. The holder may be the bank that issued the loan, a secondary market that purchased the loan from the bank, or a guarantee agency if the borrower defaulted on the loan.

Home Equity
Home equity is the current market value of the home less the mortgage's remaining unpaid principal. It is based on the market value, not the insurance or tax value. For a conservative estimate of your home's market value, try using the Federal Housing Index Calculator. See also Equity.

Horizontal Equity
The principle of horizontal equity is that families with similar financial circumstances should pay the same amount, regardless of how their assets, investments, and income are defined.

In-State Student
An in-state student has met the legal residency requirements for the state, and is eligible for reduced in-state student tuition at public colleges and universities in the state.

Income
Income is the amount of money received from employment (salary, wages, tips), profit from financial instruments (interest, dividends, capital gains), or other sources (welfare, disability, child support, Social Security, and pensions).

Income Contingent Repayment
Under an income contingent repayment schedule, the size of the monthly payments depends on the income earned by the borrower. As the borrower's income increases, so do the payments. The income contingent repayment plan is not available for PLUS Loans.

Independent Student
See Dependency Status.

Individual Retirement Account (IRA)

The IRA is one of several popular types of retirement funds. It is not legal to borrow money from your IRA to help pay for your children's education.

Installment Loan

An installment loan is a consumer loan in which the principal and interest are repaid on a regular (usually monthly) schedule. The payments are called "installments" and are all for the same amount.

Institutional Methodology

If a college or university uses its own formula to determine financial need for allocation of the school's own financial aid funds, the formula is referred to as the Institutional Methodology (IM).

Institutional Student Information Report

The Institutional Student Information Report (ISIR) is the name for the electronic version of SARs delivered to schools by EDExpress.

Insurance Fee

The insurance fee is passed on by the lender to the federal government as insurance against default. The insurance fees are charged as the loan is disbursed, and typically run to 1 percent of the amount disbursed. See also Guarantee Fee.

Interest

Interest is an amount charged to the borrower for the privilege of using the lender's money. Interest is usually calculated as a percentage of the principal balance of the loan. The percentage rate may be fixed for the life of the loan, or it may be variable, depending on the terms of the loan. As of October 1, 1992, all new federal loans use variable interest rates that are pegged to the cost of U.S. Treasury Bills.

Internship

An internship is a part-time job during the academic year or the summer months in which a student receives supervised practical training in their field. Internships are often very closely related to the student's academic and career goals, and may serve as a precursor to professional employment. Some internships provide very close supervision by a mentor in an apprenticeship-like relationship. Some internships provide the student with a stipend, some don't.

IRS

The Internal Revenue Service (IRS) is the federal agency responsible for enforcing U.S. tax laws and collecting taxes.

Lender

A lender is a bank, credit union, savings and loan association, or other financial institution that provides funds to the student or parent for an educational loan. Note: Some schools now participate in the Federal Direct Loan program and no longer use a private lender, since loan funds are provided by the U.S. government.

Leveraging

If a school offers a talented student extra financial aid, regardless of need, the student is more likely to enroll. Leveraging is the controversial practice of figuring out how much it will take to attract such students and customizing aid offers to optimize the quality of the incoming class.

Line of Credit
A line of credit is a pre-approved loan that lets you borrow money up to a preset credit limit, usually by writing checks. A line of credit doesn't cost you anything until you write a check, and then you begin repayment just like a regular loan.

Loan
A loan is a type of financial aid which must be repaid, with interest. The federal student loan programs (FFELP and FDSLP) are a good method of financing the costs of your college education. These loans are better than most consumer loans because they have lower interest rates and do not require a credit check or collateral. The Stafford Loans and Perkins Loans also provide a variety of deferment options and extended repayment terms.

Loan Forgiveness
Under certain circumstances, such as practicing medicine in a national shortage area or teaching in a rural region, the federal government will cancel all or part of an educational loan.

Loan Interviews
Students with educational loans are required to meet with a financial aid administrator before they receive their first loan disbursement and again before they graduate or otherwise leave school. During these counseling sessions, called entrance and exit interviews, the FAA reviews the repayment terms of the loan and the repayment schedule with the student.

Master's Degree
One of several degrees granted by graduate schools.

Maturity Date
The date when a loan comes due and must be repaid in full.

Merit-based
Financial aid that is merit-based depends on your academic, artistic, or athletic merit, or some other criteria, and does not depend on the existence of financial need. Merit-based awards use your grades, test scores, hobbies, and special talents to determine your eligibility for scholarships.

Mortgage
A mortgage is a loan of funds for purchasing a piece of property, which uses that property as security for the loan. The lender has a lien on the property and will receive the property if the borrower fails to repay the loan.

Multiple Data Entry Processor
A Multiple Data Entry (MDE) Processor is a company that processes the FAFSA forms submitted by students. The College Scholarship Service (CSS) and PHEAA are both MDE Processors.

National Health Corps Scholarship
The National Health Corps Scholarship (NHSC) is a scholarship program administered by the U.S. Department of Health and Human Services (HHS). It is available to medical

students studying allopathic and osteopathic medicine and to dental school students studying dentistry.

National Merit Scholarship Qualifying Test (NMSQT)
See PSAT.

National Service Trust
The National Service Trust is Clinton's national community service program. If you participate in this program before attending school, the funds may be used to pay your educational expenses. If you participate after graduating, the funds may be used to repay your federal student loans. Eligible types of community service include education, human services, the environment, and public safety.

Need
The difference between the COA and the EFC is the student's financial need—the gap between the cost of attending the school and the student's resources. The financial aid package is based on the amount of financial need. The process of determining a student's need is known as need analysis.

Cost of Attendance (COA) − Expected Family Contribution (EFC) = Financial Need

Need Analysis
Need analysis is the process of determining a student's financial need by analyzing the financial information provided by the student and his or her parents (and spouse, if any) on a financial aid form. The student must submit a need analysis form to apply for need-based aid. Need analysis forms include the Free Application for Federal Student Aid (FAFSA) and the Financial Aid PROFILE.

Need-Based
Financial aid that is need-based depends on your financial situation. Most government sources of financial aid are need-based.

Need-Blind
Under need-blind admissions, the school decides whether to make an offer of admission to a student without considering the student's financial situation. Most schools use a need-blind admissions process. A few schools will use financial need to decide whether to include marginal students in the wait list.

Need-Sensitive
Under need-sensitive admissions, the school does take the student's financial situation into account when deciding whether to admit him or her. Some schools use need-sensitive admissions when deciding to accept a borderline student or to pull a student off of the waiting list.

Net Income
This is income after taxes, deductions, and allowances have been subtracted.

New Borrower
See First-Time Borrower.

Nursing Student Loan
The Nursing Student Loan (NSL) is a low interest loan administered by the U.S. Department of Health and Human Services (HHS) and available to students enrolled in nursing programs.

Origination Fee
The origination fee is paid to the bank to compensate them for the cost of administering the loan. The origination fees are charged as the loan is disbursed, and typically run to 3 percent of the amount disbursed. A portion of this fee is paid to federal government to offset the administrative costs of the loan.

Out-of-State Student
An out-of-state student has not met the legal residency requirements for the state, and is often charged a higher tuition rate at public colleges and universities in the state.

Outside Resource
A resource is something that is available because a student is in school and is counted after need is determined. Outside scholarships, prepaid tuition plans and VA educational benefits are examples of outside resources.

Outside Scholarship
An outside scholarship is one that comes from sources other than the school and the federal or state government.

Overawards
A student who receives federal support may not receive awards totaling more than $400 in excess of his or her financial need.

Packaging
Packaging is the process of assembling a financial aid package.

Parent Contribution
The Parent Contribution (PC) is an estimate of the portion of your educational expenses that the federal government believes your parents can afford. It is based on their income, the number of parents earning income, assets, family size, the number of family members currently attending a university, and other relevant factors. Students who qualify as independent are not expected to have a parent contribution.

Pell Grant
The Pell Grant is a federal grant that provides funds of up to $2,340 based on the student's financial need.

Perkins Loan
Formerly the National Direct Student Loan Program, the Perkins Loan allows students to borrow up to $3,000/year (5 year max) for undergraduate school and $5,000/year for graduate school (6 year max). The Perkins Loan has one of the lowest interest rates and is awarded by the financial aid administrator to students with exceptional financial need. The student must have applied for a Pell Grant to be eligible. The interest on the Perkins Loan is subsidized while the student is in school.

PhD
One of several degrees granted by graduate schools.

PLAN
The PLAN is taken in the fall of the sophomore year in high school as practice for the ACT.

PLUS Loans

Parent Loans for Undergraduate Students (PLUS) are federal loans available to parents of dependent undergraduate students to help finance the child's education. Parents may borrow up to the full cost of their children's education, less the amount of any other financial aid received. PLUS Loans may be used to pay the EFC. There is a minimal credit check required for the PLUS loan, so a good credit history is required. Check with your local bank to see if they participate in the PLUS loan program. If your application for a PLUS loan is turned down, your child may be eligible to borrow additional money under the Unsubsidized Stafford Loan program.

Prepaid Tuition Plan

A prepaid tuition plan is a college savings plan that is guaranteed to rise in value at the same rate as college tuition. For example, if a family purchases shares that are worth half a year's tuition at a state college, they will always be worth half a year's tuition, even 10 years later when tuition rates will have doubled.

Prepayment

Paying off all or part of a loan before it is due.

Primary Care Loan

The Primary Care Loan (PCL) is a low interest loan administered by the U.S. Department of Health and Human Services (HHS). It is available to medical school students pursuing medicine, osteopathy, dentistry, veterinary medicine, optometry, and podiatry. Undergraduate pharmacology students are also eligible. To be eligible for this loan, you must commit to working in the field of primary care. It was formerly known as the Health Professions Student Loan (HPSL).

Principal

The principal is the amount of money borrowed or remaining unpaid on a loan. Interest is charged as a percentage of the principal. Insurance and origination fees will be deducted from this amount before disbursement.

Private Loans

Private loans are education loan programs established by private lenders to supplement the student and parent education loan programs available from federal and state governments. Some private loan programs offer terms that are highly competitive with those of the PLUS and unsubsidized Stafford loans. Most, however, are somewhat more expensive.

Professional Degree

A professional degree is a degree in a field like law, education, medicine, pharmacy, or dentistry.

Professional Judgment

For need-based federal aid programs, the financial aid administrator can adjust the EFC, adjust the COA, or change the dependency status (with documentation) when extenuating circumstances exist. For example, if a parent becomes unemployed, disabled, or deceased, the FAA can decide to use estimated income information for the award year instead of the actual income figures from the base year. This delegation of authority from the federal government to the financial aid administrator is called Professional Judgment (PJ).

Professional Student
A student pursuing advanced study in law or medicine.

Promissory Note
The promissory note is the binding legal document that must be signed by the student borrower before loan funds are disbursed by the lender. The promissory note states the terms and conditions of the loan, including repayment schedule, interest rate, deferment policy, and cancellations. The student should keep this document until the loan has been repaid.

Preliminary Scholastic Assessment Test (PSAT/NMSQT)
The PSAT is taken during the junior year as practice for the SAT. Scores on the PSAT are used to select semi-finalists for the National Merit Scholarship program. For more information on the PSAT, see the Kaplan Web page.

Reaching School
A reaching school is a school that the student would love to attend, but which isn't "guaranteed" to admit you. Every student should apply to at least one reaching school. Even very talented students should consider the Ivy League schools, MIT, and CalTech to be reaching schools.

Renewable Scholarships
A renewable scholarship is a scholarship that is awarded for more than one year. Usually the student must maintain certain academic standards to be eligible for subsequent years of the award. Some renewable scholarships will require the student to reapply for the scholarship each year; others will just require a report on the student's progress to a degree.

Repayment Schedule
The repayment schedule discloses the monthly payment, interest rate, total repayment obligation, payment due dates, and the term of the loan.

Repayment Term
The term of a loan is the period during which the borrower is required to make payments on his or her loans. When the payments are made monthly, the term is usually given as a number of payments or years.

Research Assistantship (RA)
A form of financial aid awarded to graduate students to help support their education. Research assistantships usually provide the graduate student with a waiver of all or part of tuition, plus a small stipend for living expenses. As the name implies, an RA is required to perform research duties. Sometimes these duties are strongly tied to the student's eventual thesis topic.

Safety School
A safety school is a school that will almost certainly admit the student. The college admissions process is not predictable. Even "sure admits" are sometimes rejected. Some students are admitted to all the schools to which they apply; others are rejected by all the schools. To protect yourself against the latter scenario, you should apply to at least one safety school.

Sallie Mae

Sallie Mae, formerly known as the Student Loan Marketing Association (SLMA), is the nation's largest secondary market and holds approximately one third of all educational loans.

Satisfactory Academic Progress

A student must be making Satisfactory Academic Progress (SAP) in order to continue receiving federal aid. If a student fails to maintain an academic standing consistent with the school's SAP policy, they are unlikely to meet the school's graduation requirements.

Scholarship

A form of financial aid given to undergraduate students to help pay for their education. Most scholarships are restricted to paying all or part of tuition expenses, though some scholarships also cover room and board. Scholarships are a form of gift aid and do not have to be repaid. Many scholarships are restricted to students in specific courses of study or with academic, athletic, or artistic talent.

Scholarship Search Service

A scholarship search service charges a fee to compare the student's profile against a database of scholarship programs. Few students who use a scholarship search service actually win a scholarship.

Scholastic Assessment Test (SAT I)

The SAT is one of the two national standardized college entrance examinations used in the United States. The other is the ACT. The SAT was previously known as the Scholastic Aptitude Test, and is administered by the Educational Testing Service (ETS). Most universities require either the ACT or the SAT as part of an application for admission.

Secondary Market

A secondary market is an organization that buys loans from lenders, thereby providing the lender with the capital to issue new loans. Selling loans is a common practice among lenders, so the bank you make your payments to may change during the life of the loan. The terms and conditions of your loan do not change when it is sold to another holder. Sallie Mae is the nation's largest secondary market and holds approximately one-third of all educational loans.

Secured Loan

A secured loan is backed by collateral. If you fail to repay the loan, the lender may seize the collateral and sell it to repay the loan. Auto loans and home mortgages are examples of secured loans. Educational loans are generally not secured.

Selective Service

Selective Service is registration for the military draft. Male students who are U.S. citizens and have reached the age of 18 and were born after December 31, 1959, must be registered with Selective Service to be eligible for federal financial aid. If the student did not register and is past the age of doing so (18–25), and the school determines that the failure to register was knowing and willful, the student is ineligible for all federal student financial aid programs. The school's decision as to whether the failure to register was willful is not subject to appeal. Students needing help resolving problems concerning their Selective Service registration should call 1-847-688-6888.

Self-Help Aid

Self-help aid is financial aid in the form of loans and student employment. If every financial aid package is required to include a minimum amount of self-help aid before any gift aid is granted, that level is known as the self-help level. For example, the self-help level will be $8,150 at MIT in 1995–1996 (*The Tech*, March 7, 1995, Vol. 115, No. 9, p. 1). MIT has one of the highest self-help levels of private colleges and universities, with an average self-help level of around $5,500 at the more expensive schools.

Service Academy

The U.S. Air Force Academy, U.S. Coast Guard Academy, U.S. Merchant Marine Academy, U.S. Military Academy, and U.S. Naval Academy. Admission is highly selective, as students must be nominated by their Congressional Representative in order to apply.

Servicer

A servicer is an organization that collects payments on a loan and performs other administrative tasks associated with maintaining a loan portfolio. Loan servicers disburse loans funds, monitor loans while the borrowers are in school, collect payments, process deferments and forbearances, respond to borrower inquiries, and ensure that the loans are administered in compliance with federal regulations and guarantee agency requirements.

Simple Interest

Simple interest is interest that is paid only on the principal balance of the loan and not on any accrued interest. Most federal student loan programs offer simple interest. Note, however, that capitalizing the interest on an unsubsidized Stafford loan is a form of compounded interest.

Simplified Needs Test

If the parents have an adjusted gross income of less than $50,000 and every family member was eligible to file an IRS Form 1040A or 1040EZ (or wasn't required to file a Federal income tax return), the Federal Methodology ignores assets when computing the EFC. If you filed a 1040 but weren't required to do so, you may be eligible for the simplified needs test. Details on the eligibility requirements appear on the Simplified Needs Test Chart.

Stafford Loans

Stafford Loans are federal loans that come in two forms, subsidized and unsubsidized. Subsidized loans are based on need; unsubsidized loans aren't. The interest on the subsidized Stafford Loan is paid by the federal government while the student is in school and during the six-month grace period. The Subsidized Stafford Loan was formerly known as the Guaranteed Student Loan (GSL). The Unsubsidized Stafford Loan may be used to pay the EFC.

Undergraduates may borrow up to $23,000 ($2,625 during the freshman year, $3,500 during the sophomore year, and $5,500 during the third, fourth, and fifth years) and graduate students up to $65,500 including any undergraduate Stafford loans ($8,500 per year). These limits are for subsidized and unsubsidized loans combined. The difference between the subsidized loan amount and the limit may be borrowed by the student as an unsubsidized loan.

Higher unsubsidized Stafford loan limits are available to independent students, dependent students whose parents were unable to obtain a PLUS Loan, and graduate/professional students. Undergraduates may borrow up to $46,000 ($6,625 during the freshman year, $7,500 during the sophomore year, and $10,500 during each subsequent year) and graduate students up to $138,500 including any undergraduate Stafford loans ($18,500 per year). These limits are for subsidized and unsubsidized loans combined. The amounts of any subsidized loans are still subject to the lower limits.

State Student Incentive Grants

The State Student Incentive Grants (SSIG) program is a state-run financial aid program for state residents. The states receive matching funds from the federal government to help them fund the program.

Statement of Educational Purpose

The Statement of Educational Purpose is a legal document in which the student agrees to use the financial aid for educational expenses only. The student must sign this document before receiving federal need-based aid.

Student Accounts Office

See Bursar's Office.

Student Aid Report

The Student Aid Report (SAR) summarizes the information included in the FAFSA and must be provided to your school's FAO. The SAR will also indicate the amount of Pell Grant eligibility, if any, and the Expected Family Contribution (EFC). You should receive a copy of your SAR four to six weeks after you file your FAFSA. Review your SAR and correct any errors on part 2 of the SAR. Keep a photocopy of the SAR for your records. To request a duplicate copy of your SAR, call 1-319-337-5665. Instructions for completing the SAR: http://www.fafsa.com/sar.htm

Student Contribution

The Student Contribution (SC) is the amount of money the federal government expects the student to contribute to his or her education and is included as part of the EFC. The SC depends on the student's income and assets, but can vary from school to school. Usually a student is expected to contribute about 35 percent of his or her savings and approximately one-half of his summer earnings above $1,750.

Student Loan Marketing Association (SLMA)

SLMA is the old name for Sallie Mae.

Subsidized Loan

With a subsidized loan, such as the Perkins Loan or the Subsidized Stafford Loan, the government pays the interest on the loan while the student is in school, during the six-month grace period, and during any deferment periods. Subsidized loans are awarded based on financial need and may not be used to finance the family contribution. See Stafford Loans for information about subsidized Stafford Loans. See also Unsubsidized Loan.

Supplemental Education Opportunity Grant

The Supplemental Education Opportunity Grant (SEOG) is a federal grant program for undergraduate students with exceptional need. SEOG grants are awarded by the school's financial aid office, and provide up to $4,000 per year. To qualify, a student must also be a recipient of a Pell Grant.

Supplemental Loan for Students
Supplemental Loan for Students (SLS) are federal loans for financially independent students. This program was eliminated in 1994 with the creation of the unsubsidized Stafford Loan program.

Teaching Assistantship (TA)
A form of financial aid awarded to graduate students to help support their education. Teaching assistantships usually provide the graduate student with a waiver of all or part of tuition, plus a small stipend for living expenses. As the name implies, a TA is required to perform teaching-related duties.

Term
The term of a loan is the number of years (or months) during which the loan is to be repaid.

Title IV Loans
Part B of Title IV of the Higher Education Act of 1965, as reauthorized by the Higher Education Amendments of 1992, created several education loan programs that are collectively referred to as the Federal Family Education Loan Program (FFELP). These loans, also called Title IV Loans, are the Federal Stafford Loans (Subsidized and Unsubsidized), Federal PLUS Loans, and Federal Consolidation Loans.

Title IV School Code
When you fill out the Free Application for Federal Student Aid (FAFSA) you need to supply the Title IV Code for each school to which you are applying. This code is a six-character identifier that begins with one of the following letters: O, G, B, or E. The Financial Aid Information Page provides a searchable database of Title IV School Codes.

Test Of English As A Foreign Language (TOEFL)
Most colleges and universities require international students to take the TOEFL as part of their application for admission. The TOEFL evaluates a student's ability to communicate in and understand English. For more information, see the Kaplan Web page.

Undergraduate Student
A student who is enrolled in a Bachelors program.

Unearned Income
Interest income, dividend income, and capital gains.

Unmet Need
In an ideal world, the FAO would be able to provide each student with the full difference between their ability to pay and the cost of education. Due to budget constraints the FAO may provide the student with less than the student's need (as determined by the FAO). This gap is known as the unmet need.

Unsecured Loan
An unsecured loan is not backed by collateral, and hence represents greater risk to the lender. The lender may require a co-signer on the loan to reduce their risk. If you default on the loan, the cosigner will be held responsible for repayment. Most educational

loans are unsecured loans. In the case of federal student loans, the federal government guarantees repayment of the loans. Other examples of unsecured loans include credit card charges and personal lines of credit.

Unsubsidized Loan
An unsubsidized loan is a loan for which the government does not pay the interest. The borrower is responsible for the interest on an unsubsidized loan from the date the loan is disbursed, even while the student is still in school. Students may avoid paying the interest while they are in school by capitalizing the interest, which increases the loan amount. Unsubsidized loans are not based on financial need and may be used to finance the family contribution. See Stafford Loans for information about unsubsidized Stafford Loans. See also Subsidized Loan above.

Untaxed Income
Contributions to IRAs, Keoghs, tax-sheltered annuities, and 401k plans, as well as worker's compensation and welfare benefits.

U.S.Department of Education (ED or USED)
The U.S. Department of Education administers several federal student financial aid programs, including the Federal Pell Grant, the Federal Work-Study Program, the Federal Perkins Loans, the Federal Stafford Loans, and the Federal PLUS Loans. For more information about these programs, please see the Student Guide or the U.S. Department of Education's home page.

U.S.Department of Health and Human Services (HHS)
The U.S. Department of Health and Human Services (HHS) administers several health education loan programs, including the HEAL, HPSL, and NSL loan programs.

Variable Interest
In a variable interest loan, the interest rate changes periodically. For example, the interest rate might be pegged to the cost of U.S. Treasury Bills (e.g., T-Bill rate plus 3.1 percent) and be updated monthly, quarterly, semiannually, or annually.

Verification
Verification is a review process in which the FAO determines the accuracy of the information provided on the student's financial aid application. During the verification process the student and parent will be required to submit documentation for the amounts listed (or not listed) on the financial aid application. Such documentation may include signed copies of the most recent Federal and State income tax returns for you, your spouse (if any) and your parents, proof of citizenship, proof of registration with Selective Service, and copies of Social Security benefit statements and W2 and 1099 forms, among other things.

Financial aid applications are randomly selected by the Federal processor for verification, with most schools verifying at least 1/3 of all applications. If there is an asterisk next to the EFC figure on your Student Aid Report (SAR), your SAR has been selected for verification. Schools may select additional students for verification if they suspect fraud. Some schools undergo 100 percent verification.

If any discrepancies are uncovered during verification, the financial aid office may require additional information to clear up the discrepancies. Such discrepancies may cause your final financial aid package to be different from the initial package described on the award letter you received from the school.

If you refuse to submit the required documentation, your financial aid package will be canceled and no aid awarded.

Veteran

For federal financial aid purposes such as determining dependency status, a veteran is a former member of the U.S. Armed Forces (Army, Navy, Air Force, Marines, or Coast Guard) who served on active duty and was discharged other than dishonorably (i.e., received an honorable or medical discharge). You are a veteran even if you serve just one day on active duty—not active duty for training—before receiving your DD-214 and formal discharge papers. (Note that in order for a veteran to be eligible for VA educational benefits, they must have served for more than 180 consecutive days on active duty before receiving an honorable discharge. There are exceptions for participation in Desert Storm/Desert Shield and other military campaigns.)

ROTC students, members of the National Guard, and most reservists are not considered veterans. Since the 1995–1996 academic year, a person who was discharged other than dishonorably from one of the military service academies (the U.S. Military Academy at West Point, the Naval Academy at Annapolis, the Air Force Academy at Colorado Springs, or the Coast Guard Academy at New London) is considered a veteran for financial aid purposes. Cadets and midshipmen who are still enrolled in one of the military service academies, however, are not considered veterans. According to the US Department of Education's Action Letter #6 (February 1996), "a student who enrolls in a service academy, but who withdraws before graduating, is considered a veteran for purposes of determining dependency status."

Having a DD-214 does not necessarily mean that you are a veteran for financial aid purposes. As noted above, you must have served on active duty and received an honorable discharge.

W2 Form

Employers are required by the IRS to issue a W2 form for each employee before February 28. The W2 form lists the employee's wages and tax withheld.

Work-Study

See Federal Work-Study.

Index

About the Authors

DAVID A. BALDWIN is Professor and Associate Dean for Reference and Instruction at Parks Library, Iowa State University.

DANIEL C. BARKLEY is Coordinator of Government Information/Microforms at Zimmerman Library, University of New Mexico.